1993

The Russian Literary Imagination

SOME OTHER BOOKS BY AVRAHM YARMOLINSKY:

A Russian's American Dream

Dostoevsky, His Life and Art

Literature under Communism

The Portable Chekhov (ED.)

Road to Revolution

Russians Then and Now (ED.)

Turgenev, the Man, His Art and His Age

Two Centuries of Russian Verse (ED.)

The Works of Alexander Pushkin (ED.)

THE
RUSSIAN
LITERARY
IMAGINATION

Avrahm Yarmolinsky

FUNK & WAGNALLS *New York*

The following publishers have kindly granted the author permission to reprint his introductions, revised, from the works listed below:

COLLIER BOOKS, New York: Turgenev, *Fathers and Sons,* copyright 1962 by Crowell-Collier Publishing Co.; Gorky, *Mother,* copyright 1962 by Crowell-Collier Publishing Co.; Gorky, *Autobiography,* copyright 1962 by Crowell-Collier Publishing Co.

THE LIMITED EDITIONS CLUB, New York: *Eugene Onegin,* translated by Babette Deutsch, copyright 1943 by The Limited Editions Club (the introduction also appears in a Penguin Classic, Baltimore, Md., and Harmondsworth, Middlesex, England, copyright 1964 by Babette Deutsch); Gogol, *Dead Souls,* vol. 1, copyright 1944 by The Limited Editions Club.

RANDOM HOUSE, INC., New York: *The Works of Alexander Pushkin,* copyright 1936 by Random House; *The Vintage Turgenev,* vol. 1, copyright 1950 by Alfred A. Knopf; *Two Centuries of Russian Verse, An Anthology,* copyright © 1966 by Avrahm Yarmolinsky.

THE VIKING PRESS, New York: *The Portable Chekhov,* copyright 1947 by The Viking Press.

Thanks are also due to FARRAR, STRAUS AND GIROUX, New York, for permission to reprint certain passages from *The Unknown Chekhov,* copyright 1954 by Avrahm Yarmolinsky, as well as to *The American Scholar,* for permission to reprint passages from his article on Maxim Gorky in its Winter 1941 issue, copyright 1941 by The United Chapters of Phi Beta Kappa.

The author is greatly indebted to his wife, Babette Deutsch, for her generous help in preparation of the book.

PRINTED IN THE UNITED STATES OF AMERICA

Contents

Contents

I

Alexander Pushkin

I

A QUARTER of a century after Pushkin's death a Russian critic wrote: "Pushkin is our all." The Nihilists were a dissenting voice, but with this exception the acclaim of the poet as the supreme embodiment of the national genius has been universal. In time it became usual for his compatriots to regard him as the peer of the foremost artists of the West, ranking with Shakespeare, Michelangelo, Beethoven. If the rest of the world has not been persuaded to accept this estimate, it allows that Pushkin is a literary figure not to be ignored. And yet abroad he is the least appreciated, as he is the least known, of the major Russian authors. The reason for this is not far to seek. His chief medium was verse, and, furthermore, verse that singularly resists translation, since it is weak in imagery and is innocent of intellection, relying for its magic on precision, clarity, and a verbal felicity as palpable as it is difficult to convey. There is something in Pushkin's poetry, irrespective of its substance, as Tchaikovsky observed, which enables it to penetrate to the depths of the soul—that something is its music.

The transvaluation of values that came about with the revolution, in altering the approach to Pushkin, served only to enhance his reputation and his popularity. The centenary of his death brought out the fact that both Soviet Russia and the Dispersion are eager to claim him for their own. To the émigrés he is a kind of palladium, the symbol of the nation's cultural tradition, now temporarily in eclipse, and the pledge of its renewal. To those at home in the new regime he is equally a national figure, in fact, has officially been proclaimed such, but with a difference.

In 1899, on the occasion of the celebration of the one hundredth anniversary of Pushkin's birth, an underground revolutionary organization issued a leaflet in which it repudiated him on the grounds that "he was never a friend of the people, but a friend of the Czar, the gentry, the bourgeoisie." Such an attitude is now regarded as dangerously purblind. The new society, seeing itself as the heir of all the ages, accepts him as a precious part of its patrimony. The centenary of his death spurred elaborate and most energetic efforts to bring the poet to the attention of the masses. Millions of copies of his works were printed both in the original and in the various languages of the Union. Critics were busy commenting on them, graphic artists were illustrating them, composers were setting them to music, producers were staging his plays and his tales in dramatic form, and for some time a Pushkin hour was an obligatory feature of radio programs. His writings are looked upon as the proper pabulum for youth, and as the model for young authors. Under the hammer and sickle, as under the double-headed eagle, exegesis and research center upon the poet's life and works, so that the already monumental body of Pushkin scholarship grows apace.

The new Russia, as did the old, reveres in him the greatest poet of the nation, the man who shaped the literary language and fathered its literature. But it justifies delight in him in new ways. He is found to be as congenial with the present social order as he was formerly felt to be with the old. Pushkin has always been the object of a cult, and by the same token a figure around whom legends clung. Today, in its cruder form, the legend runs that he was a rebel poet, whose valiant Muse never ceased to do battle against tyranny, and who perished at the hands of an assassin, the tool of a reactionary clique. More responsible interpreters represent him as one who, though not a man of the masses, felt with them by reason of his deep humanity, and had their emancipation at heart; as a writer whose work possessed a buoyant, life-affirming quality expressive of the attitude of a rising social class; as an author who progressed from a personal lyricism to an objective, realistic art; as a good European, a citizen of the world, a Renaissance man with universal interests; as a free spirit, unhampered by skepticism and mysticism, rejoicing in the clear light of reason, and combating, however indirectly, the powers of darkness.

The foreign reader, in making his response to Pushkin, has one advantage over the poet's compatriots: the innocency of the eye. True, what meets this eye is only a pale reflection of the original. Nevertheless, it is hoped that the outsider will be able to discover for himself something of the enchantment that Pushkin has exercised over his countrymen. The essay that follows is not so much a critical appraisal as a bare outline of Pushkin's story. The work may have more meaning when one knows a little of the man behind it.

II

Alexander Sergeyevich Pushkin was born on June 6 (May 26, o.s.), 1799, in Moscow. On his father's side, he came of an old, well-connected family, which had long been living beyond its means. Through his mother he was descended from Ibrahim Hannibal (c. 1693–1781), allegedly the son of an Ethiopian notable. At a tender age he found himself in Constantinople either as a slave or as a hostage in the sultan's seraglio. Perhaps to gratify Peter the Great's desire for a little Negro, his envoy bought or stole the lad and took him to Moscow. The Czar not only welcomed him into his entourage but had the African boy baptized and, as his godfather, bestowed his own name on him. Nor was the boy's schooling neglected: a decade later he was sent to France to study fortification. On his return to Russia he made a brilliant career as a military engineer, achieving the rank of major general and coming into possession of two estates. In the words of Vladimir Nabokov, he was "a sour, groveling, crotchety, timid, ambitious, and cruel person; a good military engineer, perhaps, but humanistically a nonentity; differing in nothing from a typical career-minded, superficially educated, coarse, wife-flogging Russian of his day, in a brutal and dull world of political intrigue, favoritism, Germanic regimentation, old-fashioned Russian misery, and fat-breasted empresses on despicable thrones." His second wife, who was of German-Swedish stock, bore him eleven children. The third son was Pushkin's maternal grandfather.

Pushkin was rather proud of his six-century-old paternal lineage —it went back to a Pushkin born in the early fifteenth century— and he also liked to refer to his African origin. He made Ibrahim Hannibal the glamorous hero of his unfinished romance, *The Negro of Peter the Great,* and when a despicable journalist hinted at the rumor that Pushkin's "black grandfather" was bought for a bottle of rum, he parried the thrust by declaring in a poem that Hannibal was "the Czar's bosom friend, not his slave." On one occasion he spoke with sympathy of the fate of those he called "my brother Negroes." It is uncertain to what degree the poet's features showed traces of his Ethiopian ancestry. That the exotic strain in his heredity partly accounts for his sensual temperament and keen feeling for rhythm is doubtful.

Like most of the gentry, the Pushkins were more Gallic than Russian in their cuture. French was spoken in the home, the children's tutors were apt to be French, and so were the books on the library shelves. Their contents were the intellectual fare of little Alexander, an impulsive, rather precocious child with a phenomenal memory. The home atmosphere was not unfavorable to the boy's literary interests. Among the people who came to the house were prominent men of letters. The father dabbled in French verse, and one of the uncles had something of a reputation as an author. Even the servants wooed the Muse. His knowledge of the vernacular and his intimacy with native folklore Pushkin owed chiefly to them, since they had charge of him most of the time. The parents were fashionable, pleasure-loving people, and the mother, "the beautiful Creole," was rather flighty. Neither took much interest in the four children they had brought into the world, least of all in Alexander. He seems to have formed no emotional ties either with his father or his mother. At heart he remained all his life a free spirit, hampered by his weaknesses rather than encumbered by pieties, filial or other.

At the age of twelve the boy entered the Lyceum, at Tsarskoe Selo (now Detskoe Selo), the Russian Versailles. This exclusive boarding school, intended to form future bureaucrats, was housed in a wing of the Great Palace and enjoyed the Emperor's special protection. On the teaching staff were some men of note, and the French instructor, curiously enough, was a brother of Marat. The curriculum included, besides the humanities, some courses in political economy and natural law, but the goal of this education was the gentleman rather than the scholar. Pushkin spent six unbroken years in this genial establishment, where he formed enduring friendships. In fact, his schoolmates stood him in lieu of family and home. An indifferent student, he profited chiefly by his reading of Voltaire and of the gayer and more elegant poets of the French Enlightenment. He also dipped into the Latin classics, though, as he confessed later, he preferred Apuleius to Cicero.

Literature was in vogue at the Lyceum. Pushkin could hardly recall the time when he was not writing verse, first in French, then in the vernacular. He had just turned fifteen when he leaped into print with a poem. In 1814 he also wrote a narrative in verse modeled on Voltaire's *La Pucelle d'Orléans*. Naturally, he contributed to the manuscript magazines edited by the pupils. He turned out a solemn ode now and then, but for the most part he scribbled anacreontic lyrics, epistles and wistful elegies, madrigals and pastorals, all derivative stuff, but couched in an unusually fluent and graceful style. The epigrams which he tossed off early won him the reputation of a wicked wit. While still at school he began to be considered the hope of Russian literature by a group of advanced young writers who met occasionally to poke fun at their stodgy elders. Never did recognition come more easily to an author.

The erotic strain in Pushkin's early verse was more than a literary manner. He was as premature in love as in letters. His amatory career began while he was still wearing the schoolboy's blue uniform with the red collar. He is said to have shared the manly pleasures of the hussars stationed in the town. His contacts with these officers may have encouraged both the libertine and the liberal in him, for the army was then the seat of opposition, as the universities were to be in a later generation. Moreover, the Lyceum was near enough to the palace for familiarity to breed contempt. The school publications sometimes contained shafts directed against the august person of the Emperor himself.

Upon graduation from the Lyceum, in June, 1817, Pushkin received a nominal appointment in the Foreign Office. The hot-blooded youth promptly began to sow his wild oats with zest. He drank, gambled, fought duels, attended the ballet—and the ballerinas—and, above all, was "a martyr to sensual love," with dire consequences to his health and rather slender purse. If we are to credit a poem of this period, this "hideous descendant of Negroes" pleased "youthful beauty" by "the shameless fury of desire." All these distractions did not hinder him from composing verse. He was beginning to write from experience, and his style was taking shape. In those days, however, he was best known for his saucy epigrams aimed at high dignitaries of Church and State, including the Czar, and as the author of a few civic poems deploring the evils of serfdom, extolling liberty and fulminating against tyranny. A certain section of the cultivated public was then agitated by the political unrest which led to the formation of secret societies and was to culminate in the conspiracy of December, 1825, so that sallies against the existing regime were apt to be warmly received. It is noteworthy that his radicalism went hand in hand with an advocacy of the rule of law, as against an arbitrary autocracy.

He was also working on and off at *Ruslan and Ludmila*, a long narrative poem. It was completed in March, 1820, and published three months later. In itself this playful tale of a princess snatched away from the bridal chamber by a magician and eventually rescued by a knight, was a puerile performance, but its appearance was something of an event. The republic of Russian letters, then a diminutive country indeed, had for some time been split into two hostile camps. The conservatives, led by a pedant who was a vice-admiral and who was to become Minister of Education, sought to rid the literary language of foreign elements and preserve its traditional connection with the archaic tongue of the Church books. They championed the dignified and decorous classicism of the preceeding century. A school of younger and more gifted writers adopted "the new style." They sought to modernize and secularize the language, bringing it nearer to the speech of polite society. They cultivated a less solemn variety of classicism and were receptive to romantic influences. Pushkin's poem, severely attacked by the diehards, was a shining example of the new poetics and contributed to the triumph of the progressives. The common reader was charmed by its light tone and felicitous lines. For years Pushkin was known as "the singer of Ruslan and Ludmila." Glinka's opera was to enhance the popularity of the tale.

III

When the little book in its colored paper cover made its appearance, its author was no longer in the capital. The previous month he had been transferred to the South to serve under General Inzov, the administrator of the colonies set up in the sparsely populated provinces of New Russia. This was deportation in disguise. Early in 1820 Pushkin had been driven to the thought of suicide by the rumor that he had been subjected to the intolerable indignity of a flogging by the police. Apparently imagining that overt punishment would rehabilitate him, he behaved in a provoking manner, thus forcing the authorities to take steps against him.

He was leaving Petersburg in a mood of mingled rage and relief. He had wearied of dissipation, and exile came as a release. He carried with him a letter in which the Foreign Minister recommended him to his new superior in these terms: "Deprived of filial attachment, he could have only one sentiment: a passionate desire for independence. . . . There is no excess in which this young man has not indulged, as there is no perfection which he cannot attain

by the high excellence of his talents." The letter further stated
that the culprit "solemnly promised to renounce [his errors] forever," and that his future now depended on the success of the
General's "good counsels."

General Inzov did not burden the *enfant terrible* either with
counsels or official duties. Instead, he lodged and boarded him,
gave him frequent leaves, lent him money, and when he was forced
to put him under domestic arrest for his escapades, visited the prisoner and entertained him with talk of the Spanish revolution.
Pushkin stayed for a while at Yekaterinoslav (now Dnepropet-
rovsk) and for two years at Kishinyov. There is a story that he
joined a camp of gypsies and wandered with them over the steppes
of Southern Bessarabia. It is certain that he traveled with some
aristocratic friends in the Northern Caucasus and in the Crimea,
spending several sunny weeks on their estate, which was situated
on the enchanted southern coast of the peninsula. He spent equally
happy weeks on another friend's estate near Kiev, where he came
in touch with several men who were to play a leading part in the
Decembrist conspiracy. Here his time was divided between "dema-
gogical discussions," as he put it, and champagne dinners. There
were few but charming women, including the beautiful and com-
plaisant hostess. He continued to fall in love with all the pretty
women in sight, although at least one of his flames believed at this
time that his sole devotion was to the Muse.

At first he rather enjoyed his new situation. A man with his
literary upbringing could not but delight in the classical associations which clung to that outer fringe of the Mediterranean world
where fate had cast him. He liked to think of himself as a second
Ovid lost among barbarians. But before long, exile began to pall.
There was the boredom and the penury, the absence of civilized
amusements, like the theater, the lack of intellectual companionship and of creature comforts. Such lines as "I've lived to bury my
desires" would point to moods of utter dejection. As his stay in the
"accursed town" of Kishinyov lengthened, he chafed more and
more under the burden of his banishment. He soon slipped back

into his old dissipated habits. In other ways, too, he proved unregenerate. His poem "The Dagger," written in 1821 to celebrate the slaying of Caesar and of Kotzebue, is on a par with the boldest political lyrics of his earlier days. To an extent, his puerile bravado, his impudent escapades, his sartorial extravagances, his cynicism, were now a protest against the constituted authorities, of whom he felt himself to be the victim.

He drew a breath of relief when, in the summer of 1823, he was ordered to join the staff of Count Vorontzov, Governor General of New Russia, at Odessa. The busy, picturesque seaport contrasted favorably with the dusty landlocked Bessarabian city. For a while he enjoyed the sun and the sea, and among other amenities, the Italian opera, the theater, and the oysters at Automne's. But he was soon complaining about his "stifling Asiatic jail" and forming plans of escape.

A new trouble was now added to the old ones: he did not get on with his superior. The Governor General had little regard for the genius of his humble subordinate. He began by offering him patronage, which the touchy poet found insulting. Then the Count attempted to force him to perform his official duties. Pushkin was outraged; he was not a Government clerk, but a professional author. True, he received an annual salary of 700 rubles, but he considered this a convict's keep rather than a civil servant's emolument. He tendered his resignation.

Count Vorontzov had for some time been making efforts to rid himself of the troublesome fellow. He may have been partly moved by jealousy, for Pushkin had fallen in love with the Countess, among others. And then the authorities got hold of a letter of his, in which he said he was taking "lessons in pure atheism" from a deaf Englishman, and that the doctrine, though disagreeable, was "most plausible." Real punishment was in order. He was expelled from the service and ordered to betake himself to the family estate at Mikhailovskoe, in the province of Pskov, and to live there indefinitely under the surveillance of the police and the ecclesiastical authorities. The disguised banishment was now an open one. He shook the dust of Odessa from his feet in August, 1824.

The four years spent in the South enriched his experience and stimulated his growth as a writer. Working as he did by fits and starts, he managed to produce a considerable amount of verse. Literature was beginning to count as a source of income for a man constantly in need of money. Some of his lyrics reveal the influence of André Chénier. His verse shows more clearly the effect of his reading of Byron, with whose work he became acquainted during this period. There was much in Pushkin's situation to feed a romantic malaise and a romantic revolt against the conventions of society.

Byron's imprint is clearly recognizable in the verse narratives that he was then writing. "The Caucasian Prisoner," the earliest of the so-called Southern Poems, is the story of a Circassian girl who falls in love with a Russian prisoner and drowns herself after helping him to escape. Another has to do with the love of a Tartar khan for a Polish princess, his prisoner, and her death in the harem at the hand of a rival. "The Gypsies" relates the story of a young man who, fleeing civilization, joins a gypsy camp, kills his rival for the favors of Zemphira, and herself as well, and is expelled from the tribe. "The Brother Robbers," like so many works of the period, remained unfinished, and is indeed a mere fragment of what was to be a long tale about outlaws. These poems contain remote echoes of Rousseauism (Pushkin was a reader of Jean-Jacques), and exhibit that sensitiveness to nature in its more exotic aspects, that mood of aristocratic misanthropy and world-weary *tristesse*, that are associated with Byronism.

Among the longer pieces completed in the South was "The Gavriliad," which is believed to have been written in 1821, during Passion Week. It is a bawdy burlesque of the Annunciation, which manages to be blasphemous and ribald in a bland, graceful eighteenth-century manner. Ever since the Lyceum days, Pushkin had occasionally lapsed into risqué verse.

His romanticism did not go very deep. He was a rebel not by

nature, but by force of circumstance. He managed to patch up a peace with life, and as he sobered down, his writings came to take on a realistic character. Some of the ideas and predilections that he retained through life indicate, however, that for all his kinship with the eighteenth century he belonged to a romantic generation.

IV

Arriving in Mikhailovskoe in August, 1824, the poet found himself in the bosom of his family. The homecoming was scarcely like the return of the prodigal. The elder Pushkin undertook to assist the local marshal of the nobility in exercising official surveillance over the young man, which involved, among other forms of espionage, opening his correspondence. As a result there were violent scenes, after one of which the father made the charge that Alexander had raised his hand against him. Pushkin was in despair: a fortress jail, a monastic prison, would be better than this domestic hell. Fortunately, the father put an end to the intolerable situation by removing himself and the rest of the family to another estate, thus leaving the field clear to his unfilial son.

The latter remained alone in the shabby little manor house, surrounded by Grandfather Hannibal's old-fashioned furniture. For company he depended partly on the servants and especially on his old nurse, who would entertain him with folk tales during the long winter evenings. He lived in the house like a guest, taking no interest in the affairs of the estate. He walked, rode horseback a good deal, visited the country fairs, and liked to mingle with the beggars who chanted the Russian equivalent of spirituals at the gates of the local monastery. He avoided the gentry, except for one neighboring estate where there was a houseful of women. He played whist with the lady of the house, teased one of her daughters, and flirted with another. Eventually both the mother and the elder daughter fell in love with him and quarreled over him. He was himself infatuated with a niece, a married woman. In a famous lyric elicited by the affair he described her as "the genius of pure beauty," but several years later in a private communication, in which he casually announced his conquest of the lady, he spoke of her as a "Babylonian harlot." He also had an affair with a serf girl which resulted in her pregnancy. Whether the child was actually born, and if so, what became of it, is one of the few things concerning the poet which the legion of Pushkinists have so far been unable to ferret out.

For the first time he had a chance to work steadily, free from the usual distractions. Always keenly aware of the gaps in his education, he read a great deal, particularly in Russian history, and he wrote. He began by completing "The Gypsies." He had brought from Odessa another unfinished manuscript: the first two chapters and a part of chapter three of a novel in verse, *Eugene Onegin,* which he had begun in Kishinyov. Since he was, as usual, in great need of money, he issued the two completed chapters in separate volumes, and went on with the tale at his leisure. To the list of his long narrative poems he added "Count Nulin," a skit in which he amused himself by parodying "The Rape of Lucrèce."

The lyrics of this period illustrate the breadth of the poet's sympathies. He took pleasure in adapting foreign material and he liked to set his stage with properties from other times and countries. On one occasion he spoke of himself as the Minister of Foreign Affairs on the Russian Parnassus. He turned into Russian several stanzas from *Orlando Furioso,* paraphrased some verses of "The Song of Songs," and composed a group of poems on themes borrowed from the Koran. It is possible that at the end of his stay at Mikhailovskoe he wrote "The Prophet," suggested by a passage in Isaiah. This lyric bodies forth the romantic notion of the poet as the divinely inspired *vates.* Generations of Russian readers have felt it to be one of the most superb examples of noble utterance in the language.

During his rustic captivity Pushkin made a new departure in composing what he described as "a romantic tragedy," *Boris Godunov.* It was completed in the late autumn of 1825. He is said to have written a comedy in French at the age of twelve, and he never ceased to take the liveliest interest in the theater. There is a dramatic element in his narrative poems, particularly in "The Gypsies." That he should next attempt a play in verse was a logical step. *Boris Godunov* is a dramatic chronicle dealing with the initial phase of Russia's Troubled Times, at the close of the sixteenth century. It is not, however, a work of political import. The upheavals of the period merely supply the material for a drama of personal ambition. The principle of autocracy is not called in question—both the elective Czar and the Pretender speak and act in its name. The treatment of the collective character "the People" is typical of an age when even extremists looked askance at the idea of a popular rising. The dramatist attributes to the populace a deep-seated moral instinct, but he sees it also as easily misguided, unconscious of its might, a blind, unpredictable, somewhat dangerous giant.

In writing his play, Pushkin hoped to give the native stage a new orientation. The theater in Russia had been dominated since its inception by French classicism. He believed that "the popular laws" of Elizabethan drama suited the Russian temperament better than "the courtly habit" of Racine's tragedy. Accordingly, he deliberately patterned his work on "the system of our father, Shakespeare." He read the plays, be it noted, in a French translation. In *Boris Godunov* the Aristotelian unities are disregarded; the action does not revolve around a single hero; tragedy and comedy are commingled, and occasionally colloquial prose intrudes upon the stately blank verse. Blank verse itself was frowned upon as not sufficiently dignified and was indeed soon to be literally outlawed by the directors of the Imperial theaters.

Pushkin did not influence Russian dramaturgy as he had hoped. In fact, he did not even make a real contribution to the native repertory. He produced not a Shakespearean piece, but a series of loosely connected scenes, dramatically ineffective and difficult to stage. Although the censor reported favorably on *Boris Godunov*, finding that the spirit of the whole was "monarchistic," the text was withheld from publication until 1831, and the first attempt to produce the play, which was made nearly forty years later, proved a failure. It remained a closet piece, and as such is held in high esteem because of its magnificent poetry. Its stage reputation it owes to the fact that it furnished the libretto for Moussorgsky's opera as edited by Rimsky-Korsakov.

The writing of the play gave Pushkin a sense of accomplishment. Further, his life at Mikhailovskoe offered other satisfactions. It held the simple pleasures that he described in the fourth chapter of *Eugene Onegin*. And yet this charming spot was, after all, but a prison, and his days were "fettered days." This banishment was more irksome than the earlier one. Again the thought of expatriation haunted him; he would settle in Western Europe; he would flee to Greece, to America. Before the end of the first lonely year he was petitioning the Emperor to allow him to go abroad for his health. Instead, he was permitted to visit the neighboring town of Pskov.

On November 19 (O.S.), 1825, Alexander I died. For a while there was uncertainty as to which of his two brothers was his legitimate successor. The secret societies, of which there were two, decided to take advantage of the confusion and carry out a military *coup d'état,* to the end of establishing a constitutional monarchy or possibly a republican government. It is said that when the news of the Emperor's death and the rumor of the rising reached Pushkin, he decided, on the spur of the moment, to rush to Petersburg. He had not been a member of either of the societies; it may be that his friends who did belong considered him too flighty to be counted on, or that they wished to spare him the danger, or perhaps his own prudence prevailed. Besides, his enthusiasm for liberty had cooled. It is probable, however, that had he been in the capital, he would have joined the insurgents on the impulse of the moment. The fact is that the exile did not break bonds. On the eve of the rising he was completing his neat and frivolous "Count Nulin," and he spent the fateful December 14 as though it were any other day. He was safe at Mikhailovskoe during the subsequent months when the Decembrists were being rounded up and tried, and he was still there when, on July 13 (o.s.), five of the rebels, with one of whom he was fairly intimate, were hanged.

The failure of the conspiracy could not but sober him further. He was now inclined to regard the existing order as a "necessity." He sincerely wished to make his peace with the government. An influential friend advised him to be patient, lie low, and write well-intentioned pieces like *Boris Godunov*, for although the authorities knew that he was not implicated, manuscript copies of his poems had been found in the possession of most of the conspirators. He obeyed, fuming inwardly at his protracted isolation, and tried to concentrate on *Eugene Onegin*. In May he petitioned the new Czar for permission to reside in Moscow or Petersburg, or to go abroad, assuring his monarch that he had no intention of opposing "the accepted order." Some days later he was writing to a friend that if freedom were restored to him, he would not remain in Russia another month, adding: "We live in a sad age, but when I picture to myself London, railways, steamboats, English reviews, or Paris theaters and brothels, my god-forsaken Mikhailovskoe bores and enrages me."

Summer came and went and still there was no change in his situation. Finally, early in September a special government courier arrived in Pskov to escort him to Moscow in great haste. Was he to be clapped into jail, or, like so many of his friends, deported to Siberia? He did not know that the government had just received a favorable report on him from a special agent who had investigated him. On reaching the capital Pushkin was immediately taken to see the Emperor. Exactly what passed between the poet and the autocrat is not known. The outcome was that Pushkin's banishment was brought to an abrupt end.

Whether or not it is true that, on being questioned by the Czar, Pushkin said frankly that, had he been in Petersburg, he would have appeared on the Senate Square with the rebels, it is certain that he promised to be a loyal subject thereafter. There is little doubt that at the time he sincerely admired Nicholas as a man and believed in his greatness as a ruler and a patriot. Shortly after his release from Mikhailovskoe, Pushkin penned a memoir on popular education, at the Czar's request. Here he expressed the hope that those who shared the ideas of the conspirators had come to their senses, and that the brothers and friends of those who had perished would perceive the necessity of the punishment and forgive it in their hearts. On the margin of the original manuscript Pushkin twice drew a gallows with five men hanging from it. He may have wanted Nicholas to believe that he forgave him for the hangings. But his true feelings were more probably expressed in his noble "Message to Siberia," written about the same time. He slipped this poem into the hands of the wife of one of the Decembrists who was leaving town to rejoin her husband in exile.* In the days that followed the first anniversary of the hangings Pushkin wrote the lyric "Arion," which carried an allusion to himself as the only survivor of the shipwrecked generation represented by the Decembrists, and later in the year he said a kind word about them in his usual commemorative poem on the opening of the Lyceum. If he had not shared their efforts and could not now sympathize with their intention, he admired their courage and compassionated their fate.

V

"Gentlemen, permit me to introduce a new Pushkin; please forget the old one." Thus the Czar is said to have presented the poet to a group of courtiers after the interview with him. But the change of heart that the Emperor discerned in Pushkin did not visibly affect his habits. After the audience, he stayed on in Moscow, basking in his newly acquired freedom and in his fame. His

---

* A poem written by one of the exiles in reply to this message enjoyed great popularity in revolutionary circles. Therein "the bard" is assured that the Decembrists are proud of their chains and live in the faith that

> Our grievous labors were not all in vain;
> A flame will yet be kindled from the spark.

The last line was the motto of *The Spark*, an underground journal edited by Lenin.

reputation was at its height, and he was being lionized by aristocratic hostesses. Soon he was again leading the disorderly irresponsible life of a gay bachelor. In fact, he was listed by the Moscow police as a notorious gambler. Once more he was burning the candle at both ends, but not with the same pleasure. He was beginning to pay the price of his precocity and his excesses. So often his days left an ashen taste in his mouth. The note of regret for wasted years recurs in his poems. The lyric "Casual Gift" which he wrote on his twenty-ninth birthday, is expressive of a bleak mood which was now assailing him more frequently.

He lived in Petersburg, lodging in a shabby hotel room, but he made frequent visits to his friends in Moscow. He was on the move a great deal, driven by restlessness and distress of mind. Sustained work was difficult. He wrote more easily during the long vacations in the country, which he took chiefly in autumn, his favorite season, staying either with friends or on one of the family estates. To a certain extent his mode of life exemplified his theory of the nature of the poet. According to his lyric "Poet" (1827), the bard, as long as Apollo does not summon him, may lead the despicable existence of a worldling and a trifler, but when the divine call reaches him, his soul rouses like an awakened eagle, and "savage and sullen," he flees in search of the proud solitude that Nature alone can offer.

He could escape to the country, but he was not permitted to go abroad, and occasionally even his trips to the provinces were frowned upon. Nominally he enjoyed the special protection of the Emperor, who undertook to be the sole censor of his writings. The tutelage turned out to be anything but a blessing. The Czar appointed Count Benckendorff, chief of the Gendarmerie, to act as go-between and as the poet's official mentor. Benckendorff assumed that the Czar's protégé would make no move without his knowledge, and when Pushkin failed to live up to his expectations, lectured him like a schoolboy. Some months after Pushkin's interview with the Czar, Benckendorff was writing to his imperial master: "Just the same, he [Pushkin] is pretty much of a good-for-nothing, but if we succeed in directing his pen and his talk, it will be useful."

In April, 1828, when war with Turkey broke out, he asked permission to join the army, but was refused. Grand Duke Constantine Pavlovich wrote to Benckendorff that the poet was guided not by patriotism, but by the desire to infect the young officers with his "immoral principles." He applied for leave to go abroad, and was again refused. That he was, in spite of everything, still a suspect character, was brought home to him with particular vividness when the police discovered in the possession of a certain army officer a manuscript poem of his with an inscription seeming to show that it referred to the Decembrist revolt. Although Pushkin explained that the lines had been written before the conspiracy, the State Council eventually made him sign a paper declaring that he would submit all his writings to preliminary censorship, and subjected him to secret police surveillance. As a matter of fact, he had never ceased to be under such surveillance. At the time when this sentence was passed (summer of 1828) he had another lawsuit on his hands. Three serfs had complained to the Metropolitan that their master was undermining their religious faith by reading them "The Gavriliad." Pushkin did not scruple to deny his authorship of the poem, but to no avail. The charge, which was a serious matter, was dropped only at the personal intervention of the Emperor, to whom the poet had addressed a confidential letter, presumably confessing his authorship and offering his apologies for having perpetrated the piece.

In what Pushkin wrote during these years there was little to give the authorities cause for suspicion. Indeed, in his forceful if ill-constructed long poem, "Poltava" (1828), he celebrates imperial Russia as Virgil did Imperial Rome. The traitor, Mazeppa, plotting the Ukraine's secession from Muscovy, is a villain out of melodrama, while Peter, the victor of Poltava, and symbol of the rising empire, is pictured as a demigod. One or two of his lyrics go so far as to express the poet's devotion to his sovereign, and on the occasion of the Polish rebellion of 1830–31, he spoke in the unmis-

takable accents of a nationalist and a patriot. For the rest, the social
motif is muted in his verse. It is upon the emotional commonplaces
in which the personal lyric is rooted that his shorter poems dwell.
There are among them manifestoes of an aristocratic aestheticism.
With Horatian disdain of the mob and its utilitarian preoccupa-
tions, he declares that the poet is born not to traffic in the marketplace or engage in life's battles, but

> *for inspiration,*
> *For sweet sounds and for prayers.*

This aestheticism carries an emphasis on the poet's independence,
which in itself was an implicit protest against the tyrannical paternalism that was strangling Russia. If only now and then, his
dissidence and his democratic leanings do crop out in his lyrics,
notably in "Secular Power." Whatever its purport, his verse was
like a breath of pure air in the stagnant atmosphere of oppression.

While he was not precisely "a new Pushkin," the years were
exercising a restraining effect on both his work and his conduct. At
the close of the sixth chapter of *Eugene Onegin,* written toward
the end of his stay at Mikhailovskoe, he had already said good-bye
to his youth. He felt that he was past his noon. It was time for him
to settle down. He ran after women as before, but now with the
notion of matrimony at the back of his head—he who had said
that marriage emasculates the soul! In the winter of 1828, at a ball
in Moscow, he was introduced to Natalie Goncharova, a sixteen-
year-old girl of rare beauty. Then, as usual, he was more or less
involved emotionally with several married and unmarried women,
including "the bronze Venus," of whom his poem "Portrait" is an
idealized sketch, and a young girl whom he had once called his
demon and whom he seriously considered marrying. Nevertheless,
Natalie made a deep impression on him. The next spring he saw
her again, and forthwith proposed to her. Since his return from
banishment he had made several moves toward matrimony, but for
one reason or another they had come to nothing. This time he received an evasive reply. He wrote to the girl's mother (the father

was in an insane asylum) to thank her for allowing him to hope, and the same day—it was May 1, 1829 (o.s.)—he started off on a long trip.

He went to the Caucasus, that romantic land which he had first visited a decade earlier, but this time he traveled into the heart of the country and further south. One day he came to the frontier and beheld, for the first time in his life, foreign land. His mount forded the river that formed the border line, and carried him onto the Turkish shore. But, alas! the territory had just been conquered by Paskevich's troops. It was Pushkin's lot never to escape from the immensities of Russia. He was now near the front—the war was still going on—and having obtained permission to visit his brother, who was in active service, he joined the army and had a taste of military life. Indeed, he took part in at least one engagement in the informal capacity of "half-soldier, half-tourist," as he described himself. By autumn he was back in Moscow, where he had to take a lecture from Benckendorff, whom he had failed to apprise of his moves. His account of this trip, is, next to his diary and letters, the most important of his autobiographical writings. His Caucasian impressions are reflected in a group of lyrics written about this time.

The distractions of his travels did not erase the image of Natalie from his mind. For her part, she was extremely chilly. He left Moscow, tried to work, and again applied for leave to go abroad or to join a mission to China. The authorities remained adamant. The early spring found him again in Moscow, and on Easter Sunday he proposed once more, and this time was accepted. It was only fitting, a friend wrote to him in congratulating him on the event, that the foremost romantic poet should marry the foremost romantic beauty of his generation.

Hectic months followed. Pushkin was marrying into a family which was living on the last crumbs of a fortune accumulated in the preceding century by a textile manufacturer who had been elevated to the ranks of the gentry. His future mother-in-law, a grasping, meddlesome, bigoted woman, soon decided that she had made a bad bargain, and kept on postponing the wedding. She obviously repented having promised her daughter, now a celebrated beauty, to this scribbler with an uncertain income, who was, moreover, under a cloud politically. To placate the Goncharovs on the latter score, Pushkin obtained a statement from Benckendorff to the effect that, far from being a political suspect, he was a protégé of the Emperor. He also bestirred himself to raise money. He wished to pay off his gambling debts, which were considerable, and to assure his immediate future, at least. His father settled on him an estate near Boldino, in the province of Nizhny-Novgorod, so that he was now a landed proprietor and the owner of two hundred male "souls." He mortgaged his property forthwith, a good part of the proceeds going to his future mother-in-law, who demanded it, so that Natalie might have a dowry. The money was spent chiefly on the bride's trousseau.

It is doubtful if at this time he saw her as she was: an empty-headed, frivolous girl, without education, intellectual interests, or even manners, whose accomplishments were limited to dancing, embroidering, and a little French. He must, however, have had no illusions about her feelings toward him. At most, she was impressed with his fame. Himself, he had, like Mme. Goncharova, his misgivings. He was thirty, and Natalie was his one hundred and thirteenth love, as he said half in earnest, half in jest (the year before his betrothal he jotted down in a girl's album a list of his flames, and the catalogue came to thirty-seven items). In spite of a passion for Natalie which allowed him to idealize her as his "Madonna," and to declare that he would sacrifice his freedom and his pleasure for her sake, more and more often he found himself thinking of the cares of matrimony and the delights of single blessedness.

In the early autumn he went off to Boldino to take formal possession of his estate and with the hope of doing some work in the country. Just before his departure, Mme. Goncharova had made a particularly distressing scene, and he had written to Natalie that she was free. As for himself, he added, he would either marry her or not marry at all.

"You cannot imagine," he wrote to a friend on arriving in Boldino, "what a joy it is to have fled far from one's fiancée and to start writing verse." The verse he wrote that autumn includes some of his most famous lyrics, such as "Elegy," "Abandoning an Alien Country," "Verses Written During a Sleepless Night," "Autumn" (early version), and "The Demons," that matchless, untranslatable evocation of a snowstorm. In one of the lyrics he sketches sharply the prosy, depressing background of his days. Cholera having broken out, he was detained at Boldino, virtually a prisoner, until early in December. Neither this nor the uncertainty about his status as a fiancé seems to have interfered with his writing. Those months, perhaps because of their total lack of distraction, were his most fruitful season. He worked on *Eugene Onegin*, putting the finishing touches to Chapters VII and VIII, and starting a new chapter, which was to remain a fragment. He also polished off "The Cottage in Kolomna," a narrative poem in that light vein which the poet never ceased to cultivate. It is a farcical piece, a trifle in the Gallic manner, delightful for its humor and its technical felicity, and unusual in that it deals with the life of the lower middle class in the capital.

The harvest of those months included also four short plays. With the exception of *The Feast in Time of Plague,* which is largely a rendering of parts of John Wilson's *City of the Plague,* they are original pieces modeled on "the dramatic scenes" of Pushkin's English contemporary Barry Cornwall (Bryan Waller Procter). *The Covetous Knight, Mozart and Salieri,* and *The Stone Guest* are objective psychological studies of three of the original sins: greed, envy, lust. The foreign setting (medieval France, Germany, Spain) is barely indicated, the interest centering on the temperamental drive which the protagonist embodies. These scenes are written in blank verse, but the style is nearer ordinary speech than is the blank verse of *Boris Godunov*. Pushkin could have said with Cornwall: "One object that I had in view, when I wrote these scenes, was to try the effect of a more natural style than that which has for a long time prevailed in our dramatic literature."

Mozart and Salieri, the only one of his dramatic compositions staged during his lifetime (in 1832), met with no success.

"The years to rugged prose constrain me," Pushkin had written at the end of the sixth chapter of *Eugene Onegin,* composed toward the close of his rustic exile. He had previously tried his hand at criticism, but it was only the year that followed his release from Mikhailovskoe that he turned to imaginative prose with "The Negro of Peter the Great." This story of the unfortunate marriage of Pushkin's Ethiopian ancestor was conceived on a large scale, but after completing the first six chapters, he abandoned it. The fragment is of considerable interest as an early character study of a Negro and also as a piece of historical fiction, couched in a style reminiscent of pre-Romantic French prose. As in "Poltava," Peter is idealized, but in a more sober fashion. Having given up the revolutionary velleities of his youth, Pushkin pinned his faith to the Westernization of Russia, and thus became an admirer of the ruler who sought so vigorously to remake the empire in the image of Europe.

It was during his seclusion at Boldino that he turned out his first finished piece of prose, *The Tales of Belkin.* It should be remembered that as a poet Pushkin had a certain tradition to build upon and depart from, while as a prose writer he was more truly a pioneer. His performance here calls for an historic rather than an aesthetic evaluation. It is less significant intrinsically than as the foundation of a tradition. He broke new ground both in his use of the language and in his imaginative response to the life around him. At one time he said that he would like to see the literary language preserve "a kind of Biblical ribaldry," adding that simplicity and coarseness suited the Russian tongue better than "European finicalness and French refinement." His own style has the clarity without meanness that Aristotle praised. He found it difficult to forego elegance, but in *The Tales of Belkin* he escaped the rhetoric of his few predecessors.

Here he looked away from historical issues and personages and attempted to deal impersonally with contemporary life as lived by people in moderate circumstances. The author chooses to conceal himself behind the pretended storyteller, who is the merest lay figure. In these stories each character is firmly drawn against his social background, but the tales do not exhibit the imaginative power or possess the psychological significance which would raise them much above the plane of the anecdote. They make agreeable reading, but they bear the same relation to the fiction of Pushkin's successors that a pen-and-ink sketch does to an oil painting.

At last he had to abandon his leisure and the literary activities it allowed. Back in Moscow he somehow made it up with the Goncharovs, but soon new quarrels started. He spent New Year's Eve with gypsy singers. A week before his wedding he was writing to a friend that he had decided to get married because it was the usual thing, but he was doing it "without rapture, without boyish enchantment," and he would be surprised if the future held any joy for him. He embarrassed the friends whom he entertained on the eve of the ceremony by his extreme dejection. He was cheerful on the day of the wedding, February 18, 1831 (O.S.), but it is said that during the ceremony several incidents occurred which the bridegroom, who was very superstitious, interpreted as evil omens.

VI

After some unexpectedly happy weeks in Moscow, the young couple settled at Tsarskoe Selo, the scene of Pushkin's schooldays. He hoped that they might live there quietly and cheaply, but he was to be severely disappointed. With the arrival of the Court in the summer, Pushkin found himself singled out for special notice by the Emperor. He was given a sinecure in the Foreign Office which carried with it a salary of 5000 rubles. Natalie too seems to have found favor in the Czar's eyes, much to her husband's annoyance. While she gave herself to the social whirl into which they were now caught up, he resented the havoc that the round of gaieties played with his work.

All that he produced during these months was a couple of folk tales in verse and a few lyrics. In the autumn, always his most fertile season, he finally wrote *finis* to *Eugene Onegin*. There is nothing in English literature which is quite comparable to it. The poem has the excellencies of eighteenth-century verse without its failings: it is sober and elegant without being didactic; it is satirical, but not viciously so; and the poet maintains a certain equanimity without ever declaring, or implying, that whatever is, is right. The tone is generally bright and fluent, that of a witty gentleman in a drawing room, though it can subside into gentle melancholy or even gravity. Spontaneity, the personal touch, and, above all, an interest in the commonplaces of experience, allies the work to the poetry of a later age. The precepts of Wordsworth are observed here: the use of common speech and the introduction into the realm of poetry of native folkways and "the things of every day," such as a baker plying his trade, a girl carrying milk to market, a small boy sledding while his mother threatens him from the window. The homely image so effectively employed to describe Lensky in death is a supreme illustration of Pushkin's freedom from "inane and gaudy phraseology." Yet the thread that connects the author of *Eugene Onegin* with the Romantics is a tenuous one. "The humble and rustic life," championed by Wordsworth, figures in *Eugene Onegin* only as the background of the picture. Pushkin eschews here everything extravagant, visionary, grand, picturesque; nor does the tale honor the Romantic doctrine of the rights of the heart. If he does yield occasionally to nostalgic reveries and tender yearnings, he is apt to smile self-consciously at the impulse. He has nothing of Keats but his fine precision. He has neither the ability nor the wish to soar into the intense inane with Shelley or to descend with Coleridge into caverns measureless to man.

There is one figure among the English Romantics whose name is always coupled with that of Pushkin. A Londoner writing home from Petersburg on Christmas Eve, 1829, described Pushkin as "the Byron of Russia." The tag, which was not new then, has stuck to the poet through the years. Indeed, he began writing his "novel in verse" with one eye on Byron. He mentioned both *Beppo* and *Don Juan* as his models, and though he departed from them to advantage, he undoubtedly owed something to these works. Like them, and unlike the long poems of his own that preceded it, *Eugene Onegin* is written in stanzaic form. Pushkin did not, however, employ Byron's octaves, but invented a stanza of fourteen iambic lines with an intricate pattern of masculine and feminine rhymes. Pushkin also followed the English poet in adopting an easy conversational manner, which allows for digressions of sorts. His own personality is decidedly in the picture. He moves in and out of the story, which readily gives place to private commentary:

> The mind's reflections coldly noted,
> The bitter insights of the heart.

He alludes to the writings of his contemporaries as well as to his own, wanders off into autobiography, and with a fine careless freedom brings in not only himself, but his friends, his enemies, his Muse, his old nurse, all in the fashion of Byron and of W. H. Auden in his Byronic moments. Obviously, he enjoyed these liberties, as there opened up before him what he called "the vista of a free romance."

Here, however, the resemblance to Byron ceased. When he was in the midst of the second chapter, Pushkin wrote to a friend that he was busy with a new poem in which he "choked with gall." He must certainly have dipped his pen into some milder stuff before he set it to paper. Occasionally his satire may be biting, but more often it is mild and playful. There is none of Byron's fire or venom or embittered rebellion. Nor does *Eugene Onegin,* in spite of its freedoms, descend to the loose discursiveness of *Don Juan.* Pushkin had a restraint and self-discipline that Byron lacked. The formal perfection that the latter admired without being able to achieve is displayed in *Eugene Onegin* throughout. Pushkin had, rather, Pope's unerring instinct of workmanship. In every mood, upon every theme, even where the subject matter is trivial or the sentiment mawkish, the verse exhibits a natural grace, a beautiful fitness, a finish, that are a source of pure delight. This is one of the reasons why Russians value the poem beyond any other work of their most cherished writer. When Turgenev asserted that he would give both his little fingers for a single line of *Eugene Onegin,* he was expressing emphatically an appreciation general enough among his compatriots. The poem's popularity was added to by the opera that Tchaikovsky based upon it.

The unique character of this "novel in verse" is due to the felicity with which Pushkin here manages to combine the charm of lyric poetry with the more solid stuff of which realistic fiction is made. Even in translation, its quality as a narrative should be apparent. Here is a story told not only with the sensitiveness of a poet, but with a novelist's psychological penetration. The men and women who move through these pages appear in their proper social settings, against the background of daily life in town or country, a background sketched in with a nice economy. Throughout the book there are vignettes of minor figures done with a cruel faithfulness rivaling that of the candid camera. The simple plot (Tatyana, a provincial girl, falls in love with Onegin, who repulses her and goes off; she makes a "good" marriage; Onegin returns and falls in love with her; she rejects him sorrowfully but firmly) hangs upon the characters. There is a strong awareness of the time factor which is prominent in much modern work. The protagonists are shown developing in obedience to the logic of their respective natures and the force of circumstances. The author's connection with Onegin alone is too close to permit him to view his hero quite objectively. Hence his presentation of this blasé young man, unwittingly in conflict with himself and possessed of a nature finer than his conduct, has a peculiar inwardness and appeal. Even more remarkable is Pushkin's understanding of the emotions of a simple-hearted young girl, and Tatyana's dream points to his uncommon insight into the workings of the subconscious. What contributes to the impression of candor left by the story is the fact that it does not evade an unhappy ending. Like Stendahl's *The Red and the Black,* which appeared at about the same time, the Russian work was a pioneer effort, anticipating the advent of the realists.

No less than the two or three novels that Tatyana found in her hero's library, *Eugene Onegin* is a book

> . . . upon every page
> Exhibiting the present age
> And modern man's true soul divulging.

"The present age" is that in which the poet passed his precocious and ebullient youth. Indeed, the accuracy with which the Russian scene in the post-Napoleonic era is delineated, the concern with contemporary manners, makes this poem something of a social document. It opens that imaginative history of Russian society that may be constructed from the richly humorous tales of Gogol, the neat fictions of Turgenev, the substantial narratives of Goncharov, Dostoevsky's tortured inventions, Tolstoy's broad canvases. This poetic narrative, rather than Pushkin's most ambitious prose effort, *The Captain's Daughter,* has long been recognized as the parent of the Russian novel, the source to which the full stream of Russian fiction must be traced. More than any other work of Pushkin's, it fertilized the imagination and impressed itself upon the mind of the public. It marks the beginning of Russia's literary maturity, the fruit of which was her chief contribution to Western culture.

As far as native literature went, Pushkin's Russia was practically virgin soil. He set his hand to many tasks, breaking new ground wherever he turned: in addition to lyrical and narrative verse, he composed poetic dramas, explored the field of folklore, writing both tales and ballads, produced a novel, historical fiction, a work of history, as well as critical essays, translated freely and fitfully from many languages. His interests being so various and his private life so crowded with distractions, it is not surprising that sustained effort was difficult for him.

Eugene Onegin is one of his few works of generous proportions. It is Pushkin's major performance and the one which gives the fullest measure of his genius. It was a work that held his attention through the years. Indeed, it occupied him most of his adult life. The cradle of *Eugene Onegin,* he said, was the Crimea, and he visited that sunny and then serene peninsula in the summer of 1820, not long after his twenty-first birthday. He began writing the poem in May, 1823, during his stay in Kishinyov, and he kept returning to it for the next eight years, his best and most productive period. Sometimes he would work at the manuscript for weeks on end, and then he would lay it aside for months, for a year. The final chapter was composed in September, 1830, all but Onegin's letter to Tatyana, which was penned a year later. The poet celebrated the completion of the work with these lines:

Here is the long-bided hour; the labor of years is accomplished.
Why should this sadness unplumbed secretly weigh on my heart?
Is it, my work being done, that I stand like a laborer, useless,
One who has taken his pay, strange to the tasks that are new?
Is it the work I regret, the silent companion of midnight,
Friend of the golden-haired Dawn, friend of the gods of the hearth?

Pushkin continued to miss this "companion" even after the book was published. His friends urged him to write a sequel, reminding him that it was a sure source of income (his marriage had placed him in greater straits than usual), and that, since Onegin was neither buried nor married, common decency demanded that the author proceed with the story. As a matter of fact, there were found among Pushkin's papers two stanzas in which he reviewed his friends' arguments and which may well have been the opening of the hoped-for sequel. This fragment, one of the many with which his desk was crammed, appears to have been composed in the autumn of 1835, a little more than a year before his untimely death.

VII

Long before the novel was completed, the separate chapters had begun to come out piecemeal, in the form of thin books in colored paper covers. The first chapter was published in 1825, when only three of them had been written. In his foreword the author said that there would probably be no further instalments. They did come at intervals of one or two years. The entire work was issued for the first time in 1833.

Eugene Onegin had grown by a process of organic accretion, as it were. The stanzas composing each chapter were not written consecutively, but more or less at the dictates of inspiration; arrangement came later. The finished product was the result of much revising, cutting, and polishing. The plot underwent several mutations; the author's viewpoint, the tone, changed with the years. The poem mirrors Pushkin's gradual sobering down, on which he harps in the body of the work. Taking leave of Onegin meant for him bidding a firm if wistful farewell to his own youth and greeting the onset of middle age.

The vicissitudes of the author's personal life not unnaturally are reflected in the poem. When he began writing it, he was, like many young noblemen, a Government employee, though serving in a minor capacity and indeed only nominally. In reality, he was a political exile whom an umbrageous autocrat had banished from the capital to the distant semi-Asiatic section of the Empire that New Russia then was. He was already famous for a number of lyrics as well as for the epigrams and civic verses that had earned him his punishment, and for several long narrative poems embodying a romantic malaise. He carried the manuscript of Eugene Onegin with him to Mikhailovskoe and eventually to the two capitals and to the several country seats that he visited. His sojourn at Mikhailovskoe left its imprint on the early chapters, while the last two owe something to his return to Moscow after he was given his freedom and to the evenings he spent in Petersburg salons prior to his marriage.

In these last two chapters events crowd upon one another more rapidly than in the earlier pages. It is as though toward the end the poet was in a hurry to have done with the tale. The separate edition of Chapter VI closes with the words "End of Part I." Presumably Pushkin intended to add at least one more part of

equal length. He may have been moved to shorten the novel because of the hostile reception accorded Chapter VII. One reviewer
went so far as to speak of the poet's "complete downfall." But if
the early critics were divided about the merits of the work, the
public—what there was of it in those days—continued to read it
avidly.

Originally a whole canto, written in 1829–30 (some stanzas
had been composed in 1825) was devoted to a description of the
journey that Onegin made after his unfortunate duel rendered
home distasteful to him. The poet took him through the Volga
region, the Caucasus, and other parts of the south, as well as
Northern and Central Russia, sketching in the dismal military
settlements run by Alexander's satrap, Arakcheyev. If Onegin does
not go abroad, it may well be because his creator never did, since
the Czar frowned on this ambition. The poet intended to have this
canto follow Chapter VII, so as to make less abrupt the transition
from Tatyana, the provincial girl, to Tatyana, the *grande dame*.
In the summer of 1831 Pushkin decided to discard the account of
Onegin's travels. He seems to have feared that it would not pass
the censor. Accordingly he altered the next chapter, which now
became the eighth and last. Excerpts from the "Travels" were
published together with Chapter VIII in 1832, and were reprinted
as an appendix to the novel when it came out in its entirety.

Before Pushkin cast his novel into its final shape he composed
another chapter, at least in part, which was to have been the tenth.
Only a tantalizing fragment of it is extant: part of fifteen stanzas
in a code, which was broken in 1910, and rough drafts of three
other stanzas in autograph. We have here apparently a chronicle
of the reign of Alexander I, and particularly of the movement
which resulted in the military uprisings of the Decembrists. This
was treading on dangerous ground, and it is not surprising that
Pushkin should have burnt the manuscript, on October 19, 1830,
preserving, so far as is known, no more than the abovementioned
fragment. The opening quatrain is an acidulous thumbnail sketch
of Alexander I:

> A monarch weak and also cunning,
> A fop gone bald, toil's arrant foe,
> Whom fame had, by strange chance, been sunning,
> Was then our monarch, as you know.

It is not clear what part this chapter was to play in the development of the plot. Was Tatyana's husband, a general no older than Eugene, to become a Decembrist, be deported, and thus leave the field free for Eugene? Or else, as was more likely, was Onegin to be drawn into the conspiracy and go down in defeat like the rest of that lost generation? Did Pushkin envision his hero redeemed, as Gogol was later to dream of redeeming the protagonist of *Dead Souls,* and Dostoevsky his Raskolnikov? Or was even the tragedy of the Decembrists to leave Onegin, in spite of his involvement, the same futile, rootless man? One can only guess. In any event, the fragment hints at the extent to which Pushkin was aware of the rebels' plans and suggests a vague sympathy with them.

The theme of rebellion fascinated him. He hated stupidity, oppression, and bigotry. His was a freedom-loving, irreverent spirit. In his early youth he had stuck out a saucy tongue at authority, earning himself a deportation, and he remained to the end under police surveillance. Onegin's maladjustment, his weary cynicism, his attitudinizing, may be interpreted as a protest against the slave-owning society of which he was the product. It is, however, an indirect protest, the meaning of which was probably not clear to Pushkin himself. Although he has been officially crowned by the Russia that issued out of the Revolution, he was no revolutionist. The story of Eugene and Tatyana is at bottom a story of failure and wasted lives. The man obviously runs into a dead end. The woman, whose life is outwardly fortunate, is clear-eyed enough to perceive the weakness of the man she loves, and though this does not destroy her love, it ruins the possibility of fulfillment for her. Yet this story of defeat is told by a man who has accepted life on its own terms and resigned himself to it.

VIII

During the winter of 1831 Pushkin followed the Court to Petersburg, where he was to spend most of his time during the half dozen years that remained to him, his trips to the country being rarer than in his bachelor days. He was married a little over a year when his wife presented him with a daughter, and she bore him a son the year following, but the cares of motherhood nowise lessened her eagerness for the more glittering side of society life. The poet found himself reduced to accepting the role of the husband of a prima donna. He spent his time escorting the dazzling Natalie to interminable balls, dutifully swallowing ices and suppressing yawns. He was attracted by other women, including one of his sisters-in-law, and occasionally he sought entertainment in the fashion of his bachelor days, but if he aroused his wife's jealousy, on the whole he was a devoted husband, and one who had ample reason to be jealous on his own account. He was annoyed by the attentions shown his coquettish wife and irritated by the company of aristocratic knaves and fools into which he was thrown. As he did not always conceal his sentiments, he made enemies in high places.

Pushkin's sinecure allowed him free access to the archives. He took advantage of it to engage in historical research and indeed was thought of as an official historiographer. The past had always attracted him, perhaps because he felt himself less restricted in dealing with it. The subject he finally chose to investigate was the Pugachov Rebellion, the bloody jacquerie which swept across Eastern Russia under Catherine the Great. In the latter part of 1833 he escaped from the hateful social round, spending several months in a tour of the Pugachov country.

He had barely returned when the new year brought him an insulting gift in the shape of an appointment to the post of Gentleman of the Bedchamber, an honor usually accorded younger men. Pushkin was certain that this rank had been conferred on him so that his wife might attend Court balls without impropriety. The poet was now a courtier. He hated his uniform, and referred to it as a jester's motley. He hated the Court, and called it a cesspool. Nevertheless, he wore the uniform and he attended the Court functions. Furthermore, he accepted a subvention from the Czar in order to publish his history of the Pugachov Rebellion. Financially, his affairs were going from bad to worse. His father having become completely insolvent, he accepted the burden of managing the family estates. He had no means of securing money save by his pen. In order to write, he needed the leisure and the peace that the life he was living denied him. But Natalie would not think of burying herself in the provinces, nor could he offend the Czar by running off to the country. It was a vicious circle. To add to his vexations, he discovered that his letters to his wife were being opened by the police.

He must put an end to this intolerable dependence, for which, after all, he had himself to thank. In June, 1834, he made an ineffectual attempt to resign from the service, which only humiliated him further. A year later he made another effort to free himself from his entanglement. This time he pointed out to the Czar that during his married life he had incurred debts amounting to 60,000 rubles, and pleaded for a four years' leave of absence, so that in retirement he might be free to write, and thus mend his fortunes. He had to accept a four months' leave and a sum of 35,000 rubles which was only nominally a loan. The Czar thought it safer to keep the poet under his eye. The more Pushkin struggled, the more firmly he became enmeshed. The financial assistance was of little help. Living beyond his means, he was reduced to pawning his valuables, and he owed money even to his own valet. He was aging. He was irritable. Work was more difficult than ever. The year 1835 was particularly sterile. He had no paucity of ideas, but he kept passing from one thing to another, unable to finish anything. The one piece he had to show for his labor was a medley of prose and verse, "Egyptian Nights," in itself the merest fragment. The critics were burying him. Was he indeed played out?

His productivity was diminished during these years. But his finest prose work was just ahead of him, and it was not long since he had written some of his most powerful verse. One thinks of "The Bronze Horseman," technically one of his supreme works, which he composed in less than a month in the autumn of 1833. Like "Poltava," it celebrates Peter the Great. Incidentally, it is a paean to the city that he had erected on the marshes in defiance of Nature and as proof of his indomitable will. Yet the poet sees not only the greatness of the man who represents Russia's manifest destiny, but also the pitiableness of the small individual crushed by Leviathan. The vain revolt of the elements, symbolized by the Neva flooding the city, is paralleled by the equally futile threats that the crazed little clerk launches at Peter's statue. In the end the reader's feelings are divided between sympathy for the helpless clerk and admiration of the mighty Czar. Whether or not the censors found such sympathy subversive, they held the piece to be objectionable, and indeed it became accessible in unexpurgated form only in the present century.

And then there were his verse renderings of folk tales, which are among the most precious literary heirlooms of the nation. Pushkin had always been interested in the songs and stories of the unlettered peasantry, and had a keen ear for the peculiar turns of folk speech. This gift, combined with his humor and his craftsmanship, allow these five fairy tales to rank with his best work. "The Tale of the Pope and His Workman, Baldà" is the gem of the collection, but "The Tale of the Golden Cockerel" is better known because of Rimsky-Korsakov's opera, *Coq d'Or,* which is based upon it. It may be of interest to note that Pushkin derived the story of the magic weathercock from a chapter in Washington Irving's *Alhambra,* a French translation of which was in his library. About this time, notably in 1832–33, Pushkin also wrote "The Songs of the Western Slavs," which testify to his delight in folk balladry. Many of these pieces are free versions of poems by Prosper Mérimée which he passed off as Serbian folk songs. In spite of their spurious origin, Pushkin's Songs have the authenticity of poetry.

In his final period his chief medium was prose. "The Queen of Spades," written in 1833–34, might have been included among *The Tales of Belkin,* yet it has more body and much greater psychological depth. If there is filiation in literature, this story may be regarded as the humble ancestor of Dostoevsky's subtle masterpiece, *Crime and Punishment.* "Dubrovsky," an earlier tale, introduces the note, somewhat muffled it is true, of protest against injustice, which was to be echoed so resonantly by later writers, beginning with the author of *A Sportsman's Sketches.* The story is far less important as a Russian variation on the Robin Hood theme than as the earliest story about rural Russia in which the iniquity of the courts and the evils of serfdom are so presented as to suggest that something may be wrong with the system. Perhaps because he realized that it could never pass the censors, Pushkin was content to leave the story, as it has come down to us, in the rough.

The piece that shows Pushkin at his best as a prose writer is "The Captain's Daughter," practically the last thing that he published. It bears the same relation to his prose that *Eugene Onegin* does to his verse. An historical romance which resurrects the age of Catherine, it interweaves a family chronicle with an account of the Pugachov rising. The story of young Grinyov's love affair and marriage is a tale such as Pushkin had said he would compose when, in defiance of Apollo, he ceased to speak the language of the gods. One can understand why Tolstoy considered it the poet's greatest achievement. Rudimentary and occasionally melodramatic though it is, it has, in its small way, some of the qualities of *War and Peace:* the balance, the soundness, the affirmative attitude. It has too the best character drawing that Pushkin ever did, and is couched throughout in a chaste and simple style which has been a happy influence upon generations of Russian writers.

Pushkin casts a kind of glamor over the figure of the impostor, Pugachov, in this novel. Instinctively he sides with the daring rebel, be it the peasant leader of a jacquerie, or an outlawed gentleman, as in the case of Dubrovsky, or an heroic bandit like Kirdjali in the story of that name. Yet the social implications of the rebellion, which forms the background of "The Captain's Daughter," are slurred over, the most realistic details of the conflict occurring in a portion of the story that was omitted from the final text. Here, as in his scholarly study of the rising, Pushkin's viewpoint is inevitably that of a representative of the class against which Pugachov had taken up arms. "Heaven save us," he has his narrator exclaim, "from seeing a Russian rebellion, senseless and ruthless." In another place he interrupts the narrative to remind his reader that the best and most lasting changes are those which result from a gradual improvement in manners and customs.

In his last years he felt more strongly than ever that the country stood to gain nothing from a violent upheaval. He had the inclinations of a liberal, and his sympathies were with the downtrodden, but he had his doubts about democracy and on at least one occasion he spoke with great scorn of the American experiment. Government by gentlemen, a kind of enlightened absolutism, was not without its appeal for him. He could exalt the free individual, bowing to none, living at his own sweet will, admiring Nature and the arts, and having no care to meddle with such matters as the making of wars and the imposition of taxes. This naïve attitude is expressed in some detail in a didactic poem which is among his last. In another lyric, however, written at about the same time, indifference gives way to indignation against what he calls "secular power." And when he came to sum up his life-work (in "Unto Myself I Reared a Monument"), he spoke not as the aesthete who is above the battle, but rather as a humane libertarian, basing his claim to enduring renown on the fact that with his lyre he had roused kindly sentiments and in a cruel age had "celebrated freedom."

IX

The beginning of 1836 brought the distressed poet a ray of hope. He had long been wanting to publish a magazine, and after much delay he was at length permitted to do so. The enterprise, he thought, might prove quite profitable, enabling him to pay off his debts and free himself from his embarrassing dependence on the Czar's bounty. It was his intention to establish, with *The Contemporary,* a solid periodical, at once a literary miscellany and a journal of ideas, head and shoulders above the public prints of the day. He took for his pattern the English periodicals, such as the *Edinburgh Review.* He knew that he could count on the support of a group of authors, some of them young men like Gogol, but chiefly writers of the older generation. Naturally, he was to be not only the editor, but a contributor as well, writing special articles and drawing upon his unpublished work.

Though he was engaged in the highest type of journalism, Pushkin felt that his undertaking exposed him to all manner of indignities. He had therefore to safeguard the more carefully the venerable name he was bequeathing to his children, of whom there were now four. It was the Devil's doing, he wrote to his wife about this time, that he, a man with talent and a soul, had been born in Russia. He was now more touchy than ever on the subject of his honor. In May he barely avoided a duel with a gentleman who had been overheard talking frivolously with Natalie. She was then giving him another and more serious cause for anxiety. Already in the winter of 1835–36, which was a particularly brilliant season, gossip was coupling her name with that of a certain Georges d'Anthès. This dashing young officer of the Guards was a French émigré who was soon to be adopted by Baron Heckeren, the Dutch Ambassador to the Russian Court. Although Pushkin trusted his wife, her coquetry and the young man's persistent attentions created a trying situation.

The summer was a dismal one. The review proved a sore disappointment. There was not a sufficient public for a serious quarterly such as he was issuing. Moreover, some readers felt that he was no longer in the literary vanguard. The money that was needed so badly failed to materialize, and what with the censorship and the work connected with the magazine, it was only a source of vexation. His debts were mounting and the demands made on him by his relatives were increasing. Furthermore, when autumn came, he had to forego his customary retreat to the country. He was unable to work, and he was in a state of irritability which was doubtless aggravated by jealousy of d'Anthès. The latter, in pursuing Natalie, had the help of his adoptive father, who seems to have played the part of pander while spreading rumors to the effect that Natalie was having a liaison with the Emperor. Scandal-mongers were eager to enlarge upon the Pushkins' quarrels and infidelities.

On November 4 (o.s.), Pushkin received an anonymous letter informing him that the Most Serene Order of Cuckolds had elected him coadjutor to the Grand Master, as well as historiographer. It was plain that the purpose of the communication was to insinuate that the new member of the Order had the Czar to thank for his horns. Pushkin's first step was to make an ineffectual attempt to repay the loan he had received from the Czar, as a preliminary to severing his relations with the Court. Assuming that Baron Heckeren was responsible for the letter, he then challenged d'Anthès to a duel. The challenge was accepted, but Pushkin withdrew it on learning that a match had been arranged between his sister-in-law, Catherine Goncharova, and his opponent. When pressed to do so, Pushkin declared that in proposing to Catherine, d'Anthès was acting as a man of honor, but privately he held to the belief that the marriage was a cowardly dodge to avoid the duel and perhaps intended as a cover for clandestine relations with Natalie. There is some reason to believe that d'Anthès had previously had a liaison with Catherine and that there was urgent cause for hurrying the nuptials, which occurred on January 10, 1837 (o.s.).

After the wedding d'Anthès continued to press his attentions upon his newly acquired sister-in-law, acting with a boldness that was bound to provoke Pushkin, and aided as before by Heckeren. An anonymous letter informing Pushkin that his wife had had a rendezvous with d'Anthès incited him to write a violently abusive letter to the old baron. As a result, d'Anthès challenged Pushkin to a duel, which took place on February 8, 1837 (January 27 o.s.). His opponent was only slightly wounded, but Pushkin was seriously hurt. Two days later death freed him from Benckendorff's officiousness, from the Czar's burdensome generosity, from the pangs caused by Natalie's careless frivolity, from malice and intrigue, espionage and calumny, from his own crippling weaknesses. He loved life too well, however, to have welcomed the bullet which gave him his romantic congé. And although he made a Christian end, one cannot be certain that he had the comfort of a belief in an afterlife. Yet he achieved immortality, of the kind that poets desire—"on the lips of living men."

I I

Gogol's Masterwork

I T should by now be a matter of common knowledge that *Dead Souls* belongs among the major Russian novels. Indeed, it is the first of them, as it is also Gogol's most significant work and the one on which his renown chiefly rests. Upon this novel his thoughts centered during the better part of his life as a writer. He was twenty-six years old when he began it, in 1835. He then had to his credit three books, made up of short stories and miscellaneous essays. He had also written a comedy, *The Inspector General,* but this was still to be staged. It was to become a mainstay of the Russian repertory, and ultimately afford material for Danny Kaye. His reputation, a not inconsiderable one, was that of a regional writer, for in his tales he evoked chiefly the landscape, the folk, the lore, the history of his native Ukraine (born into a family of Cossack gentry, he had not left the South until he was nineteen). As yet, however, he had not made up his mind that literature was to be his life-work, the field in which he was to seek to satisfy his vaulting ambition.

Gogol himself set down an account of the conception and the long gestation of *Dead Souls*. He did this in a revealing piece of self-vindication which he called "An Author's Confession" and which he penned half a dozen years before his seemingly self-willed death.

The comic vein that showed itself in his early writings was the result, he explained, of an inner compulsion: he was subject to fits of unaccountable depression, and he found relief in inventing funny characters and absurd situations. Yet aimless foolery could not long content a man of his essentially serious nature, one who, indeed, had believed himself from early youth a dedicated spirit. He began to feel that he must put his gift for caricature at the service of a worthy cause. This he first attempted to do by holding corrupt officialdom up to ridicule in *The Inspector General*. When the comedy was staged, in 1836, the impact it produced made Gogol more keenly aware than ever that laughter was a mighty power. "Laughter," he wrote, "is a great thing: it deprives you of neither life nor property, but before it the guilty is like a hare with its legs tied." Moreover, he felt that the time was now ripe for him to undertake a work of major proportions. His friend Pushkin had been urging him to engage in something of the sort.

Indeed, Pushkin, who was, in his own words, "the godfather" of *The Inspector General,* presented Gogol with the story which was to be the germ of his masterpiece. It had to do with a man caught buying dead "souls" (*i.e.,* male serfs) in the vicinity of the Pushkin estate. The rogue was interested, of course, merely in the title to this "baptized property," which could then be mortgaged for a substantial sum. In Gogol's time, it should be noted, a serf was carried on the tax list long after his demise, often until the next general census, his owner in the meantime having to pay the poll tax for him. As a matter of fact, illegal transactions involving "dead souls" were not a very rare occurrence.

Gogol began the book without having worked out a definite plot and without having conceived the characters clearly. He had hoped that as his hero, Chichikov, traveled about the country in further-ance of his little scheme for getting rich quick, men and women would spring into view and grateful situations develop. But the story refused to take shape. The author was perpetually teased by questions as to the role of this or that character, the meaning of one or another scene, and the purpose of the whole. He came to the conclusion that only when he had satisfied himself on the score of the usefulness of his work and its value as a public service, would he be able to become genuinely interested in it and get a good grip on it. Eventually convinced that in his capacity as a writer he too could serve his country, he turned to his task in a more exalted and exacting frame of mind, and devoted himself body and soul to his book.

To free himself from every distraction, he laid aside all thought of civil service or teaching and even gave up his friends—his ties with his family were slight. Finally, to achieve the detachment he required and to gain perspective on the country to which his thoughts and affections were riveted, he expatriated himself. In 1836 he went abroad, and for the next half dozen years he led an ascetic existence, wandering over Western Europe with his manuscript, upon which he worked briefly in Rome. He took some time off for a few minor tasks, rewriting a tale that he had published earlier and composing one of the most influential of short stories, "The Overcoat," but his main preoccupation was the novel. He finished the first Book in 1841, and this volume was published in the spring of the following year under the title *Chichikov's Adventures, or Dead Souls*. The first title had been supplied by the censor, the second was of Gogol's own choosing. It was relegated to a subordinate place because it was suspected to be a disguised attack upon the immortality of the soul, or, what was as bad, a detraction of the institution of serfdom.

A remote and subdued descendant of the picaresque romance, *Dead Souls* is made up of a series of incidents strung together by the device of the journey, and carries with it the elementary pleasure that attaches to such an adventure. The reader readily accustoms himself to the easy pace at which the novel moves, and he certainly has no difficulty in following the simple plot. As the story opens, Pavel Ivanovich Chichikov, a bachelor, whose pleasing appearance gives no hint of his shady past, drives into a provincial capital in his own carriage, attended by his coachman and his valet. He puts up at an inn and proceeds to pay his respects to the local dignitaries, from the Governor on down. He has an affable manner and the air of a man of substance, and so ingratiates himself with everybody. But while, seemingly without a care in the world, he basks in the hospitality generously tendered him, he is quietly intent on furthering his own little stratagem. Having struck up an acquaintance with the country squires of the neighborhood, he visits their manors as well as the estates of one or two other landowners whom chance throws in his way. His object, behind the screen of sociability, is to buy up those of their serfs who had died so recently that their names had not yet been stricken from the register. His purchases made, Chichikov returns to town to have the documents relating to them properly executed. By mortgaging his ghostly acquisitions, he hopes to come into a tidy sum that will enable him to settle down as a man of property in good earnest, with flesh-and-blood serfs, a suitable wife, and, eventually, a brood of little Chichikovs. The transactions are successfully completed, but Pavel Ivanovich, for all his tact and charm, manages to offend the ladies at a ball, and, to make matters worse, rumors of his queer purchases get about and the place soon becomes too hot for him. He has his carriage brought round in haste, and is on the road again. Therewith the book comes to an end.

There is little tension here, and none of the emotion that attends upon a birth, a death, a love affair. The story moves on the prosy level of questionable business dealings, and the major crisis at the close does not chill the blood. Indeed, there is something of a static quality to the book, awareness of time's passage playing a minimal part in it. The novel exhibits rather the feeling for space that E. M. Forster prizes in *War and Peace*. The sense of enormous stretches of land, a vastness that both oppresses and challenges, haunts the pages, and is one element that makes for the peculiarly Russian atmosphere of *Dead Souls*.

The book's chief claim to attention, then, lies in the comedy at the heart of it and in the various men and women who people it. They are from different vantage points: some are glimpsed briefly at a distance, others occupy the middle ground, and a few, mainly the squires with whom Chichikov drives his bargains, are so much in the foreground that one sees every wart. As for Chichikov, it takes the reader no time at all to perceive what manner of man he is. Complacency, affability, levelheadedness, all enter into his makeup, but he is ruled by an acquisitiveness that knows no scruples. Here is one of the sharpest projections of the "economic man" of our civilization, a projection the more remarkable since Gogol caught the middle-class type when it was barely hatched and before its beak and claws were quite discernible. So plausible is this compound of stubborn appetites and wavering aspirations that one finds, as the author did, something of Chichikov in each of us.

There is less complexity in the other characters who are portrayed at full length: the mawkish daydreamer, Manilov, the brutish Sobakevich, the wastrel and mischief-maker, Nozdrev, the old dame, Korobochka, as thrifty as she is stupid, Plushkin, the pathological miser. They are drawn by an artist who, seizing unerringly upon the characteristic gesture, the individual accent, combines a gift for mimicry with a strong sense of the grotesque, a preference for exaggeration and overemphasis. Yet all these creations are solid pieces of humanity, images that come to inhabit the mind as though they had always belonged there. They are flesh of the flesh and bone of the bone of Russia, but they have more than a local validity.

The book deals chiefly with a section of the landed gentry. The provincial bureaucracy is also drawn, but in lesser detail. The officialdom presented here is of a piece with that at which the author pokes fun in *The Inspector General*. As for the lower walks of life, Gogol scarcely ventures into them. He had no doubt a considerable knowledge of the common people and some sympathy for them. On one occasion Chichikov, examining a list of dead serfs he has just acquired, meditates, with a wistfulness quite out of character, on what the lot of each of them had been. Neither the author nor his hero, however, wastes any sentiment on the living specimens of the class, nor are they seen otherwise than as lazy louts who must be kept in hand.

The novelist insisted that his fictions were based on a close acquaintance with observed facts. His mind, he would have us believe, worked not by invention but by induction from a mass of concrete details painstakingly assembled. Indeed, he talked like the Naturalists of a later era, with their zeal for documentation, though of course he did not use their pseudo-scientific jargon. At the same time he avowed that he built his characters by examining himself, that they were, in fact, projections of actual or potential tendencies in his own psyche, and that when his readers laughed at his protagonists they were really laughing at him. In writing the book, he was parading his own faults and thereby freeing himself of them by a kind of spiritual catharsis. Early on he recognized that the most effective way of exorcising his devils was not by representing them as monsters horned and hoofed but as petty miscreants. It was natural for him to do this because, as Pushkin said, he possessed to a supreme degree the gift for evoking *poshlost:* sleek vulgarity pretentiously masking a vacuous conformity.

It was this double process of observation and introspection that allowed Gogol to furnish *Dead Souls* with characters who are at once individuals and recognizable types. Manilov and Sobakevich, to name only two instances, are each of them as much a byword in Russia as Mr. Micawber and Scrooge in the English-speaking world. Indeed, one finds much in Gogol that is akin to Dickens. He has the same eye for the eccentric, the same streak of lyricism, the same passion for reform, though Dickens wanted to change institutions, while Gogol felt that nothing could be accomplished without changing the heart of man. True, the Russian lacks the Englishman's large geniality, yet on the other hand never descends to the depths of his bathos.

In any event, what gives its tone to the book is not simply that the people in it are presented in those terms of the low and the ugly that Aristotle declared appropriate to comedy, but that these comic figures are patterns of mediocrity, that the lives they live are humdrum and paltry, that if any of them show prowess, it is only at the table. The lesser officials are rapacious enough, but their superiors are less knavish than doltish. Here are no criminals, no villains out of melodrama, but ordinary people in whom the moral impulse has become paralyzed or flabby through want of exercise.

Even the rascality of Chichikov is presented as of a relatively venial kind. Whatever he may have done in the past, when we see him in action, he is merely plunging his hand into the grab bag like so many others, and the author is at some pains to point out extenuating circumstances, such as the influence of foul upbringing in the case of Chichikov and of sorry old age in that of Plushkin. There is in Gogol a strain of quasi-sympathy with Chichikov that softens the satire. Apparently the novelist was not steadily subject to the anesthesia of the heart that Bergson held to be essential to the triumph of the comic spirit.

While acknowledging that Chichikov is a specimen of the banality of evil, the author suggests that there is more in this little man than meets the eye, and hints that a remarkable change may yet take place in him. The careful reader will note other more or less discreet allusions to a broadening and deepening of the narrative and to the possibility of its taking on "a majestic lyrical flow." Gogol intimates that the story may yet bring forward "someone worthy to be called a man," a figure of noble stature, or a Russian girl "such as is not to be found anywhere else in the world." There are further passages in the nature of poetic digressions which are utterly at variance with the tone of the book. Thus, in the course of an evocation of the "exposed, desolate, and flat" native landscape, Gogol apostrophizes Russia, asking where, save in this limitless expanse, could a Titan arise and a boundless idea take shape. The book concludes with another equally rhapsodic passage, a paean to the troika, which becomes a symbol of Russia itself, as it dashes past the other nations of the world toward a grand, mysterious goal. As a matter of fact, this ecstatic outburst is occasioned by the speeding up of the troika occupied by no more admirable specimens than Chichikov, in flight from retribution, and his two retainers, the unsavory Petrushka and the oafish Selifan. Here is a striking non sequitur. One can understand Gogol's incongruously proud vision only when one realizes that long before he had concluded this volume, his conception of the "epic" as a whole had undergone a wonderful transformation.

The novel that developed from a mere anecdote came to assume in the author's mind the proportions of a grandiose work. Early in the writing he decided that all of Russia, the lights as well as the shadows, the shame as well as the glory, would be reflected in his novel. He would laugh out of court the foibles and brand the vices of his fellow citizens, but he would also reveal the virtues inherent in the Russian character, so that none could fail to recognize, admire, and emulate them. As he proceeded, another idea seized upon him: he would depict nothing less than the regeneration of man. Book One was peopled with the spiritually blind, halt, and lame. More truly than the buried serfs, they were all "dead souls." But these dry bones would live again. New figures would appear, of a higher order than those in Book One and some, indeed, radiant with moral beauty, but the main theme would be the re-education, the rebirth of Chichikov and of the sad crew with which he was surrounded. The Czar himself was to play a part in reforming him, and the "epic" was to close with Chichikov drawing his first breath as an honest man.

Thus the book would be a kind of *Pilgrim's Progress,* a work which, without having the taint of didacticism, would instruct and edify. But Gogol, acutely conscious of his own failings, felt that such a task lay within the gift only of an author who had himself achieved spiritual health. His mission as a writer, therefore, was at one with his duty as a Christian intent on saving his soul. By reading the Gospels, praying and fasting, he prepared himself for his great undertaking, and to ask a blessing upon it even made a pilgrimage to the Holy Land—it proved a dismal experience. When he was sunk in depression or overcome by illness (he repeatedly felt himself to be on the verge of death), he took refuge in the belief that God would preserve this frail, cracked vessel for the sake of its precious contents.

Dead Souls was to be, like *The Divine Comedy,* a trilogy, with Book One corresponding roughly to Dante's *Inferno.* Gogol dismissed it as merely "a porch hastily constructed by a provincial architect," leading to the magnificent "palace" that was to be.

While he was putting the finishing touches to the first part, he started the sequel that was to occupy him during the decade that remained to him. He wrote and rewrote draft upon draft. By 1845 he had finally completed Book Two, but only to consign it to the flames. If his book was wanting, it was because he was not close enough to moral perfection. Another explanation that he offered of his act was that while he had portrayed human excellence, he had failed to show how the generality of men might achieve it. This pietist was concerned about ethical techniques.

It was all the more painful for him to destroy his manuscript, since he had hoped that it would correct the misapprehensions that Book One had aroused in the public mind. Like *The Inspector General* before it, *Dead Souls* had beeen taken as a condemnation of the existing order. Nothing could have been further from the author's thought. He was a firm believer in the sanctity of established institutions. All that was necessary for the achievement of both spiritual and material welfare was for each man to do his duty in the position in which God had seen fit to place him. This credo Gogol felt he must publish to the world. To express it, however inadequately, he allowed some excerpts from his correspondence to be printed. And then, in anguish of mind and heart, he started his Penelope work on *Dead Souls* all over again. He kept at it desperately, although he was beginning to question both his ability as a writer and, under the influence of a morbid asceticism, the ethical propriety of literature itself. On the night of February 23, 1852, he burned what may have been another complete text of Book Two. Ten days later he died, during an acute attack of the morbid depression to which he had long since been subject.

In spite of repeated burnings, two versions of a fragment of Book Two have been preserved, one early and one of later date. Although in his last years Gogol was obviously sick in mind as well as in body, the fact that he destroyed his manuscript would seem to indicate that his critical judgment remained intact. He must have had shattering periods of awareness, when he realized that he was incapable of the task that alone seemed to him to justify him as a writer. Affirmation was beyond him. When he tried to sing hosannas, his voice went flat. The figures that were to exemplify the strength and nobility of the Russian character, like the lovely Ulinka, the industrious Skudronzhlogo, and the devout millionaire, Murazov, are as lifeless as they are virtuous. Nor was Gogol successful in his efforts to show a man rising on the stepping-stones of his dead selves to higher things. All these attempts reveal Gogol's weaknesses, his intellectual blind spots, his curiously deficient moral sense. There are some excellent passages in what remains of Book Two, but they are no different from what is to be found in Book One, and depict the same unregenerate humanity: a shyster lawyer, a gentleman farmer with a mania for administrative machinery, a country squire remarkable for the Homeric feasts that he spreads. What chiefly redeems the tedium is the presence of our old friend, Chichikov himself, who, until nearly the very end, is the same amiable swindler that he was earlier.

After all, *Dead Souls* must be judged by the first volume, the only one that Gogol completed to his satisfaction. One cannot read it without recognizing that its unhappy author belongs in the company of those masters of comedy, Aristophanes and Cervantes, Molière and Mark Twain. As far as his own country was concerned, the novel was a landmark in more senses than one. It contributed, though this was unintentional and indeed in spite of the author's wishes, to the discrediting of the ancestral order. Young Russia, chafing under the tyrannical paternalism of Nicholas I and already dreaming of a democratic way of life, drew conclusions from the book that the novelist was at pains to repudiate. The portrayal of a stupid and corrupt officialdom was regarded as an indictment of the political system. The picture of the gentry was taken as a powerful if indirect plea for abolition. In the comedy that Gogol unfolded, the liberal public was struck by the incongruity between the superior status of the serf-owners and their failure to function in any socially useful fashion. What were they but a set of conscienceless parasites, wasting or grossly devouring what they had not produced, mere cumberers of the earth?

The novel laid the foundation for the critical realism that flourished down to the end of the century and that is so distinctive a trait of Russian literature. Gogol's successors lacked his humor, but like him they seized upon the seamy side of things, out of a desire to see reality reshaped after an image of perfection. Eager to have literature bear directly upon life, they appear to have inherited his peculiarly keen sense of the writer's civic responsibility. Although they appreciated, as he did not, the importance for good or evil of the institutions under which man lives, their works carry implicitly the injunction with which Gogol opened the unfinished testament jotted down in his last days: "Be living souls, not dead souls!"

I I I

Turgenev–A Revaluation

III

Turgenev—A Revaluation

I N his student years Turgenev, who was slow in discovering his
true medium, broke into print with some verse. Then he tried
his hand at writing for the stage. He failed to achieve distinction as a poet. Although he made at least one permanent contribution to the Russian repertory with *A Month in the Country,*
his interest in drama did not persist. He grew to dislike his plays
and he kept his poems out of his collected works: a poem, like an
oyster, was worthless, he said, if it was less than perfect. The alle-
gories, fantasies, and lyrical pieces which make up the work of his
old age, *Poems in Prose,* are examples of a hybrid genre lacking
both the form and the substance of poetry.

In his late twenties he published several romantic stories, which
passed unnoticed. His work began to attract attention only when
he started publishing serially, under the general title, *A Hunter's
Notes,* better known as *A Sportsman's Sketches,* short pieces ranging from sketches with a factual slant to more formal stories. They
are held together by the device of presenting them as accounts of
the narrator's experiences during his excursions in pursuit of game.
Turgenev wrote many of them abroad, where he had gone to be
close to Pauline Viardot, the prima donna with whom, on her first
visit to Russia, he had fallen desperately and permanently in love.
His great reputation dates from the publication of the *Sketches* in
book form in 1852, when he was a man of thirty-four.

The work owed its great initial success in part to the fact that it
was taken as an attack on serfdom, the abolition of which was then
a burning issue. It is hardly an abolitionist tract, however. Turge-

nev abominated serfdom, but he was not a crusader by temperament, and could no more engage in propaganda than he could stand on his head. In half the pieces the dangerous subject is not touched upon at all. It may be noted that when the book was in the writing the author inherited from that domineering dowager, his mother, fifteen thousand acres and two thousand male "souls," and that until the Emancipation he remained the owner, an uneasy one, it is true, of what his friend Herzen called "baptized property." It is certain, nevertheless, that the book did materially help to create an atmosphere hostile to the perpetuation of serfdom, and may indeed have played a part in disposing the Emperor in favor of the peasant reform.

The movement against Russian serfdom is a battle long ago. Yet after the lapse of more than a century *A Sportsman's Sketches* still makes uncommonly good reading. It has an evergreen freshness. An outdoor, wholesome book, it is written out of an intimate knowledge of and sensitiveness to the natural scene, its shapes and colors, its sounds and odors. Felicitously these pages evoke the landscape that Turgenev knew best, that of Central Russia, where the forest gives way to the grasslands. It is a landscape with figures. The author's main concern here, as in the bulk of his work, is with human beings. The book is, indeed, more than anything else, an album of likenesses, each sharply visualized, whether silhouettes or full-length portraits. Some are of the peasantry. There was much in simple people that attracted Turgenev, not least their spiritual wholeness and their ability to face life with instinctive stoicism. His sympathy for the underdog does not blur his vision. The serfs are drawn with full appreciation of their humanity, but there is no attempt to gloss over the brutalizing effects of their position or to conceal the fact that, given half a chance, they can turn into ruthless despoilers of their fellows. But among the villagers who catch the author's eye are those who possess dignity and moral resources, and, with some alloy of superstition, a certain spirituality. The masters lose in comparison with the men. Not evil by nature, they are hopelessly corrupted by unlimited power over the human beings they own. Quietly but firmly, sometimes by a casual remark, the author lays bare their sense of caste, their grossness, their cruelty toward their serfs, and, most emphatically, their managerial ineptitude.

Turgenev's attitude here is, as it will continue to be, that of a bystander observing the scene before him. He keeps a distance between himself and his material, which allows him perspective, but which often makes for a somewhat chilling detachment. At the same time this observer has an immense curiosity about people and is, furthermore, able to set down what he sees with a sure, if delicate touch. Because of its easy style, its candor, its apparent freedom from all contriving, *A Sportsman's Sketches* gives the impression of complete authenticity. A work that, for all its parochialism, has something universal about it, it is a supplement to, all but a match for, Gogol's *Dead Souls*.

With the publication of *A Sportsman's Sketches* in book form, Turgenev decided that he had come to the close of a period of his life as an author, and must strike out in a new direction. "I am done with extracting the triple essence of human character," he wrote to a friend, "pouring it into small bottles: 'Sniff it, please, gentle reader, uncork it and sniff it; it has the Russian bouquet, hasn't it?' Enough, enough!" He must adopt a new manner. He must put his mind to a studied piece of work, on a large scale, a novel. But was he capable of "something great and calm"? He knew he couldn't tell until he tried.

In the thirty years that were left him he did produce several long narratives that are usually classed as novels. At the same time he continued to write short pieces. He curbed an inclination to flippancy and a weakness for odd characters, but his manner underwent a less clearly discernible change than his matter. Men and women of the people practically disappeared from his fictions, except as accessory figures, kept well in the background. True, the very year that *A Sportsman's Sketches* was published he wrote two peasant tales. One, which Carlyle pronounced the most pathetic story in the world, is the widely anthologized "Moomoo," an account of the miseries of a gentle giant of a serf, deaf and dumb, almost a symbolical figure. Furthermore, many years later Turgenev added to *A Sportsman's Sketches* a piece about a peasant woman reduced to little more than a living corpse, yet accepting her bleak lot with a meekness and fortitude more than human. Henceforth he was to draw his models from the middle class: members of the gentry and people whom education had raised above their unprivileged status.

Not many of his thirty-odd stories have the concentration and simple charm of "The Tryst," "The Singers," "Bezhin Meadow" (in *A Sportsman's Sketches*), but if there is little more by way of plot, they do have more substance. A distillate of character continues to be their main ingredient. In one of his few public addresses Turgenev elaborated a theory of personality, the gist of which was that mankind consists of Hamlets and Don Quixotes, or, more exactly, of persons in whom the hamletic and the quixotic elements are mixed in varying proportions. This view of human nature was useful to him in the construction of his characters, though a healthy instinct kept him from applying the formula with mechanical rigidity. Of course, his best creations refuse to be pigeonholed. Himself a man with a hamletic streak in his makeup, he satisfied his urge to project men and, more especially, women of the opposite temper. Yet it is significant that even his strong characters are not shown as having realized their ends. Either they die young, their work undone, or their achievements are merely mentioned as a thing of the future.

A variant of the hamletic type appears in an early narrative which was not included in *A Sportsman's Sketches*, "The Diary of a Superfluous Man." This is a characteristic piece of writing, though it does not show the author at his best. Like so many of his tales, it is a story of frustration and failure, enveloped in an atmosphere damp with pathos. Indeed, pathos is the earmark of Turgenev's art. The diarist is defeated in love and, as a victim of consumption, he is defeated in a more elementary, biological sense.

Both he and his lucky rival are unworthy of the young heroine. Woman's superiority to man was a belief at which Turgenev arrived early in life. The theme of woman's moral supremacy haunts him as a recurrent dream haunts the mind. It is present in that singularly malformed tale "A Quiet Spot," in which a high-minded young beauty is passionately involved with an amiable weakling, who eventually succumbs to drink. The author's skill in portraiture renders plausible both characters, but not the suicide of the girl: he seldom manages drastic action effectively.

"A Quiet Spot" offers in passing a glimpse of the confined, uneventful, leisurely existence of the provincial gentry. It is a tale of unrequited passion, a love story, like nearly all of Turgenev's fictions. Nothing so fascinates him as does this force welling up from irrational depths. Now it floods the heart with "the gay terror" of impending happiness. Now its enchantment creates a new personality. It can clothe the world in glory, it can give a man wings, but it can also act on him like a disease. It "seizes a human being as a hawk does a chick. . . ." It may exalt or crush the finer instincts. Be it good or evil, Turgenev's preoccupation with it is basically in terms not of sensuality but of sentiment. And never does he show fulfillment. He is content to paint the dawn and occasionally the afterglow of love.

His particular delight is to celebrate the secret inception and first stirrings of young love, all compact of expectation and foreboding. Thus in "First Love" he succeeds in capturing the bliss and torment of a schoolboy passion, seen retrospectively in that mood of melting nostalgia to which he not seldom yields. The most striking backdrop for the action here is what Russians call a "sparrow night": a short summer night tremulous with heat lightning, which is peculiarly appropriate to the mood of the piece. Memories of a dead love are also the substance of "Asya." This haunting story revolves about a rather likable youth who, like so many of Turgenev's male characters, is lacking in ardor and tenacity. At the psychological moment he fails to respond to the feeling he has aroused in the moody, passionate heroine. Fate intervening, their first embrace is also the last—a situation that recurs in Turgenev's work. The youth thus misses his chance of happiness. The story might take as its epigraph the remark of a character in one of Turgenev's later novels: "Man is weak, woman is strong, chance is all-powerful."

The pleasant young man with a fatal flaw in his make-up reappears in that rather mawkish tale "Torrents of Spring." Sanin falls in love with an angelic, ravishingly beautiful girl, but ignominiously betrays her by allowing himself to be seduced by a hardly more credible predatory siren. Although his enslavement lasts only a few years, his life is wrecked. Like the protagonist of "Asya," he is doomed to drag out the existence of a lonely old bachelor. It is tempting to relate this emphasis on joyless celibacy to a personal predicament of the novelist's. Because of his lifelong attachment to Pauline Viardot, the exact nature and history of which will probably never be known, he had no family of his own, and, moreover, was an expatriate during the last twenty years of his life. He had an illegitimate daughter by one of his mother's laundresses, but she did not live with him. The situation nourished his self-pity and the sense of unfulfillment that shadows his pages.

Other stories of his dwell on the irrationality and the power of love. That it is the most unfathomable of life's mysteries is the conclusion reached by the narrator in "A Hapless Girl," a somber, melodramatic tale with a tragic finale. The familiar thesis is illustrated more successfully in "The Brigadier," which, in spite of its meanderings, has the verisimilitude of a case history. In a totally different genre is his last story, "Clara Milich." An unconventional young actress falls in love with a backward, characterless youth, and, when he fails to reciprocate, poisons herself. Dead, she succeeds where alive she failed: the ghost takes possession of Aratov. Turgenev was never more emphatic in assigning the active role in the relationship to the woman. Aratov dies (of "a fever complicated by inflammation of the heart"), with a blissful smile on his lips, his fingers clutching a strand of his phantom bride's hair. His last words are that love is stronger than death. Turgenev would have been glad to believe this, but his work offers abundant evidence that he did not.

In quite a few of his stories everyday life is invaded by the supernatural. Like Hawthorne, he is careful to leave a loophole for a natural explanation, yet the impression these narratives are apparently intended to leave is that there are more things in heaven and earth than are dreamt of in positivist philosophy. Turgenev kept circling about the occult and peering beyond the gates of the unknown. But for all his romantic streak, he was a man of realistic temper, secular, sober, skeptical. His spectral tales are the nadir of his art. In almost all of them only the creaking machinery of the supernatural is present. An admirable reporter, he could seldom write convincingly about matters outside the range of his experience.

One turns with relief from these apparitions and prophetic dreams, from mesmerism and Oriental magic, to the clear-eyed bitter realism of "A King Lear of the Steppes." In this magnificent story the wicked daughters, far from suffering punishment, attain to power and authority, and, furthermore, lead happy lives. Equally compelling is that fine character study "Old Portraits." One of Turgenev's last stories, it is based on memories of his early years. Indeed, a reminiscential strain pervades many of his shorter narratives. Thus, "Old Portraits," one of the best of them, evokes the charm of the placid past when the foundations of the ancestral order were still firm, but does not gloss over its horrors. The story ends on a note harsher than any sounded in the peasant tales. A serf, a gay little fellow who is made much of as an accomplished dancer, comes into the possession of a master who goads him cruelly. One day the gentle soul splits his owner's skull with an axe. "Those were good old days—but let's be done with them," are the closing words.

"A King Lear of the Steppes" may be classed as a novelette, and "Torrents of Spring" comes closer to the proportions of a novel. Turgenev himself dignified by that name only six of his tales, all written between 1855 and 1876: *Rudin, A House of Gentlefolk, On the Eve, Fathers and Children, Smoke,* and *Virgin Soil.* They are poles removed from the huge, sprawling, tumultuous novels of Dostoevsky. Nor does any of them approach *War and Peace* in sweep and massiveness. *Rudin* hardly achieves the stature of a novel. Only *A House of Gentlefolk* and *On the Eve* exhibit an economy, coherence, and compactness that gives them a formal beauty. The other novels, particularly *Smoke,* do not hang together so well. Henry James, who admired Turgenev this side idolatry, and whose work shows traces of his influence, considered his finest novel to be *On the Eve. Virgin Soil* is ampler, and *Fathers and Children,* though structurally less satisfactory, what with the comings and goings crowded into the few weeks during which the action unfolds, has passages of greater depth than any other of Turgenev's novels.

His method, generally, is to concentrate on one or more crucial episodes and to report briefly the antecedent and subsequent developments which serve to round out the cycle of the lives involved. As a rule the stories are told by an omniscient narrator, the author or another. Objective though he is, he can never keep himself completely out of the picture. Now and then he offers on obtrusive generalization or puts in a gnomic remark. Rarely, however, does he introduce a character who functions as his mouthpiece. Exceptions are the argumentative Potugin in *Smoke* and Uvar Ivanovich, the penetrating old glutton who acts as a tongue-tied commentator, in *On the Eve.* Turgenev practically never explores the sensibilities of his characters through the consciousness of an observer, the author's alert but not all-knowing deputy. The action is usually slight and takes place within a short period of time. There is no concern for suspense. The design is simple, its dominant principle being antithesis: the strong woman versus the weak man, the pure virgin versus the Jezebel, the idealist versus the philistine. Except for *Virgin Soil,* these novels give the impression of expanded short stories. They argue shortness of breath on the author's part. Can it be that Turgenev's genius, like

Chekhov's after him, was most at home with the minor form? He himself seems to have thought so. "Who looks for a novel in the epic sense of the word," he once remarked, "needn't come to me. . . . No matter what I write, it will always be a series of sketches." Fortunately, there is room for novels that are not epic in character.

As might be supposed, "the great constrigent relation between man and woman" plays an important part in the novels, as it does in the rest of Turgenev's work. Here, as nearly everywhere else, he dwells on the romance of love, rather than on passion or durable affection. Even in *Fathers and Children,* a novel of ideas, it has a prominent role. Arkady's entanglement with the two sisters is delineated with all the delicacy and understanding of which Turgenev was capable in dealing with young lovers. Alone in *Virgin Soil* is the love motif somewhat muted. It is paramount in *A House of Gentlefolk.* Steeped in pathos, the story of Liza and Lavretzky is framed to illustrate the evanescence of happiness, which is no sooner grasped than it escapes. With this theme goes another motif dear to Turgenev's heart: the melancholy wisdom of renunciation. Time was when countless hearts were wrung by the sorrows of this ill-fated pair. In our dry-eyed age few tears are likely to be shed over a heroine who takes the veil to expiate the sin of having fallen in love with another woman's husband, whom she had mistaken for a widower, and over a hero who accepts this decision without protest. Yet though some of these pages have a faded look, it is not difficult to surrender to the art with which the progress of the brief romance is traced in this finely wrought period piece. In *Rudin* the love affair serves as a test of the protagonist, "a man of words, but not of deeds," a test that he ignominiously fails. The involvement here is the familiar one of the high-hearted girl with a weakling of a man.

There are in these novels specimens of conventional girlhood and motherhood, "emancipated" members of the sex, one or two aged harpies and delightful old ladies, and several horrible women: the promiscuous creature who is Lavretzky's first wife;

the seductive society belle of easy morals who nearly captures Litvinov (in *Smoke*); the unscrupulous wife of Nezhdanov's employer (in *Virgin Soil*). Unique in Turgenev's gallery is the undersexed lady of the beautiful shoulders (in *Fathers and Children*) through whom Bazarov learns that love is not all a matter of physiology. The center of the stage, however, is usually occupied by a lovely woman of exceptional moral stature, who has the wisdom of the heart as well as of the mind. It is to her that the novels owe their special fragrance and sometimes their meaning. She appears in various guises, all having a family resemblance. These spiritual sisters are idealistic creatures with an intense nature controlled by a firm will. Their stories, which are paralleled in the shorter narratives, form a legend of good women, as true in love as any of Chaucer's, but with no Cleopatras or Medeas among them.

The most vital example of the type is Yelena (in *On the Eve*). Before our eyes this dreamy girl turns into a woman, singleminded, intransigent, faithful unto death and beyond. She has the bearing of an Antigone. That she should give herself to her lover before their marriage (a bold stroke for so Victorian a novelist) and start with her husband for the hardships and dangers of an alien land might be put down to nothing more unusual than the impulsiveness of a romantic girl deeply in love. But when her husband dies before they reach their destination, the young widow knows neither despair nor confusion. She does not weakly return to her people and her own country. Instead, she resumes her journey to the savage Balkans, resolved to carry on the work to which her husband had dedicated himself: the freeing of his countrymen from the Turkish yoke.

Yelena throws in her lot with a militant Bulgarian nationalist. She plays Ruth to her Insarov's Naomi. For Russia had not bred— not yet—fit mates for her kind: her suitors had been a mercurial artist, a timid pedant, and a soulless bureaucrat. In *A House of Gentlefolk* Liza too is wooed by a young official who is a shallow, self-seeking worldling. But she does meet a Russian who is all but worthy of her. Among philistines and scoundrels, fools and toadies, the author places in a prominent position not only hamletic characters like Rudin and like Nezhdanov (in *Virgin Soil*), but also men of the type of Lavretzky. These members of a gentry that has had its day are honest, well-intentioned, sensitive, and, at least potentially, useful citizens, but they are no towers of strength. Rising head and shoulders above them are only Insarov, the dedicated soul who lives for a cause, Solomin (in *Virgin Soil*), a man of broad social vision and firm purpose, and, of course, Bazarov, the "Nihilist."

The times favored "engaged" literature; they demanded of the author that he embrace his age and contribute to its self-knowledge. The public looked for guidance to writers of fiction and expected to find in their works an echo of its fears and hopes, a confrontation of the *Zeitgeist*. Though his natural bent was toward the intimate rather than the public theme—he protested that he had no *"politisches Pathos"* and that "to a man of letters politics is poison"—Turgenev tried to live up to these expectations. His novels, unlike his shorter narratives, show a concern for the political questions of the day. The ultimate relevance of the short stories is one of personal morality. They carry no social message, fly no programmatic flag. They have to do with individuals in their private capacity, facing the problems of the inner life and meeting their separate fates. The protagonists of the novels, on the contrary, have a social dimension. These are pages from the history of Russia during the middle decades of the past century, when the country was in the throes of the revolutionary change from a serf economy to one based on free labor.

Thus *Rudin* reflects a phase in the development of the Russian intellectual. The hero's failure on the personal level, in his relationship with Natalya, is seen as symbolic of the inadequacy of the generation to which he, and his creator, belonged: "the idealists of the thirties." Scions of the gentry, nurtured for the most part in a hothouse atmosphere of German Romantic literature and philosophy, they were volubly devoted to the good, the true, and the beautiful. But they were apt to be strangers in their own country, rootless men, unfit for action and incapable of feeling, given as they were to an excess of self-analysis. Before the story comes to an end, the author make a valiant attempt to arouse our sympathy for Rudin. The man, he argues, has high moral standards, and his rhetoric, since it can kindle the young with enthusiasm for lofty principles, is a power for good. And the poor devil comes to a quixotic end—an afterthought of Turgenev's, the account of Rudin's death on a barricade in revolutionary Paris on June 26, 1848, appearing only in the second edition of the tale, several years after it was first published.

A man of Rudin's stripe appears in *A House of Gentlefolk,* which is also set in the forties. This "Poltava Demonsthenes" is, however, a wholly subsidiary figure. The leading character, Lavretzky, is not a seedy, déclassé intellectual, but the owner of many "souls" and broad acres, a likable, cultivated, well-intentioned man. For a few rapt hours he had believed that he would mend his broken life with the aid of Liza's love. We catch our last glimpse of him when, after a lapse of years, he returns, a lonely, aging man, to the scene of his brief bliss. Yet he faces existence with serenity, a serenity born of renunciation: he has given up hope of personal happiness and learned to find contentment in useful work. The moral of the tale is not without faint social overtones. Attention is called to the fact that Liza, whose character had been formed by her peasant nurse, talks to a villager without a trace of condescension. In managing his estates, Lavretzky, whose mother had been a serf, has at heart not only his own interests but also those of his peasants. It is in character that, in an argument with Liza's odious suitor, he should demand reverence for the moral values (*pravda*) cherished by the Russian masses.

On the Eve opens on a summer's day in 1853. Before it closes, the guns have spoken, and Russia is in the midst of a war, the end of which will usher in the period of great reforms. Living up to its title, the novel reflects the anticipatory spirit of the years that opened into the stormy sixties. This is something other than the atmosphere of futility dominating *Rudin* and the aura of nostalgic melancholy enveloping *A House of Gentlefolk*. Insarov dies without striking a blow in the fight for which his life had been a preparation. Yelena, his widow, goes off to carry on his work and is lost to view. The story ends on a mournfully meditative note. Nevertheless, this novel breathes the tonic air of promise. To the contemporary reader it was both a reproach addressed to a remiss generation and a pledge that the time was near when Russia would breed men, like the Bulgarian, possessed by the will to fight for the freedom of their country. It was more than a pledge: Yelena became the model for the young women who in the next generation were to lay down their lives for the Revolution.

The months that Turgenev spent on writing the novel were those of the historic year during which the terms of the abolition of serfdom were finally formulated and the decree made public. The epoch-making Emancipation Act, which dealt a severe blow to the ancestral order, was promulgated in the early spring of 1861. *Fathers and Children* was completed that summer and printed in February, 1862, in a single issue of the leading Moscow monthly. The appearance of this work was of major significance.

As the title indicates, it is a variation on the stock theme of the antagonism between the generations. That motif is essential to the pattern of the novel but the heart of it is the emergence of democratic radicalism. What gives the book its weight is the fact that it brings into focus the initial phase of opposition to the existing sociopolitical order in mid-nineteenth-century Russia. The action is set in the summer of 1859. The intelligentsia was then beginning to lose its upper-class character. Its ranks were being infiltrated by educated commoners. Not unnaturally, some of them were prominent in the incipient revolt against the Establishment, which rested on the triple pillars of the Church, the Throne, and serfdom. The typical plebeian iconoclast is represented by Bazarov, the principal character in *Fathers and Children*.

Bazarov exhibits to the full Turgenev's power to give body and breath to his characters. The budding medico's impulses and convictions are made as real to us as his long face with its sandy sideburns and his cool green eyes. From the moment when he is first seen in no haste to offer his red hand to his host to the moment, several months later, when this atheist lifts an eyelid in horror as he is made to receive the last sacrament, he is the center and pivot of the tale, literally its hero. Tough-minded and hard-fisted, a model of steadfastness, he is unique among Turgenev's male characters, dominating the action and throwing the other *dramatis personae,* all of them marvels of portraiture, into the shade. If he is brash, arrogant, boorish, it is perhaps because he finds himself among people who are incapable of understanding his ideas, who are out of sympathy with them, and who, worst of all, do not take them seriously. The reader fancies that he behaves differently when he is among those who share his views. The indication is that such a congenial group does exist. His is not a lone voice crying in the wilderness.

In an early scene he shocks his wellborn middle-aged hosts by announcing that he and those of like mind reject "everything," and he is willing to call himself and his kind "Nihilists." He spurns religion, lashes out at poetry, music, the romantic conception of love and marriage—in short he discards the ways of thinking and feeling that he associates with the gentry, a class that this grandson of a serf, who is proud of his background, hates with all his heart. What he affirms is also eloquent of his scorn for gentility. Empirical, crudely materialistic science has his fanatical allegiance. He champions utilitarian ethics, holds society to be responsible for the moral and physical ills of its individual members, exalts the virtues of labor. ("Nature is not a temple but a workshop, and in it man is a toiler.")

Bazarov's "Nihilism" is not a matter of ideas and theories only. In taking leave of his young friend, who is a parlor Nihilist, he declares, "Your kind can't get any further than high-minded meekness or high-minded fuming, and that's fiddlesticks. For one thing, you won't fight, and yet you fancy yourselves capital fellows —but we want to fight. Furthermore, our dust will make your eyes smart, our filth will soil you, and, besides, you haven't grown up to our level, involuntarily you admire yourself, you take pleasure in damning yourself. That bores us—give us others to damn! We need to smash others!"

In censored pages it was not possible to specify whom and for what "we" meant to fight. Turgenev came close to supplying the answers in a private letter that he composed shortly after the appearance of the novel. "My entire tale," he wrote, "is directed against the gentry as a leading class." About his conception of Bazarov's personality he had this to say: "He is called a Nihilist, read: a revolutionary. . . . I envisaged a somber figure, savage, huge, only half emerged from the soil, strong, bristling, upright— and doomed to perish, because he stands only on the threshold of the future—I dreamed of some strange match to Pugachov and his like." It must be admitted that our Nihilist has little in common with the Cossack adventurer who, giving himself out to be the Emperor Peter III, led a vast peasant rebellion against the land-lords in the reign of Catherine the Great. But there is in Bazarov the stuff that goes to the making of a wrecker, a destroyer, a revo-lutionary: intolerance, lack of squeamishness, scorn for moral scruples, a large capacity for hatred, contempt for moderation and patchwork, reliance on the arbitrament of force. Rudin, like Lavretzky, can be fully understood only in the context of his age and country. As a projection of the radical temper, Bazarov, though profoundly Russian, is a figure possessed of universal validity.

Turgenev himself was not a revolutionary either by tempera-ment or conviction. Quite the contrary. A democrat and a professed gradualist, he pinned his faith to education and peaceful reform as the only way for Russia to achieve a free, open society. But he was instinctively attracted to the rebellion of which he was himself incapable, returning to the subject of the Russian Revolution in his last novel.

Turgenev spoke of Bazarov as his favorite brainchild, and he managed to communicate his own fascination to generations of readers. He consigns his hero to an untimely end in order to underline the fact that, as he said, Bazarov was born too soon. The Nihilist's last days and his parents' grief are depicted in pages that belong to the most expressive and moving in fiction. The young man dies of a stupid accident—illustrative of Russia's backwardness—without striking a single blow in the fight to which he looks forward so eagerly; but his creator must have known intuitively that the Bazarovs were destined to a long and fateful career.

In the novels considered thus far, particularly the last two, the private difficulties of the characters are seen against the larger predicament of the country itself, of this vast, dark, inert Russia. Whence will salvation come? Turgenev's answer in *Smoke* is that of a good European who knew no other remedy for the ills of society than "the homeopathy of science and civilization." Alone slow, patient, "pedagogical" activity conducted at the grass-roots level can help. The Russians must learn the rational methods, the habits of industry and efficiency that have produced the civilization of the West. And it behooves them to be humble. The diatribes of Potugin, Turgenev's mouthpiece, against patriotic self-vaunting make timely reading today.

In spite of his "kowtowing to the West," Turgenev, as a Russian classic, has not been put on the Index (from 1918 to 1955 thirty-six million copies of his works in fifty-two languages were printed in the Soviet Union). The twenty-eight-volume Moscow edition of his works and letters, begun in 1957, was completed in time for the celebration of the hundred and fiftieth anniversary of his birth on November 9, 1818 (N.S.). His writings, along with those of other Russian authors in the liberal tradition, must be exerting their humanizing influence at home.

The message of *Smoke* is underscored by its satire. Gall drips from the pen of this mild man. His animus is directed against two sets in the Russian summer colony at Baden: on the one hand, the titled aristocrat yearning for the fleshpots of serfdom (the action is laid in the year following the Emancipation), and, on the other, the lunatic fringe of the radical camp. The reactionaries, with their stupidity and illimitable egoism, and the fire-eaters, ridden by a doctrinaire fury, are shown as brothers under the skin, equally alienated from the people. Not that the mystique of Populism, whether of the Slavophil or the socialist variety, could be acceptable to Turgenev. The rights of the individual were paramount with him.

The Westernist credo and the political caricature are dovetailed, not very skillfully, into a love story, a tragic variant of which will appear several years later as *Torrents of Spring*. The satire is heavy-handed, the love story convinces. In spite of its title, which of course refers to Litvinov's meditation on the insubstantiality of all things human, *Smoke* is by no means another monument to futility. And this not only because the novelist allows his hero eventually to rebuild his personal life and engage in honorable, useful work, thus, for once, providing a happy ending. Litvinov is one of those competent, practical, public-spirited men who, being pioneers of civilization, are Russia's hope, and, Turgenev suggests, whose number is growing. Finally, there is the boon of Emancipation. Litvinov, at last returning to his estates, finds disorder and confusion. Yet, above the troubled waters of Russian life, "moved, like the spirit of God, freedom."

Virgin Soil, the last of the novels, is the most explicitly political of the lot. It deals with the inchoate revolutionary movement of the late sixties. The two young people who are the central characters are drawn together by a community of ideals that they mistake for love. Marianna's devotion to the cause of Populism (*narodnichestvo*) is depicted with the feeling with which Turgenev usually celebrates the personal relation. She is a virginal, dauntless creature, ready to die for her convictions. Nezhdanov, on the other hand, is another variation on the hamletic theme, a frustrate and divided soul, involved in revolutionary action only through adventitious circumstances and eventually losing faith in it.

In the end Marianna finds her true mate in Solomin. It is upon the strong plebeian shoulders of men like this hard-headed, hard-working engineer, the author implies, that the future of Russia rests. Like the conspirators who consider him one of their own, he hates the decaying feudal class and the equally predatory bourgeoisie which is bound to supplant it. But he does not share his comrades' belief in the imminence of the agrarian revolution. "A gradualist from below," anticipating the Fabians, he envisages a long, peaceful preparatory process of an essentially educational character. The epigraph to the book speaks of the necessity of tilling virgin soil with a plow that cuts deep. Turgenev meant not violence, but enlightenment. The lesson offered here is the same as that of *Smoke*. And again the beneficiaries of the existing order, whether frankly reactionary or hiding behind a spurious progressivism, are given no quarter. On the other hand, some of the freaks and crackpots who plot peasant uprisings and actually precipitate an ill-starred miniature *Putsch,* are treated with a certain amount of affection. In no other piece of fiction does Turgenev so unmistakably show his democratic sympathies.

The weakness of the novel is apparent when it is contrasted with Dostoevsky's work on virtually the same theme: *Devils* (better known as *The Possessed*). This book, born of fear and wrath, in spite of its distortions gets at the heart of the matter in revealing the possibilities of perversion in the process of revolution. It is clear that the subject is alien to Turgenev. Just as in some of his short stories there are the mechanics of the supernatural without its atmosphere, so here we have the apparatus of conspiracy without its animating spirit. Nevertheless, there are some fine touches in the book. Turgenev properly finds in a sense of injury, inferiority, failure, a mainspring of the revolutionary mood. Paklin, the unhappy fellow traveler, is one of the novelist's most subtly conceived characters. The facts regarding the movement are depicted with more accuracy than might be expected, considering that the author was an expatriate who got his information about underground activities at second hand.

Just as Dostoevsky intended a sequel to *The Brothers Kar-*

amazov, so Turgenev in his last years began a novel that was to be in the nature of a continuation of *Virgin Soil.* He started writing it in 1881 and promised a translation of it to the London *Century Magazine,* but the severe illness to which he was to succumb prevented him from going on with the work. In his obituary of Turgenev, W. R. S. Ralston, the novelist's translator, summarizes the plot of the tale, which he was to translate under the author's supervision, as follows. A Russian girl with Nihilist sympathies settles in Paris, where she meets and eventually marries a French socialist. For some time the couple are happy. Then the wife makes the acquaintance of a young compatriot of hers who is an émigré revolutionist. He opens her eyes to the deep differences between Western socialism and its Russian counterpart. To her horror, she recognizes that in thought and feeling an abyss divides her from her husband. "How the story was to end," Ralston admits, "I know not." Other accounts of the plot have the heroine falling in love with her compatriot and leaving her French husband. This finale would suggest that at the end Turgenev toned down his Westernism, and also became more friendly toward the cause of militant *narodnichestvo* than he showed himself to be in *Virgin Soil.* Several persons are said to have seen fragments of the work in progress, but none has come to light so far.

Looking back on his novels, Turgenev wrote in 1880, three years before his death: ". . . I strove, within the limits of my powers and ability, conscientiously and impartially to represent and incarnate in appropriate types both what Shakespeare called 'the body and pressure of the time' and the rapidly changing countenance of educated Russians, who have been the predominant object of my observations." The artist speaks here in the accents of the memoirist or the social historian. Indeed, their procedure was not uncongenial to Turgenev. Some of the pieces in *A Sportsman's Sketches* straddle the borderline between fact and fiction. "The Brigadier" contains the text of a letter that Turgenev had found among his mother's papers. As one reads the long dossierlike digressions in his novels, one feels that a first-rate biographer was lost in him.

"Every line I have ever written," he told an American visitor, "has been inspired by something that has actually happened to me or come within my observation." He had the huntsman's eye and ear, as well as a prodigious memory upon which he leaned heavily. He insisted that he discovered rather than invented his characters, drawing them only after they had, in the Russian phrase, "calloused his eyes." George Moore acutely remarked that Turgenev's imagination was illuminative rather than creative. Naturally, he transmuted the empirical data with which he worked, and at some point in the process of composition the unconscious put its hand to the wheel. Indeed, he asserted that he wrote *Fathers and Children* almost in a trance, so that he was sometimes surprised at what came from his pen.

The body of his work is of unquestionable documentary value and adds more richly to knowledge than this implies. Within its confines the student will find much that is flesh of the flesh and bone of the bone of "the strangest and most wonderful people in the world," as Turgenev in an expansive moment described his compatriots. To open his books is to enter a lost world under the guidance of one of its inhabitants. Over it hangs a breath of decay. Perhaps for that reason he tends to hark back to his early years, when the old order was less rickety, and to carryovers from a more remote past. "Old Portraits," as also the eighteenth-century vignette, a miniature masterpiece, in *Virgin Soil,* shows how skillful Turgenev could be in animating amiable fossils. But for all his nostalgia, nothing was further from his mind than the wish to turn the clock backward. The existing order is doomed, he knows, but a better society lies within man's grasp. All that is needed to obtain the conditions of justice and freedom is persevering work carried on in an atmosphere of enlightenment. There were, however, recurrent moments of dejection when he doubted the possibility of such work or of such an atmosphere.

To a generation that has seen what ours has seen there is something unreal about pages that imply the meliorist position dictated by the liberal's faith in reason and science. Turgenev has little to say about the evil in the heart of man. He does, however, convey a sense of Fate's malfeasance in some of his most memorable scenes: that, for instance, of Insarov's end in Venice, and particularly the description of Bazarov's death, one of the cruelest as it is also one of the tenderest things in literature. Characteristically enough, this powerful, ruthlessly veracious passage is not allowed its full force. It ends on a pietistic note that rings hollow. Turgenev has his lapses of taste. Reading "First Love," for example, one of his best stories, is an experience similar to that of walking along a firm road with a fine view and suddenly stepping into a boggy place.

In a kind of credo that he set down in 1875 at the request of a friend, he wrote: ". . . I am, above all, a realist and chiefly interested in the living truth of the human face." A modern reader is apt to find Turgenev's realism not sufficiently penetrating, a little bloodless, rather timid. He tends to be too explicit. His habit of leaving no loose ends in his narratives gives them a look of spinsterish tidiness. He sees each character in detail, he scans the features, he looks into the heart. The rest of the anatomy is largely neglected. How these men and women came to be what they are is not shown, but reported in factual digressions on which his imagination had not gone to work. He keeps his nose too close to the evidence to permit the vision of far-off things. There is pity in his pages, but no terror. Here is an intelligence that does not soar or dive, and if it thus avoids risks, it also misses opportunities for discovery.

One returns to his work for the sake of observing characters sometimes subtly, almost always firmly drawn, against an appropriate background. Here are a few full-length portraits, and any number of neat sketches, intriguing cartoons, delicate line drawings. One recognizes the nicety of his insights into human feelings and foibles, yields to the moods that he creates, senses, too, even

when one is strange to them, the beautiful authenticity of his settings. He has the power to conjure up the genius of a place, to give
the very breath and being of a moment in a moonlit garden, on a
country road, in a room of a dilapidated manor house smelling of
kvas, apples, and leather.

The scene of practically all his writings is rural or semirural.
Rusticity is his element. He prefers the diffused light of the out-
doors to the theatrical glare of spots. His dramas are played out
against a background of earth and sky that has the charm of a
Corot and the fine fresh detail of a Constable. What he wrote as a
young man remained true to the end: "I should prefer to contemplate the precipitous movements of a duck's wet foot as it scratches
the back of its head on the edge of a marsh, or the long and
glistening drops of water slowly falling from the muzzle of a mo-
tionless cow that has just drunk from a pond in which she stands
knee-deep, rather than all that the cherubim can behold in
Heaven." Occasionally, however, Turgenev betrays a certain un-
ease in the presence of Nature. He asks whether men feel at a loss
before her because her completeness mocks their insufficiency. Or
he reflects somberly that she maintains her equilibrium in indifference to man's imbalance. But he is not at home with abstractions,
is not given to dialectics, and falls back readily into a stasis of
resignation or appreciation.

Whatever his attitude, the felicity of Turgenev's style is something even a mediocre translation must suggest. The dialogue,
except in the admirable interchange between peasants, may be too
literary; but the narrative and descriptive passages are couched in
a prose never startling yet both precise and emotional, moving with
an ease and grace that has the effect of cool music. The writing
flows along smoothly and is punctuated by the deliberate simile
rather than the flashing metaphor.

Realist though he is, the lyric touch comes naturally to Turgenev.
Exploration, analysis, are not his forte. The thinking of this con-
firmed rationalist is fraught with feeling. As often as not, he
swings between a mild elation and a gentle melancholy. The tone

of his fictions is often elegiac. They dwell on "the agitated sadness of expectation in the young, the impassive sadness of regret in the old." When Turgenev touches, as he often does, on the annihilation of the individual, he strikes the chord of despair, but he does not hold it. His positivist armor is not without chinks. Furthermore, granted that human existence is a brief interval between two darknesses, it nevertheless admits of luminous moments. For him they were not only those of love or of music. They could be something as ordinary as the sight of the bright wet muzzle of a cow standing knee-deep in a pond. The very evanescence of such experiences moves him to contemplate them with a jealous delight that his art, at its best, renders contagious.

Anton Chekhov–Humane
to the Tips of His Fingers

THOUGH generally reticent about his personal history, Chekhov never attempted to conceal the sordidness of his beginnings. On one occasion he gave a fairly clear hint at what his early environment had been. As a successful young writer he made this suggestion to a fellow author: "Write a story of how a young man, the son of a serf, a former grocery boy, chorister, high school lad and university student, who was brought up to respect rank, to kiss priests' hands, to revere other people's ideas, to give thanks for every morsel of bread, who was whipped many times, who without rubbers traipsed from pupil to pupil, who used his fists and tormented animals, who was fond of dining with rich relatives, who was hypocritical in his dealings with God and men gratuitously, out of the mere consciousness of his insignificance—write how this youth squeezes the slave out of himself drop by drop, and how, waking up one fine morning, he feels that in his veins flows no longer the blood of a slave but that of a real man. . . ." He was talking about himself.

Perhaps he did not quite squeeze the last drop of the slave out of himself. Certainly he never felt that he was in any sense a master of life or of art. But he was a freedman. He bought his freedom at the cost of persistent effort, by a process of self-education, so that morally as well as economically he was a self-made man. In the end, this boy who had been born into the meanest and the most backward section of Russian society, the lower middle class, and who had not been immune to its vulgarities, managed to make his

way into what E. M. Forster happily describes as "the aristocracy
of the considerate, the sensitive, and the plucky."

Chekhov was indeed the son of a serf and would have been
born one himself, had not his grandfather, an acquisitive peasant,
managed to purchase the family's freedom. His father rose in the
world, becoming the owner of a grocery, or rather of a general
store, which also dispensed liquor. This was in the wretched little
southern seaport of Taganrog, where Anton was born on January
17, 1860 (O.S.), the third child in a family that was to include
five boys and a girl.

The grocer was a strict disciplinarian who administered beatings
to his children as a parental duty and forced them to attend church
services, of which he was himself passionately fond. He was the
kind of person who uses religion to make those about him miserable. In addition to attending endless masses, little Anton, though
he had neither ear nor voice, had to sing in the church choir organized by his father. As he stood in the chancel under the admiring eyes of the congregation, the high-spirited boy felt like a little
convict, and he came to associate religious education with torture
behind unctuous smiles. "It is sickening and dreadful to recall,"
he once wrote to his eldest brother, "the extent to which despotism
and lying mutilated our childhood." He grew up to abhor every
form of deceit and coercion.

The population of Taganrog included a great many Greeks,
some of them wealthy importers. They maintained a one-room
parish school of their own for the children of the poor, which was
presided over by an ignorant and brutal master. Anton was sent
there in the hope that he might eventually obtain the position of
bookkeeper with one of the Greek merchants. After a year's at-
tendance, during which he did not learn as much as the Greek
alphabet, he was transferred, at the age of nine, to the local
gimnaziya, a combined grammar and high school. There he gave a
poor account of himself, partly perhaps because he had little time
for study. Among other things, he had to play watchdog for his

father at the store, where he became familiar with all the tricks of short-weighting and short-changing.

Anton was sixteen when the store failed and his father escaped debtors' prison by absconding. He went to Moscow, where his two older sons were studying. The rest of the family soon followed, except Anton. Left to shift for himself, he continued at school, earning his way by tutoring and getting some help from relatives. His situation was not a happy one, but at least his natural gaiety was no longer restrained by an oppressive domestic atmosphere.

After graduating from high school, he joined the family and, having a small stipend from the Taganrog municipality, entered the university as a medical student. The Chekhovs were in a sad way. Anton became virtually the head of the house, and it was to him that the family looked for support, as it was to go on doing through the years. That winter, the story goes, in order to buy a pie for his mother's birthday, he wrote a piece for a comic weekly. That brought him his first literary earnings.

"Oh, with what trash I began," Chekhov once said, "my God, with what trash!" He supplied the humbler public prints with fillers of all sorts: jokes, legends for cartoons, advertisements, aphorisms, recipes, mathematical puzzles, all in a comic vein. He wrote sketches, theatrical notices, miniature essays and stories. He even produced, on a bet, a romantic tale purporting to be a translation, and a full-length thriller, in which a *femme fatale* is murdered under baffling circumstances. (Unlike some other of his early pieces, this novel was not allowed to lie decently buried in the files of the paper in which it first appeared, but sixty years later was seized upon by the ghouls of Hollywood.) He also tried his hand at journalism. This was not yet serious writing, but it meant being occupied with serious subject matter. He was turning out a great amount of copy, being able to scribble under any conditions, whenever and wherever he pleased, and sometimes dashing off a sketch—such as "The Siren"—without a single erasure. The stuff wrote itself. For the most part it was farce, innocent banter, calculated to raise a good-natured laugh and be forgotten.

Occasionally, however, a note of bitterness, a suggestion of civic feeling, a hint of sympathy for the underdog crept in. And, though his work did not show it, the humorist had his moods of self-disgust. The hacks with whom he associated were an unsavory lot. He hated to think of himself in that galley. "A newspaper man is a crook at best . . ." he wrote to one of his brothers. "I am one of them, I work with them, shake hands with them, and people say that at a distance I have begun to look like a crook." At any rate, he told himself he would not die a journalist. Although he could not quite see himself as a doctor, perhaps medicine would be his salvation.

On receiving his medical diploma, he was for a while in charge of a hospital in a small town. Even earlier he had begun accumulating the knowledge of the peasant patients and provincial doctors who figure in his stories. After a few months he returned to Moscow to hang out his shingle. He was a hard-working and conscientious physician, but medicine did not prove his salvation, certainly not in a financial sense. His patients were mostly poor people, and in any case he regarded healing the sick as a humane duty, scarcely a means of livelihood. He continued to rely chiefly on his pen for his earnings and although he went on writing at a great rate, only the worst of the worrying and pinching was over. In time he came to take a certain satisfaction in having two occupations. "Medicine is my lawful wife," he wrote to a friend when he had been a doctor for four years, "and literature is my mistress. When I get fed up with one, I spend the night with the other. Though it is irregular, it is less boring this way, and besides, neither of them loses anything through my infidelity." Eventually the mistress came to supplant the wife.

There were times when he felt that medicine somewhat hampered him as a writer. A doctor has few illusions and that, he said, "somehow desiccates life." But his better judgment was that medical training helped his writing, giving him a more perceptive and penetrating knowledge of men and women, guarding him against the pitfalls of subjectivity, one of his bugbears. There are few clinical studies among his stories. And even when he deals with a case of typhus or with a woman having a miscarriage, however precise the delineation of the symptoms, he observes the patient for the sake of the human being, never the other way about. Basically his concern is not with illness, but with health.

Meanwhile there began to turn up among his writings, and with increasing frequency, pieces that gave promise of the harvest to come: bits of pure comedy, sharp character sketches, little master-pieces of pathos, candid studies of the folly of the heart. He was maturing, slowly, unevenly, yet unmistakably. To his astonishment he was discovering that he had a public and that, indeed, he was the object of critical consideration, in spite of the fact that he had not yet made the dignified "stout" monthlies. When, early in 1886, he scraped together enough rubles to take him to Petersburg, the intellectual and publishing center of the country, he was received "like the Shah of Persia." And then came a marvelous letter from Grigorovich, one of the Olympians, telling him that he was the foremost of the younger writers and pleading with him to take his talent seriously. Toward the end of the year when he again visited the capital he found that he was "the most fashionable writer" there. In the interim he had brought out a second and successful book of stories (the first had passed unnoticed), and had begun to write for the great daily *Novoye vremya* (New Time), which meant better rates and greater prestige.

He was developing a literary conscience. Formerly, he joked, writing had been like eating pancakes: now when he took up his pen he trembled. The man who had started out as a hack, care-lessly exploiting a comic vein that was not of the richest, was de-veloping into a conscientious, responsible artist who was to become a writer of major stature. He was now anxious to undertake some-thing serious, something that would engage all his powers and that he could work at without haste. In the summer of 1887 he fulfilled at least the first of these wishes by writing a drama, which he called *Ivanov* after its unhappy hero. He had always loved the theater and had written plays even as a schoolboy. *Ivanov*, however, was a failure, which he was in haste to forget, and he was soon at work on his first serious long narrative, "The Steppe." For this leisurely, tender, evocative "history of a journey" he drew largely upon childhood memories of the great southern plain. But the vein of comedy was not to dry up all at once. In a few days he dashed off *The Boor*, which he described as "an empty Frenchified little vaudeville piece." It proved to be a box-office hit that was to entertain generations of Russians, and foreigners as well. He was to write several more such skits, most of them dramatizations of his own early stories, but henceforth the comic spirit was practically absent from his fiction.

To his surprise, as much as to his delight, in the autumn of 1888 he received the Academy's Pushkin Prize for distinguished literary achievement. He was tasting the full sweetness of recognition. But there were times when he felt that he did not deserve it. "The Steppe" he had worked at slowly, "the way a gourmet eats woodcock." And yet, although its publication centered all eyes on him, he suspected that there was something radically wrong with it: it was not an organic whole, but a sequence of tableaux. "The Name-Day Party," which he wrote the same year, he had killed with hurry. He had a father and mother, a sister, and younger brothers on his hands, living together in a two-story house that had to be kept up, and to pay his bills he had to meet deadlines. Shortly after he had received the prize he was writing to a friend that his literary activity had not yet begun in earnest. He was a mere apprentice, worse, "a complete ignoramus." He must start from scratch, learn everything from the beginning. If he were to spend forty years reading and studying, then perhaps he might fire such a cannon at his public that the skies would tremble. "As it is, I am a lilliputian like everybody else," he concluded.

Novoye vremya, the daily to which Chekhov began contributing in 1886, was an organ of reactionary opinion. He had no scruples about appearing in its pages, and he contracted a close friendship with its owner and editor, the renegade liberal Alexey Suvorin.

During his school and university years he had remained untouched by the radicalism that flourished among the students. He moved largely in conservative circles and shared the prejudices current there against socialists, "troublemakers," and even, to some extent, against Jews. A couple of years after the beginning of his association with Suvorin's paper, he was writing for the monthlies, which belonged to the opposite camp. He was commencing to abandon political conformity, as he had earlier rid himself of the coarseness, servility, and hypocrisy to which he had also been bred. And yet he was far from having achieved a consistent outlook. He was on the hither side of thirty when he observed that he changed his political, religious, and philosophical *Weltanschauung* every month. He seems to have been at this time under the spell of Tolstoy's ideas. Some traces of this influence, which lasted several years, are to be found in his works.

But Chekhov was not the stuff of which disciples are made. In reaction against the authoritarian spirit of his upbringing, he developed a skeptical independence of judgment. In the end he discovered that he couldn't share Tolstoy's faith. He put his trust in science; he loved culture, by which he meant, he wrote on one occasion, carpets, a carriage with springs, wit. Between being whipped as a matter of course and not being whipped there was a gulf that compelled him to believe in progress. He came to feel that there was more love of one's fellow men in steam and electricity than in chastity and vegetarianism. Once the spell of Tolstoy's influence was broken, he was in the position of a man whose house, as he put it, was left empty. No new tenant came to occupy it. His mind was not doctrinal, much less dogmatic. The nearest he came to formulating a positive credo was in a letter to a friend in which he remarked casually: "My holy of holies is the human body, health, intelligence, talent, inspiration, love and absolute freedom—freedom from violence and falsehood, no matter how the last two manifest themselves."

He had come by freedom the hard way and he prized it all the more highly. It was one of the few certainties in a world of shift-

ing values, a firm principle, a guide for the perplexed. And freedom seemed to him to be menaced not so much from the Right as
from the Left. It was this camp, he felt, that harbored a spirit of
partisanship and intolerance that he recognized as a threat to his
liberty both as man and writer. In a mood of prophecy, rare with
him, he remarked that a time would come in Russia when "toads
and crocodiles," giving lip service to "science, art, and free
thought" would outdo the horrors of the Spanish Inquisition.

He might have added another article to his credo. He put no
stock in classes or institutions, he had no faith in the intelligentsia
or the proletariat, or for that matter in the peasantry, although he
shared the Populists' belief in the essential moral soundness, indeed
superiority, of the masses. He was the least dogmatic as he was the
least politically-minded of men. He owed allegiance to no ready-
made ideology, no class, no party, no institution, be it of Church
or State. The only dictates that he recognized were those of his
own conscience. His concern was always with the man, the woman,
the child, as a person. To portray them simply, inwardly, and,
above all, honestly, was, he believed, his whole duty.

Little of the rebel as there was in him, he learned not merely to
hate coercion in private relations, but to look quizzically at government itself. He saw no reason why the State should be excused
from the decencies required of its subjects. In any case, as a writer
of fiction he was little concerned with social questions and less
with political matters. It should be noted that the greater part of
his work was produced in the period of discouragement with political action following upon the failure of the inchoate radical
movement of the seventies which culminated in the assassination
of Alexander II. A sensitive writer could not help taking on to
some degree the color of this twilight age.

Without being political-minded, Chekhov was yet fully aware
of social evils and had a strong sense of civic responsibility. Here
too he felt that what counted was individual initiative, personal
effort. This attitude makes intelligible a somewhat puzzling epi-

sode in his life. On May 3, 1890 (N.S.), he left Moscow, abandoning his manuscripts and his practice, his family and his friends, to travel six thousand punishing miles to the penal colony on the island of Sakhalin, where he arrived on July 23. The exhausting, not seldom dangerous, journey was made by train, by steamer and boat, by sledge, on murderous roads by coach—this was before the construction of the Trans-Siberian Railway. En route Chekhov set down an account of his trip and dispatched the record in installments to a Petersburg newspaper. The sketches, which were called *Across Siberia*, have been available in English since the middle fifties. They dissatisfied the author, because he felt that they said more about his own reactions than about Siberia. But the account does not strike one as inordinately subjective. Of course, the personal note is unavoidable in writing of this kind, and one is grateful for it. The emphasis, however, is on the external world— the natural scene and the country's inhabitants: the old settlers, the convicts, the deportees, the no less unhappy recent immigrants, and the officials. Interlarded with the descriptions of his adventures are passages in which Chekhov expresses his private opinions, such as opposition to the life sentence for criminals, and voices his high hopes for the future of Siberia.

He spent three months on Sakhalin, making an intensive study of the penal colony, visiting every settlement and practically taking a single-handed census of the convict population. He returned home by way of the Indian Ocean and the Black Sea. This was a leisurely journey and one that formed a glowing contrast with his trip to the dismal island and his stay there.

When he stopped off at Hong Kong, he wrote a letter home which contains the following passage: "Wonderful roads, tramways, a funicular railway, botanical gardens; no matter where you look, everywhere you see the tenderest care of the English for their employes, there is even a club for sailors. I rode in a jinriksha, bought all kinds of trash in Chinese shops, and was indignant hearing my Russian fellow travelers rail at the English for exploiting the natives. I was reflecting: yes, the Englishman exploits the

Chinese, Sepoys, Hindus, but he gives them roads, running water, museums, Christianity; you, too, exploit, but what do you give?" (These lines are expunged from the Soviet edition of Chekhov's works and letters [Moscow, 1944–51, 20 vols.], described as the first *complete* collection of his writings. It is indeed a most comprehensive edition, provided with a scholarly apparatus of ample notes and commentaries, variant readings, information about changes and excisions due to pre-Revolutionary censorship. Nevertheless, the volumes of Chekhov's correspondence bear traces of expurgation reflecting the anti-Western rage of the period—deletions remaining hidden.) Not before late December was he back at his desk in Moscow. He had brought with him material for a substantial study of Russia's Far Eastern prison island.

The fruit of Chekhov's investigation of convict life on Sakhalin was a rather poorly organized, if meaty and scrupulously candid book: a cross between personal memoir and a lumbering sociological monograph. After having been serialized in a periodical, it came out separately in 1895. The work, recently translated into English under the title *The Island,* contains anecdotes, thumbnail portraits, and lives of individual convicts and settlers, but also population statistics, weather tables and other geographical data, and scraps of historical information. There are, too, passages that rival Dostoevsky's *Notes from the House of the Dead* in their picture of the degradation to which a human being can be reduced. It is noteworthy that Chekhov did not use any of his Sakhalin impressions in his fiction. He built "with the blocks quarried in the deeps of his imagination and on his personal premises," as Henry James declares an artist must. Siberia and Sakhalin were not Chekhov's personal premises.

There is at least one complete story, a true one, in *The Island.* It is told by Yegor, a peasant convicted of murder, but it is not clear that he is actually guilty. The uncouth talk is rendered in all its earthy crudity with dictaphone faithfulness; there is no attempt to reshape the raw stuff in hand. The peasant in the case is rather unlike the tillers of the soil whom Chekhov usually depicts. The man is caught in the machinery of the State but is not crushed by it. Asked if he is homesick, he says no, but adds, "There's only one thing—I'm sorry for the children. They have no sense." To the next question, of what he was thinking when he was being taken to the steamer that was to carry him to Siberia, he replies that he was "praying to God." "What for?" "That he should put sense in the children's heads." A solid figure, calling to mind Platon Karatayev in *War and Peace,* he has a toughness and resilience one has learned not to expect from Chekhov's characters. Yet this true story bears a curious resemblance to the narratives of his invention. There is something about it that is essentially Chekhovian. It is not so much a certain inconclusiveness, due to the doubt as to whether Yegor is guilty of the murder for which he is serving time or is the victim of a miscarriage of justice. Rather, it lies in the fact that these few pages, as unemphatic as they are artless, suggest the cruel power of accident, that they leave with the reader the sense of the inherent pathos of man's lot.

Before his departure for Sakhalin, Chekhov had given his friends several conflicting and rather unconvincing reasons for his venture. It has been surmised that in undertaking the arduous journey—one that, given the state of his health, was hazardous as well—to that manmade hell, he was trying to escape from an involvement with a married woman. There is reason to believe, however, that a strong motive was his desire to acquaint the public with the fate of a segment, perhaps the most wretched segment, of Russia's convict population. He knew that in the prisons throughout the country numberless men and women were being depraved and destroyed "carelessly, thoughtlessly, barbariously," as he put it in a letter, and he blamed not the authorities, but himself and all of his compatriots for their silent acquiescence. Hence he felt it to be his duty to try, on his own, as was characteristic of him, to do something about prison reform. What could be more effective than telling people truthfully what he saw with his own eyes of the workings of the system? He belonged to a generation that had not lost faith in the power of enlightenment. "Man will become better," he wrote in one of his notebooks, "when you show him what he is like."

His quixotic gesture did not rouse the public, and seems not to have done anything for the convicts. It was in vain that where so many had been driven, he had gone alone freely, already suffering from incipient tuberculosis, traveling thousands of miles and living under grueling conditions. It can only be imagined that his sacrifice helped him to feel that he had made a brave effort to pay his debt to society. He was glad to have written the book and proud to think of "this coarse convict garb" hanging in his literary wardrobe.

He made other attempts in that direction. Early in 1892 he traveled into the famine-stricken provinces to organize relief, and was nearly lost in a blizzard. Later in the year, when Central Russia was threatened with cholera, he acted as medical supervisor of the district in which he was living. With characteristic candor he confessed to a friend that he was in the vexing position of being able to read of nothing but cholera, to think of nothing but diarrhea, while feeling indifferent to the people he was treating. It was equally characteristic that he should give up every other activity for an entire summer in order to help them. He took an active part in the building of village schools near his home and interested himself in a project of founding a settlement house in Moscow. In 1897 he was a volunteer census-taker, going from one log cabin to another, in spite of illness.

Two years after his return from Sakhalin, Chekhov settled in the country. Since his student days he had summered there, for much as he loved the bustle and the human contacts of the city, he relished the solitude and serenity that the rural scene offered. Now he bought an estate of six hundred acres near the village of Melikhovo, in the province of Moscow, and made a home there for his parents, his sister, and his younger brothers. One reason why he wished to leave town was that his health was poor. He said he was like an old cupboard coming apart. He had never been strong.

For years his digestion had been poor, he had been suffering from piles, and since his early twenties he had had a persistent cough and from time to time had spat blood. Though he resolutely ignored these symptoms and would not let himself be examined by a physician—he was the opposite of a hypochrondiac—he supposed that the country might benefit his health. Besides, living might be cheaper there, and perhaps he would be able to write less and in a more leisurely and painstaking fashion. Again, there would be fewer visitors and other distractions.

Some weeks after he was installed at Melikhovo he was telling a friend that what with the chores and the fresh air, he was getting so husky that if the place were brought under the hammer, he would hire himself out as a circus athlete. But he was soon forced to realize that the change was doing him little good. He may have lacked a certain spontaneity of feeling and his relations with people may have been pretty much on the surface, but he was incorrigibly gregarious, so that there were as many guests as there had been in Moscow and they were harder to get rid of. Then, too, life in the bosom of the family had its drawbacks. Again there were the patients: in a year nearly a thousand peasants were treated by him, free of charge. It was delightful not to have to pay rent, but the expenses had nowise decreased. In order to buy the property he had gone into debt, and he was driven to fresh exertions by the oppressive thought of the money he owed. Some of it he had borrowed from Suvorin, who, though Chekhov no longer contributed to *Novoye vremya*, continued to publish his books.

He had scarcely made himself at home at Melikhovo when he was complaining that while his soul wanted to expand and soar, he had to go on scribbling for lucre, without respecting what he wrote, and that his only solace was medicine, which he practiced without thought of money. He had grown up among people with whom money played "an infinitely great role," and that, he confessed on another occasion, had terribly depraved him. He should take a sulphuric acid bath, he said, so as to have his old skin eaten away and then grow a new hide. But if his soul had few opportunities to expand and soar, he knew moods of animal contentment here, when he neither regretted yesterday nor anticipated tomorrow. Spring in the country was so exquisite that he could not but hope there would be spring in paradise. On a walk across the snowy fields he felt as detached, as remote from the humdrum and the hurly-burly as if he were on the moon. At moments he was so happy that he would superstitiously bring himself up short by recalling his creditors.

Even at its best, the place could not hold him. The master of Melikhovo was a restless man, craving new impressions, eager for all that was strange and fresh. He made frequent trips to Moscow, where he was profusely fêted. He visited friends in the provinces, sailed up and down the Volga, traveled to the Crimea and the Caucasus, and in Suvorin's company saw France and Italy. European comforts, European culture made Russia seem more drab and dingy than ever. His return from Sakhalin by the Orient route had whetted his appetite for the exotic. He longed to go to South America. He wanted to see Chicago. Lack of funds and lack of courage, according to him, prevented him from realizing these dreams. Probably lack of health also had a good deal to do with it.

On one of his trips to Moscow he was dining in a restaurant with Suvorin when he had a severe hemorrhage of the lungs. With his usual nonchalance, he went about his business as soon as the bleeding stopped, only to suffer a relapse three days later. He was taken to a hospital. This was in March, 1897. An examination—the first he had permitted—showed that he was far gone in consumption.

While he was in the hospital he was correcting the proofs of his story "Peasants." It was the fruit of that intimate knowledge of the people that life in the country had helped to give him. The years at Melikhovo had not been as productive as the Moscow period had been. Nevertheless, it was then that he wrote most of his long stories and some shorter ones that are among his best. As for "Peasants," he had planned a larger canvas, which was to deal with the hopeless miseries of the poor and ignorant, urban as well as rural. In the end, he limited the scope of the tale to the lives (and deaths) of the villagers. Only a short fragment is extant of the sequel retailing the fortunes, or rather the misfortunes, of a peasant's widow and little daughter who beg their way through the countryside to Moscow, where the mother obtains service in a miserable boarding house and the little girl stays with her aunt, an old prostitute. The fragment of the sequel is worthy of the long story that preceded it. "Peasants" is one of Chekhov's strongest, most revealing, and compelling pieces.

The doctors prescribed a strict regimen, country air, and residence in a southern climate, and they forbade him to practice medicine. He was not the man to take their orders seriously. But that autumn he did go abroad for his health. He settled in Nice, and in the spring went up to Paris. The Dreyfus case had recently been reopened, and he became interested in it. He took his stand with the Dreyfusards. He was full of admiration for Zola. *Novoye vremya* stank in his nostrils; anti-Semitism smelt to him of the slaughterhouse. What particularly disgusted him was that the paper reviled Zola in its editorial columns while pirating one of his novels in its supplement. Chekhov stated his position frankly enough to Suvorin, and their former intimacy became impossible, but he did not break completely with the old reactionary. He continued to count Suvorin among his friends, who included Tolstoy, the Christian anarchist, and were soon to be joined by Maxim Gorky, the revolutionist.

He could not stay abroad indefinitely. Whatever interest the foreign scene had for him, and that interest paled since he was ill, the pull of home was a strong one. On his return he was forced to give up Melikhovo and go to live in Yalta, in the mild air of the southern coast of the Crimea.

He had visited the resort once or twice before, and it had depressed him profoundly. Now he was condemned to live in the Godforsaken place, where, he said, even the bacilli were asleep. It was exile to a warm Siberia, a balmy Devil's Island. When he had been there over a year he wrote that he still felt like a transplanted tree hesitating whether to take root or begin to wither. Eventually he resigned himself to Yalta, but he never got to like it, in spite of the fact that he had the companionship of several fellow writers there, including Tolstoy, whom he revered.

The exile did not do for him what it should have. He did not get the proper diet or nursing, and he kept breaking away to take trips that cannot have benefited his health. His condition grew steadily worse. Nevertheless he was able to write. Such memorable stories as "The Man in a Shell," "Gooseberries," "The Darling," "On Official Business," "The Lady With the Pet Dog," were composed during those years. He also prepared his collected works for the press—not an unmixed pleasure, since he was dissatisfied with much that he had written and disgusted with his early stuff. They were issued in ten volumes in 1899–1901 under the imprint of A. F. Marx. He had sold his works to that publisher for 75,000 rubles, becoming, as he said, "a Marxist for life."

It was during these years that Chekhov composed his better-known plays. He had made a fiasco of his first attempt at playwriting with *Ivanov*, which was written and staged in Moscow in 1887. Two years later he rewrote the play for a revival in Petersburg and found the work of revision excruciating. He decided that he was no playwright. "Shoot me," he wrote to a friend, "if I go mad and occupy myself with what is not my business." In its revised form *Ivanov* proved a success, but his next piece, *The Wood Demon,* put on the same year, fell flat, and he disliked it so much that he refused to have it published. It was six years before he tried his hand at playwriting again. *The Sea Gull* was produced in Petersburg in 1896. Its failure verged on a scandal. The unhappy author swore that he would never attempt a play again. Yet in 1898 his *Uncle Vanya,* a revised version of *The Wood Demon,* was produced in the provinces and met with a favorable reception. At the close of the same year a newly formed company which went by the name of The Moscow Art Theatre performed *The Sea Gull* with great success. This was the beginning of the association between

Chekhov and the Art Theatre, which persisted in spite of the fact that he was not wholly satisfied with the way in which his plays were interpreted. All of them, including the last two: *The Three Sisters* and *The Cherry Orchard,* became the very backbone of the repertory of the Art Theatre, which, in fact, adopted the gull as its emblem.

The role of Irina in *The Sea Gull* was played by Olga Knipper. Chekhov met the actress at a rehearsal. Within less than three years, on May 25, 1901, they were married. He was then forty-one and his bride thirty-one. They spent their honeymoon in a sanatorium.

Some years earlier when Suvorin had been urging him to marry, Chekhov had declared, "Very well, I'll get married, if you wish. But my conditions are: everything must remain just as before, that is, she must live in Moscow and I in the country, and I'll go to see her. Happiness continuing day after day, from morning to morning, I shan't be able to stand. . . . I promise to be a splendid husband, but give me a wife who, like the moon, will not appear in my sky every day." He found precisely such a wife. To keep her engagements, she had to winter in the two capitals. His illness tied him to his southern place of exile. He went to see her in Moscow, occasionally she visited him at Yalta, or they would have a few weeks together elsewhere. They exchanged letters almost daily. Writing to her, before their marriage, of the fate that kept them apart, he said that neither of them was to blame: "It's the Devil who has put the bacillus in me and the love of art in you." After they were married, he assured her that she need feel no pricking of conscience if she could not be at his side, that he didn't feel cheated, that all was going well with them, and that they were indeed a model couple, since they didn't interfere with each other's work. The arrangement, however, had its drawbacks. He missed her more than he had imagined possible. Separation was not a matter of choice: it was enforced by his ill health. On that account he was not with her when she had a miscarriage; she promised him a son the following year, but they were never to have the child that both longed for. There was something pathetic about this union, for all the insistent gaiety that marked his resigned acceptance of the situation.

The year before his marriage Chekhov was elected honorary member of the newly created Section of Belles Lettres in the National Academy of Sciences. He was at this time the most outstanding literary figure in Russia, next to Tolstoy. He did not long wear the academic laurels, however. In 1902 Maxim Gorky was accorded the same honor, but as he was then under indictment for a political offense, the authorities succeeded in having the election annulled. Thereupon Chekhov resigned from the august body. Though his protest was not a public one, the gesture was significant for a man of his temper. He had long since abandoned any attachment to the ideas that Suvorin championed in his paper. For at least a decade Chekhov's public—and that meant all literate Russia —had been taking it for granted that he belonged in the liberal camp. He still had no patience with cut-and-dried ideologies, owed no allegiance to any political group, nor did he show any leanings toward socialism. On occasion he would bracket "sulky-faced Marxists" with police inspectors. But he was now definitely with those who looked forward to the speedy downfall of the autocratic regime. What cropped up in the writings of his last years was something above and beyond millennial hopes: a dissatisfaction with quietism, a welcoming of the violent change that he saw on the way. At twenty-eight he had asserted that there would never be a revolution in Russia. At forty he believed differently. The country, he felt, was emerging from its torpor and beginning, as he put it, "to hum like a beehive." He wanted to catch this new mood of wakening energies. Indeed, in his last story, "Betrothed," a girl breaks away from her confining home environment and goes out into the world, and it has been stated that in the first draft Nadya, the heroine, joins the revolutionists. Chekhov also spoke of wanting to write "a buoyant play." He did not write it. His last play, *The Cherry Orchard,* first staged the year before the upheaval of 1905, tolled the knell of old Russia rather than rang in the new. Nor did he witness its aborted start.

What with his trips north and the excitement attendant upon the production of his plays, his mode of living was scarcely what the doctor ordered. After he was married, he grew rapidly worse. The first night of *The Cherry Orchard* was set for January 17, 1904, the playwright's forty-fourth birthday. His friends turned the evening into a celebration of the twenty-fifth anniversary of his literary activity, although he had actually broken into print in 1880, twenty-four years previously. Shaken with coughing, Chekhov was hardly able to stand up to receive the ovation and listen to the addresses. He was critically ill that spring and yet, with the war against Japan in progress, he talked of going to the front as an army doctor. In June he was rushed to a health resort in the Black Forest and there, on July 2, he died. His body was taken to Moscow in a refrigerating car for the transportation of oysters. The last trick that Fate played on him was of the sort that it would have amused him to jot down in his notebook.

Toward the end of his life Chekhov remarked to a friend that people would stop reading him a year after his death. As a matter of fact, his vogue kept growing steadily until the cataclysm of 1917 and his position as the major figure of the Silver Age of Russian literature was becoming increasingly secure. During the harsh, strenuous revolutionary years his reputation suffered a partial eclipse, but by now it has regained its former luster, and his work is valued not alone for its intrinsic quality but also for the light that it throws on a dead past. Just when his compatriots, coping with the tasks and hardships of the new order, were looking away from Chekhov, the Western world, especially England and America, was enthusiastically exploring him as a remarkable discovery. Indeed, shortly after the First World War, the homage paid to him in certain literary circles verged on a cult. That first fine careless rapture has since died down, and something closer to a just estimate of his significance can be arrived at.

*　　*　　*

As a playwright Chekhov made a virtue of his limitations and so brought something new into the theater. He lacked the dramatic instinct. His plays want the sense of crisis, the heightened tension, the clear-cut clash of wills that one was wont to expect on the stage. There is something loose and amorphous about them. Of the five full-sized pieces that he wrote, *The Cherry Orchard* alone comes closest to answering the traditional demands of the theater. It is also the play which has had the greatest box-office success. The supersession of the landed gentry by the mercantile middle class, which is its theme, is obviously one with abundant dramatic possibilities. The auctioning off of Mme. Ranevskaya's ancestral estate affords a definite climax toward which the action rises and from which it declines. The more important characters are drawn in such a fashion as to offset one another, and there is a good deal of suspense, first as to the fate of the property, and second as to whether the new owner will propose to the daughter of the house.

Not that the other plays are wholly wanting in theatrical moments. In fact, they are punctuated by pistol shots, accounting for two suicides, one fatal duel, and one attempted murder. But these outbursts of violence are of little dramatic significance and merely serve to underscore the static conditions into which they irrupt. They are like stones flung into a stream and soon covered by the waters. With the exception of a few indurate egotists, the characters in all the plays are unhappy, defeated, and mostly futile, though restive, individuals, caught in situations that are pathetic and that skirt tragedy by suggesting what is irremediable in life. Aware of their failings, these people reach out for the meaning of their sufferings and on occasion dream of a glorious and distant future which would compensate for their wasted lives. For the rest, they are ordinary men and women, typical of the strata of society to which they belong, chiefly the intelligentsia and the rural gentry. The characters engage in much anguished talk about the shortcomings of Russian life and hold up work as the salvation of the country, but the heart of the plays lies not in action or in programs, but rather in states of mind, in the ebb and flow of feeling, in the nuances of inner experience. The frustration, the self-prob-ing, the emotionalism, the starry-eyed aspiration—all this, with the enveloping mood of wistful musing, relieved by a saving touch of the grotesque, bathes the plays in an atmosphere peculiarly their own, gives them a lyrical quality which to a large degree com-pensates for their lack of drama.

Russian audiences are still receptive to the spell of Chekhov's plays, though one imagines that it is difficult for them to identify themselves with his weary, lackadaisical heroes. The foreign spec-tator, too, is apt to surrender to the emotional tone of *The Three Sisters* and *The Cherry Orchard,* especially. As for the reader, by an imaginative effort he should be able to establish rapport with this elegiac poet of the theater.

Chekhov's stories are by far the larger and the more rewarding, as well as the more influential portion of his work. He limited himself to the short narrative not without a struggle. When his writing first assumed a serious cast, he was harassed by the feeling that he was doing less than his best. Characters, situations, scenes were crowding his mind, begging to be realized: what weddings, what funerals, what splendid women! The unborn figments were jealous, as he put it, of those that had seen the light. But he was hoarding this wealth, he was not going to throw it away on trifles, he was going to save it for some substantial work, for a novel. And he did start the novel. He kept mentioning it in his letters. He called it *Stories from the Lives of My Friends.* In spite of the suspicious title, he insisted that it was not going to be a patchwork, but a composed whole. He even chose a dedicatee. And then, about 1891, all references to the work cease, and no trace of the manu-script has been found to this day. Now and again in later years his desire to write a novel would reawaken, and indeed he did produce several long narratives, but not one of them quite achieves the stature of a novel.

Perhaps to account for his failure, Chekhov threw out the rather dubious suggestion that the writing of novels required a degree of cultivation, a mastery, a consciousness of personal freedom possessed only by members of the privileged classes, and that the art was beyond the powers of plebeians like himself. Aggravating the sense of his inadequacy was the belief that he belonged to a generation of epigoni, unworthy descendants of giants like Turgenev, Dostoevsky, Tolstoy. In any case, the short story remained his vehicle to the end. It offered a form admirably suited to his genius.

With few exceptions, the locale of his tales is the native one, their time that in which Chekhov himself lived, their approach realistic. Within these limits, their variety is enormous, taking in, as they do, men and women, old and young, rich and poor, people in every station: peasants, landowners, priests, policemen, schoolteachers, prostitutes, doctors, merchants, government officials. The human comedy, at least a large part of it, is enacted in a series of short scenes, some of them farcical, many of them deeply tinged with pathos, a few verging on tragedy or having a touch of irony. The interest may attach to a simple situation, as in "Vanka," or it may lie in a complex of relations, as in "The Name-Day Party," or again it may center on a psychological type, as in "The Man in a Shell."

In his notebook Chekhov entered this quotation from Daudet: " 'Why are your songs so short?' a bird was asked. 'Is it because you are short of breath?' 'I have a great many songs and I should like to sing them all.' " Aside from trifles, he wrote some four hundred and fifty narratives that have left a signal mark on the art of the short story. Practically all his work, except some early bagatelles, is available in English.

Where he attempts a story involving action and suspense, one with a plot, a sharp point, a neat solution, the result is apt to be wanting in distinction. Probably his lack of dramatic instinct was responsible for this. Where, however, he uses the method that he made peculiarly his own, though it had been employed before his time by Turgenev and other Russians, he is one of the masters.

The most characteristic of Chekhov's stories lack purely narrative interest. They no more bear retelling than does a poem. Nothing thrilling happens in them, nor are the few reflective passages particularly compelling. Some of the tales, having neither beginning nor end, are, as Galsworthy put it, "all middle like a tortoise." Others have a static quality, with no more progression than there is in a dance. Instead of moving toward a definite conclusion, they are apt to trail off or drop to an anticlimax. And yet they manage to take hold of the imagination in an amazing fashion. Precisely because of the lack of invention and contrivance, the absence of cleverness, the fact that the loose ends are not tucked up nor the rough edges beveled, and that they remain unfinished in more senses than one, they have the impact of a direct experience.

It lay within Chekhov's gift to create characters who have come to be a byword in Russia. And this although the creatures of his imagination are somewhat shadowy, since he is inclined to sketch a type rather than to paint the portrait of an individual. He had an intimate understanding of the complexities, the non sequiturs of the mind and particularly of the heart. His was an observant eye for the telling detail of appearance or behavior, for whatever would contribute to placing his characters within the proper physical or social setting. His stories have an atmosphere as distinct as an odor.

Chekhov's preoccupation is with existences that are commonplace, drab, narrow. The life he pictures is one in which there is cruelty, want, boredom, misunderstanding, with only an occasional interval of happiness or serenity, a rare intimation that justice and goodness may ultimately prevail—in sum, an unintelligible and largely painful business. A man and woman are involved with each other and can live neither together nor apart. A cabman loses his son and can find no one to whom to pour out his grief but his horse. A woman wastes her youth in the provinces. Human beings are broken by the machinery of the State. Chekhov's characters may long for something that would lend meaning and beauty to their existence, yet they do not act to bring that consummation nearer. Their frustration is apt to be the result of their own helplessness. Often we encounter them in the midst of their feeble struggles, or, already defeated, facing an impasse. Chekhov preached the gospel of work as the panacea for his country's ills, and his heart went out to nonconformists and to enterprising, courageous men, such as the explorers of the Russian North, and yet he was incapable of projecting successfully a fighter, a rebel, a man of steadfast purpose. It is as though he were so suspicious of power, associating it with its abuse, that he looked upon weakness with a forgiving, almost an affectionate eye. The situations he usually presents are at the opposite pole from melodrama, as is his style from the melodramatic. His language is simple, rather slovenly, with rare strokes of bold imagery, sometimes very expressive, always free from the emphatic, the rhetorical, the florid.

A man of a sober and naturalistic temper, Chekhov was dogged by the thought that our condition in this uncomfortable world is a baffling one. He liked to say that there was no understanding it. And, indeed, his writings heighten that sense of the mystery of life which is one of the effects of all authentic literature. At the same time they tend to discourage the view that existence is a meaningless play of chance forces. In "A Tedious Story," a work of his early maturity and one of the most somber pieces to have come from his pen, an old professor discovers to his deep distress that there is nothing in his thoughts and feelings that could be called "a general idea, or the God of living man." Chekhov's writings pay covert homage to such a life-giving idea. In the semblance of the image of beauty, of the impulse toward justice, of the ideal of saintliness, it glimmers through the daily commonplace. His men and women sometimes reach out for something "holy, lofty, and majestic as the heavens overhead." On a few occasions he allows his characters intuitions tinged with mysticism. Thus "The Black Monk" is concerned, however ambiguously, with madness as the gateway to transcendental reality, and the examining magistrate in "On Official Business" is haunted by the thought that nothing is accidental or fragmentary in our existence, that "everything has one soul, one aim," that individual lives are all parts of an organic whole.

Like the student in "A Nervous Breakdown," Chekhov had a "talent for humanity"—a generous compassion that went hand in hand with understanding and with a profound regard for the health of body and soul. Asked to give his opinion about a story dealing with a syphilitic, he wrote to the author that syphilis was not a vice but a disease, and that those who suffer from it needed not censure but friendly care. It was a bad thing, he went on to say, for the wife in the story to desert her husband on the ground that he had a contagious or loathsome illness. "However," he concluded, "she may take what attitude she likes toward the malady. But the author must be humane to the tips of his fingers." Chekhov lived up to this precept.

Next to his humanity, his supreme virtue is his candor. He is no teller of fairy tales, no dispenser of illusory solaces or promises. He does not tailor his material to fit our sense of poetic justice or to satisfy our desire for a happy ending. In his mature years he clung to the conviction that a writer was not an entertainer, not a confectioner, not a beautician, but a man working under contract who was bound by his conscience to tell the whole truth with a chemist's objectivity and indifference to bad smells. At the same time he was plagued, as has been seen, by a feeling of his insufficiency. He lived, he protested, in "a flabby, sour, dull time," and he had, like the rest of his generation, no goals toward which to lead his readers, no enthusiasm with which to infect them. And so he assigned to himself the modest role of a reporter, a witness, a man who, without presuming to solve any problems, merely posed them or recorded, to the best of his ability, the way others posed them.

He was indeed an incorruptible witness, but he did not remain in the witness box all the time. Implicit in his writings is a judgment against cruelty, greed, hypocrisy, stupidity, snobbery, sloth—all the slavish traits he had been at pains to squeeze out of himself, against whatever degrades man and prevents him from achieving his full stature. Notwithstanding his protestations of objectivity, and though his attitude toward evil was not so much active hatred as abhorrence, there is indignation and indictment in his pages, a thinly veiled criticism of life. He even succumbs to the Russian weakness for preachment. There is no doubt that eventually he came to expect a corrective influence from his plays and stories. By telling the truth, he said to himself, he would help men to live more decently. And the truth, in his view, as Frank O'Connor has pointed out, was that a venial sin, lack of consideration, meanness, self-indulgence, petty cowardice, is death-dealing and hugely reprehensible. One need not have faith in human perfectibility to acknowledge that there is something liberating and exalting in a frank facing of man's estate.

Just before the Second World War, Somerset Maugham remarked, "Today most young writers of ambition model themselves on Chekhov." Unquestionably the Russian's influence helped to direct public taste in the English-speaking countries toward the acceptance of a rather shapeless kind of short narrative implying the forlornness of man, morally flabby creature that he is, in a world he never made. Whatever the literary fashion, people are likely to keep returning to a writer who, in addition to his other virtues, came as close as any of his fellows to being humane to the tips of his fingers.

Maxim Gorky–Soviet Laureate

❦

ALTHOUGH born into a fairly comfortable lower-middle-class family, Gorky found himself in the gutter at the age of ten. His early writings—he began his career in the nineties—grew out of the experiences of a boyhood and youth spent in the lower depths of society. Those stories of unskilled workers and vagrants owed their immense success partly to the fact that he was offering the public glimpses of an unexplored world. Others before him, Dostoevsky among them, had shown the lives of the poor but none had written so brutally, so challengingly, and out of such intimate knowledge. Morever, his work implied a criticism of the system that produced the outcasts he described. It carried an undercurrent of revolutionary sentiment in consonance with the times. The recklessness of his characters, their raw passions, the savage circumstances of their lives stimulated a generation that needed courage for its task of throwing off the shackles of an oppressive political order.

As a short-story writer—the medium with which Gorky began continued to attract him almost to the end of his career—he has serious faults. Aside from his weak narrative sense, he has, literally speaking, bad manners; one is never sure when he will make a *faux pas*. He is likely to fall into bathos and indulge in rhetoric or fanciful imagery, he cannot refrain from sophomoric commentary, and he sometimes intrudes himself inopportunely, marring what would otherwise be an effective piece. From the first he had a leaning toward romanticism of the Hugoesque type and a fondness for orotund prose. He felt the need, as he wrote to Chekhov in 1900, of heroic utterance. Repeatedly he tried to write poetry and one of the sorrows of his life was the recurrent discovery that he could not. The nearest he came to success in this genre was the prose poem "The Song of the Stormy Petrel," a transparent allegory of the Revolution, written in the days when the tempest was still beyond the horizon. Unfortunately, he is at his worst when he thus engages in heroics or when he is lushly allegorical. He does not do too well when he tries to psychologize, which luckily does not often happen. He comes off best when he deals directly with things he has seen and that have moved him to tenderness or indignation. Among these more satisfying stories one must count such pieces as "One Autumn Evening," "Twenty-six Men and a Girl," "Notch," "Birth of a Man," and above all the incomparable, heartbreaking "Lullaby," the story of a cheap whore and her son, exquisite in its humanity.

With the notable exception of his early play *The Lower Depths,* which belongs with his hobo stories, Gorky achieved no outstanding triumph with his dramatic efforts. They deal with broad social themes, such as the class struggle, the decay of the bourgeoisie, the abyss between the intellectuals and the masses, the impending revolution. He has the playwright's ear for natural conversation and particularly for folk speech; but like the intellectuals in his play *Summer Folk,* many of his characters might say of themselves, "We do nothing, and we talk abominably much." His pieces are Saroyanesque—for the most part sequences of scenes not built up to a climax and lacking a suitable dénouement. They show the same want of plot as his short stories. In his very last years Gorky wrote two plays, constructed around one group of characters, the final scenes, with symbolic symmetry, placed against the background of the February and the October revolutions respectively. There is tension in them, especially in *Bulychev and Others,* an imperfect but bitter and powerful piece. The new life is only vaguely adumbrated in it. The central figure is an old man, incurably ill and in the end dying, who obviously embodies the old order. Yet, curiously enough, this tycoon is not the capitalist of the caricatures. He belongs to the race of full-blooded, blunt, forceful men whom Gorky depicted with an instinctive sympathy which overcame his ethical scruples.

As a democrat and a socialist, Gorky had every reason to abominate malefactors of wealth, the conquistadores of commerce and industry, who in Russia were a particularly unlovely breed. He made it quite plain that they were captains in the enemy's camp. Yet this type of man had a strong and durable attraction for him; he was drawn to them by their vigor, their capacity for living strenuously and building energetically, even when their energy was directed toward predatory ends. His very first novel, published at the turn of the century and dealing with wealthy merchants and shipowners, was a story of big business. Likewise the last long narrative he finished pictured three generations of a family of industrialists.

During the quarter of a century separating these two novels he produced half a dozen others, all concerned with the small folk of the provinces, the proletariat, and the lower middle class. The earliest of them, a story of the vain struggle of the poor against an implacable social order, closes symbolically with the chief character, in flight from the police, dashing his brains out against a wall. The work that followed it is in sharp contrast. The note of despair has changed to one of hope; Gorky in the meantime had had a taste of prison and revolutionary activity (during the upheaval of 1905), experiences which seemed to have been fuel for the flame of socialist faith that burns in every line of *Mother*.

This novel has the distinction of being the only Russian literary work of note to have been composed on American soil. *Mother* was written, in part, during the summer of 1906, while Gorky and the Russian actress who was his companion were guests of John Martin, an American friend, in Martin's country place in the Adirondacks. The author had arrived in New York in April of that year as an emissary of the Bolshevik faction of the Social Democratic Party. His mission was to collect funds for the Party, carry on propaganda for revolution in Russia, and agitate against an American loan to the Czar's government. He had his hands full with these tasks, but nevertheless managed to do a good deal of writing. Among other things, he tossed off an unflattering account of his impressions of New York. The first of its four sections is entitled "The City of the Yellow Devil." He intended to write an essay to "prove" that the mental age of all Americans, including millionaires, senators, and professors, was thirteen to fifteen years. In October he sailed for Europe, settling at Capri, where he finished *Mother*. He remained in Italy as a refugee for seven years.

The December, 1906, issue of *Appleton Magazine* carried the first installment of the book, and within a year it was available in a dozen languages. The original was issued in 1907 under a Berlin imprint. In Russia the complete, unexpurgated text was not published until 1917, the year of the Revolution. A habitual reviser of his writings, Gorky made certain changes in the novel before including it in his collected works, which were printed in 1923–27. Thus, the heroine's religiosity was toned down and an important secondary character's humanitarian tirades were curtailed, presumably to satisfy the demands of ideological orthodoxy. The style, too, was altered somewhat, and the number of subsidiary figures cut, reducing the cast to a mere hundred.

Mother is a tale glorifying the revolutionary movement in old Russia. That movement had its origin in the mid-nineteenth century, the epoch of reforms, chief among them having been the emancipation of the serfs in 1861. For decades insurgency had been a matter of loosely connected, small, clandestine groups, consisting for the most part of youthful intellectuals and semi-intellectuals. Professing a native variety of agrarian communism tinged with anarchism, which went by the name of Populism, they either made feeble and futile attempts to rouse the peasants against the landlords by peaceful propaganda, or they plotted— and carried out—equally ineffectual acts of political terror, which culminated in the assassination of Emperor Alexander II. But by the turn of the century the movement, now led by two antagonistic socialist parties, was beginning to gain in numbers, partly by attracting wage-earners. Furthermore, the Populist ideology had now a strong rival in Marxist socialism. In scattered cities and industrial towns revolutionary cells, in addition to carrying on undercover activities, organized strikes and public demonstrations against the Government.

On May Day, 1902, such a demonstration took place at Sormovo, a factory suburb of Nizhny-Novgorod, the city which was Gorky's birthplace and which was eventually to be renamed for him. As a matter of course, the crowd was manhandled and dispersed by the police and the military, while the ringleaders, including Pyotr Zalomov, a worker who had carried a red flag, was arrested, imprisoned, and deported to Siberia. At the trial they made impassioned speeches, which were reported at length in the underground press. Gorky followed these events closely. Indeed, he was acquainted with some of the people behind him, including Zalomov and his mother, who, remarkably enough, was an active member of the revolutionary cell.

Here was the germ of his novel. Its two protagonists, Pavel Vlassov and his mother, were modeled on the Zalomovs, mother and son, and the events at Sormovo furnished the pattern for the climactic episodes in the narrative: the May Day demonstration with the red flag and the trial of the leading demonstrators. A Marxist critic objected to *Mother* on the ground that the heroine was an invented, atypical figure. The author retorted by pointing to the "propaganda value" of the image he had fashioned: a factory hand's elderly, illiterate widow, crushed in spirit, if not in body, by her husband's brutality, drawn into "the movement" through her affection for her son and gradually undergoing an amazing metamorphosis—becoming a fearless, ardent, dedicated activist. Gorky added, however, that this woman was not exceptional, that he knew of others like her, and he cited the case of a member of the Bolshevik Central Committee who, during a house search, hid the Committee's seal in her hair. Gorky had the realistic novelist's concern for the factual. He played with the idea of writing a sequel to *Mother* which would deal with Pavel Vlassov's lot in Siberia and his later experiences; he gave it up, he said, because, living as he did in Italy, he lacked the necessary knowledge of factual details.

Mother depicts the activities of the revolutionary underground as it existed at the opening of the century, and delineates some of the individuals who engaged in them. These are pictured as the embodiment of sweetness and light; the people against whom they are pitted are the image of evil and darkness. The forebodings of bloody upheavals are faint and fleeting. It is clear that in presenting the situation the author did not aim at precision, balance, psychological penetration. What he wanted to do was to infect his readers with his own hatred of the autocracy and of predatory capitalism, his own enthusiasm for socialism and faith in its triumph, his own admiration of the martyrs and soldiers of the Revolution. He was also seeking, he said in retrospect, to counteract the failure of nerve caused by the fiasco of the Revolution of 1905.

Did Gorky succeed in his purpose? Soviet commentators, heedless of the novel's defects as literature, have praised it to the skies as a model specimen of what was later called "socialist realism." A biographer of the novelist declares *Mother* to be "a book indispensable to the international proletariat." Lenin, meeting the author in London in 1907 at a Party Congress, congratulated him on having written a useful and timely book. But as the years went by he found its author an unreliable fellow. You could never be sure where you would have him next. A year or two after producing so useful a work as *Mother* he delivered himself of *The Confession,* a novel in the mystical vein then fashionable. True, it set forth no drawing-room religiosity but rather wedded religion to collectivism; and yet the whole book, with its faintly hagiographic style, centered on the idea of man's quest for God. On the publication of this novel Lenin held his peace. Some years later, however, when in the course of an essay Gorky opposed to the current search for God the idea that He must be achieved by creative effort, Lenin gave vent in no uncertain terms to his indignation at this

dalliance with divinity. He told Gorky in a letter that "any defense
or justification of the idea of God, however refined and well-
intentioned, is a justification of reaction." Whether or not Gorky
was persuaded, he did not sustain his interest in religion.

The best passages in his novels have an earthy quality derived
from his closeness to the common people and give off a warmth
that may have had its source in his fervent faith in humanity. His
fictions as a whole are marred, however, by an insidious didacticism, a weakness of invention and a rough-and-ready treatment of
character. Writing to Romain Rolland in a self-analytical mood,
he described himself as being easily overwhelmed by external impressions, a ready prey to the objective world, and thus as having
no eye for the mysteries of the soul. His gaze was turned outward
rather than inward and his memory served him better than his
imagination.

His faults show up least and his gifts are displayed to the
greatest advantage in his autobiographic trilogy, *Childhood, My
Apprenticeship,* and *My Universities.* Although he began planning this work early, it was not until he reached middle life that
he executed it. The greater part of these reminiscences was written
during the seismic years of the First World War and the Revolution. The three volumes are obviously the work of a man who had
a phenomenal gift for storing up every telling detail that touched
his senses. It is not the kind of autobiography that focuses attention on the development of the central character. Indeed, the narrator, for all his uninhibited frankness, tells the reader more about
his companions than about himself; he gives one a set of crowded
canvases of old Russia, full of a fine particularization and suffused
with a glowing humanity. This autobiography is Gorky's sturdiest
work, and although its high level is not sustained to the end, it is
the most likely of his books to endure. Indeed, it belongs with the
major Russian books of our time.

"I know Russian life and Russian literature fairly well, and I
shall say, not without regret, that no one invents less than I." He

wrote thus in a letter dated 1910, when he was a celebrated fiction writer and playwright. He was blessed with self-knowledge. The connection between his personal experiences and his tales is far more direct than is usually the case. We have his word for it that he could document what appears incredible in his stories, naming actual persons and places.

Small wonder, then, that the idea of setting down his reminiscences without any pretense of fiction began to haunt Gorky at an early age. As far back as the spring of 1893, a few months after the appearance of his first short story, the twenty-five-year-old author made a rough draft of two autobiographical sketches. The one bearing the bizarre title "An Account of the Facts and Thoughts the Interaction of Which Withered the Best Pieces of My Heart" has to do with his childhood. In the autumn of 1906, while in the United States, he wrote to his publisher that he was thinking of undertaking his autobiography. He added, in jest one must suppose, "It is said that the Americans are offering a lot of money for it: no less than one hundred thousand dollars." It was not until half a dozen years later, when he was at the height of his powers, that he carried out his plan to chronicle his days. *Childhood* was serialized in a newspaper in 1913. A sequel, *My Apprenticeship,* followed within two years, and the final volume, entitled ironically *My Universities,* was published in 1923, bringing the story down to the end of his second decade. Together with a few short stories, this frank and intimate account of Russian realities forms the most noteworthy part of the large body of writing that Gorky left.

Alexey Peshkov, age three, his father, an upholsterer, having died of cholera, is taken by his mother from Astrakhan to the old city of Nizhny-Novgorod, where her family lives. These Kashirins own a dyeing establishment. The child stays with them, on and off, under more than one roof, until, at the age of eleven, now motherless, he is sent out into the world by his grandfather to earn his bread. At that point the initial volume comes to a close. You follow the external events in the life of the little boy who will eventually become known to the world under his most famous pen name, Maxim Gorky (Russian for "bitter"). You learn what the middle-aged memoirist can tell you as to how Alexey's experiences during his most impressionable years molded his body and his mind. But the book is much more than the history of the spirited, refractory child and the raw youth who grew up to be "a satellite of the Revolution," as Trotsky put it, and in the end a spokesman for Bolshevik ideology and the Soviet regime. Attention is focused less on the vicissitudes that Alexey endured than on the social setting in which he found himself: at first the world of impoverished tradespeople, later the lower depths of Russian society in the 1870s and 1880s.

The *Autobiography* is a work written out of a keen interest in human beings, especially eccentrics, nonconformists, independent, questing souls. It is a gallery of unmistakably Russian portraits, some sketched with a few sharp strokes, others drawn in detail. The pages of *Childhood* teem with men, women, children: members of the Kashirin household, boarders, tenants, neighbors, acquaintances, the local idiot, Alexey's chums. The mother, seen like the rest through the eyes of her little son, remains shadowy. But not so is dour old Kashirin, who, you feel, is portrayed to the life. But the figure on whom the memoirist concentrates most fully and on whom he lavishes all his powers of evocation, was the guardian angel of his early years, the person who, as he tells us, was closest and dearest to his heart and who exercised a profound and lasting influence on him: Grandmother. Indeed, at one time Gorky proposed to entitle the first part of his autobiography *Babushka*. This illiterate crone—with her limitless kindness and forbearance, her strength of body and spirit, her joyful acceptance of life and complete faith in a just and merciful God—is a truly unforgettable character, all the more impressive because she is an actual individual, only partly transfigured by the idealizing work of memory. While she dominates *Childhood*, there are memorable pages about her in *My Apprenticeship,* and in *My Universities* there is a description of how the news of her death affected her grandson, then nineteen years old and working as a baker's assistant in Kazan:

I did not cry. But—I recall—it was as though an icy wind swept over me. Sitting on the woodpile in the yard, that night, I felt a great longing to talk to somebody about Granny; to tell them how kind she was, and wise, and a mother to all. For a long time I carried this heavy longing in my heart; but there was no one I could talk to of such things, and it finally burned itself out, unsatisfied.

These days came back to mind when, many years later, I read A. P. Chekhov's splendidly true tale of the cabman who talked to his horse of his son's death. And I regretted that, in those days of bitter grief, I had not had a horse to talk to, or a dog. I regretted that it had not occurred to me to confide my sorrow to the rats. There were many of these in the bakery, and I was on the best of terms with them.

The little Alexey witnesses scenes of gaiety, more rarely of tenderness, and acts of kindness even by others than his grandmother. Later, when he is on his own, he comes to know several generous-hearted people. Such is the cook on the Volga steamer on which the boy works as a dishwasher; "Queen Margot," who helps him in his blind struggle for an education; the activist in the revolutionary underground who befriends the youth shortly after—in a fit of disgust with himself and with life generally—he attempts suicide. But the bright spots merely accentuate the bleakness of the over-all picture. Few books evoke so candidly and vividly the squalor, the wanton brutality, the naked greed, the drunkenness, dishonesty, cynicism, that prevailed in Russian life during Gorky's childhood and early youth, and not only at the bottom of the social pyramid. True, the *Autobiography* also brings out the warm radiance of humanity that fitfully illuminates the darkness. Emphasis, however, is on the "abominations." Gorky goes out of his way to point out that these should be brought to light because they have not been extirpated from the people's "distressing and shameful" existence "to this very day." These words were written on the eve of the First World War. He was in Petrograd when it broke out, since an amnesty granted in 1913 to political offenders had allowed him to return to Russia.

The "accursed" war harrowed him, but he was heartened by his faith in the Russian proletariat. He hailed the collapse of the autocracy in March, 1917, but not the seizure of power by the Bolsheviks half a year later. Not at first. Like many intellectuals of his generation who were of a radical and democratic temper, he met the October Revolution with hostility, despite his previous support of the Bolshevik faction of the Social Democratic Party. Writing on November 29, 1917, in the newspaper *Novoya zhizn (New Life)*, of which he was then editor, he referred to Lenin, Trotsky, and their followers as "blind fanatics and conscienceless adventurers." In the same editorial he called Lenin "a cold-blooded conjurer who spares neither the honor nor the lives of the proletariat." He believed that his former friend was leading the working class into a bloody anarchy bound to end in bloodier reaction. And he likened Lenin's methods to those of the terrorist Nechayev, that moral monster. If Lenin, so Gorky wrote, allowed himself to carry out a futile and cruel experiment on the Russian people, it was because he had all the characteristics of a "leader," including amoralism and the pitilessness of the master class. (When Gorky was canonized by the regime this page of his biography was expunged from the official record.)

Yet though he was disgusted by the conduct of the Revolution and appalled by the brutalities and the vandalism it brought in its train and that he recorded in his newspaper, he was quick to sense that in those days of mud and blood a new Russia was being born. His attitude was not unlike that of Alexander Blok, save that he lacked the poet's vision of the messianic significance of the Revolution. At all events, he did not emigrate; indeed, toward the end of 1918, when things were at their worst for the new regime, he buried the hatchet. Describing his meeting with Lenin, Gorky said that Lenin gave him the look a shepherd gives a strayed sheep. He never strayed so far again.

Having constituted himself the guardian of the remnants of Russian culture in a period of destruction, he was the good angel of those intellectuals at home who else would have perished in the general chaos, and he stood between some of them and starvation. His humanity extended even to aristocrats and former high officials, for whom he interceded. Through his good offices people obtained railway tickets, clothing, medicines, writing paper, remission of prison sentences; old men received false teeth and infants, milk. He headed the equivalent of the American Writers' Project, the child of the Depression, and took the initiative in founding the so-called Houses of Men of Letters, of Scholars, and of the Fine Arts. Although there was dislike and distrust on both sides, he worked with the authorities and in public praised Lenin. And then in 1921, at the start of the New Economic Policy, he left the country. The official version of his career, broadcast at his decease, was that he went abroad for the sake of his health, on Lenin's advice. Unofficial testimony would seem to indicate that he left the country because he could not adjust himself to the new regime.

Gorky stayed abroad eight years. While he was in Germany he edited a review in which he attempted the impossible task of bringing together émigré and Soviet writers. Publicly he remained a friend of the new Russia and his writings continued to appear in the Soviet press, but privately he was critical of the Kremlin. Indeed, in protest against the removal of certain works, including Tolstoy's tracts, from Soviet libraries, he considered giving up his citizenship. He did not do so. In the summer of 1928 he visited Russia, just after his sixtieth birthday had been elaborately celebrated there. The following year he repatriated himself. Whatever misgivings he may have had he effectually silenced. He is said to have made his peace with the Government in order to preserve the grand illusion of his life: that he was the bard of the Revolution and the proletariat.

In the years that followed Gorky's repatriation he embraced the Soviet regime wholeheartedly, choosing to disregard the seamy side of life under it. He occupied the place held by Tolstoy in the early years of the century. Both alike were not only honored as imaginative writers but were looked to for moral guidance. Yet there was an essential difference in their attitude. The sage of Yasnaya Polyana, while not ranging himself on the side of the revolutionaries, was in opposition to the autocracy and the Church. The ex-hobo was not only the dean of Russian letters but the Soviet laureate. Having aligned himself with those in power, he was the acknowledged spokesman of the regime, a man clothed with authority. He headed committees, he dispensed blessings in the form of prefaces, he edited magazines, including the one characteristically entitled *Our Achievements.* He helped to initiate such various enterprises as a record of the events of a single day throughout the world, a history of Russian factories, an institute for the study of man in sickness and health. He had always kept a fatherly eye on promising young writers with a proletarian background and now he could nurse along fledgling talent on a grand scale. He was affectionately caricatured as the All-Soviet Incubator of Literary Chicks. He was decorated with the Order of Lenin and showered with signs of official recognition. His name was bestowed on streets, factories, theaters, airplanes, institutions for homeless children; the ancient city of Nizhny-Novgorod, his birthplace, as well as the province of that name, became respectively Gorky and the district Gorky. The first time that he had to address a letter there he found the change "embarrassing and unpleasant."

At the first plenary session of the Organizational Committee of the Union of Soviet Writers, which took place late in 1932, Gorky, the honorary chairman, was acclaimed the originator of "socialist realism," and, indeed, he had been the first to use the term publicly earlier in the year. As a matter of fact, this self-contradictory formula was thought up by a Party functionary and endorsed by Stalin. Regarded, of course, as stemming from the teachings of Marx, Engels, and Lenin, it was defined as the "basic method" of producing imaginative literature and critical comment faithfully reflecting reality, and at the same time imbuing the readers' minds with devotion to socialism and to the way of revolution.

What with his romantic streak, Gorky muddied the already turbid waters of doctrine by opining that "socialist realism" was essentially an alias for revolutionary romanticism. "Our art," he wrote, "must rise above reality and elevate man above it." He advised writers to stress the good and slur over the evil, not in order to make propaganda for the regime but because he believed that this would help people to improve themselves and their lives. He thus unwittingly sanctioned the "lacquering" of reality and the insistent hallelujah note that became such offensive characteristics of Soviet writing. In his speech at the First Congress of Soviet Writers in August, 1934, Gorky condemned propaganda in literature and called for attention to craftsmanship. He paid a tribute to the regime by declaring that while the traditional position of realistic writers was that of judges and critics, Soviet writers had gained the further right to "participate in the construction of a new world and in the process of changing the world." His function as a critic, to which he alluded in his address, was largely inoperative. He seems never to have questioned the Party's privilege of tutelage over arts and letters. Nor did he speak against the imposition on these of "socialist realism" that from the first unmistakably showed signs of being a veritable strait jacket.

To a compatriot remaining behind in exile who asked him how he could give full assent to the dictatorship, he replied in substance that the new regime was justified by its works, that it had brought out the constructive potentialities of the people and furthered their intellectual growth. He cited as a specific instance the case of a hand in a sugar refinery who was reading Shelley in the original. What marked Gorky's outlook then as always was the awed respect for "culture" often felt by self-taught men. If he had at one time looked suspiciously at the Revolution, it was because he feared it might prove a bull in the china shop of Russian culture. Books, knowledge, learning, science, were magic words for him. Moreover, to this least puritanic of men, culture was a matter of disciplined labor, an outgrowth of work. Because of their dark heritage of slavery and oppression, he held, the Russians had not learned to work. He insisted that if they could become fully aware of the civilizing, unifying, "religious" values of toil, their life would be fabulous and a lesson to the rest of the world. He had come to believe that the Revolution was the educational power that would be the instrument of this miracle. The revolutionary process was to him "a struggle of the rationally organized will of the laboring masses against the elemental forces of nature" as well as against the antisocial individualism that is the product of a competitive society. He saw the conflict as synonymous with "the struggle for culture and for the creation of culture." One feels in Gorky not so much a savage indignation flowing from an offended sense of justice as delight in creative energy. He welcomed the new order because he saw it liberating energy by freeing men from the tyranny of their fellows and their own brute instincts.

The concept of work as the mother of culture dominated his thinking about art also. He saw it as the instrument of social action. Art, he held, rises above the conflicts of the hour to get a wider view of the battlefield and from that vantage point direct operations. Literature should show things as they are only to enable the working class, future ruler of the world, to understand what must be destroyed and what must be built. He assigned to the writer the dual function of being the midwife of the new order and the gravedigger of the old.

He was, of course, no intellectual either by nature or by training, although like his *bête noire,* Dostoevsky, he was given to injecting philosophical discourses into his fictions. He shared with the greater man the belief that a writer's significance is in large part dependent on his success as a missionary. There was hardly a time, except perhaps in his youth, when he was content with the role in which Chekhov cast the artist—that of a veracious and impartial witness. And yet his own gifts were fundamentally those of a faithful recorder of things seen and heard.

It is noteworthy that although the Soviet laureate exclaimed over, and even lent a shoulder to shifting, the Soviet scene, he did not choose to deal with it imaginatively. Was this the instinctive wisdom of the artist who knows not only what to take but what to avoid? For years before his death the new order had his complete allegiance, yet it remained a thing to celebrate: he could not yet, as the writer must, take it for granted. He never tired of repeating that the working class was in the process of engendering "a new mankind and a new attitude toward the world." He defined the attitude as one of considering the world to be at once man's possession and man's field of endeavor, but he failed to body forth this attitude imaginatively.

The fictional work to which he gave his last decade was a four-volume reminiscential novel, which remained unfinished. Its general title, *The Life of Klim Samghin,* and its subtitle, *Forty Years,* are clues to its character. Like the several French narrative cycles begotten by Proust's masterwork, it is at once the biography of an individual and of the generation to which the author belonged. It by no means measures up, however, to the novels of Roger Martin du Gard, Jules Romains, or Georges Duhamel. Indeed, it is a singularly unsatisfactory performance, not least because it is so boring. Some incidental figures, especially plain folk, are solid and memorable; but for the most part it is thronged with people who are indistinguishable one from another, except for the few who impress themselves on the reader because of their presence on interminable pages. Samghin's personal history is only mechanically connected with the chronicle of the forty years preceding the Revolution, and aside from the few chapters dealing with the Moscow rising of 1905, the chronicle is helpless, throwing a fitful and uncertain light on what goes forward.

Death stopped Gorky's hand in 1936, just when he had brought Samghin's story down to the March Revolution. Had he lived to carry the narrative beyond the October Revolution it is clear that, whatever he might have written, it would not have burned with the indignation he had felt as, in the days that shook the world, he watched power begin its work of corruption. If at the last, as the personal dictatorship grew before his eyes, he suffered a revulsion of feeling, it remained a secret between him and his conscience. He died ostensibly at peace with the regime, one of the most revolting tyrannies the world has known. After his death the honors accorded him during his lifetime were succeeded by an official cult. On the third anniversary of his death the foremost Moscow daily editorially pronounced him "a giant of thought and a magician of the word" and asserted that "now as in his lifetime he determines the development of all Soviet literature." His work is fairly buried under unctuous commentary and exegesis, without a grain of critical salt to the heap.

Gorky was an uneven writer, with some serious faults. In a period of violent change he sought to work with the forces that he conceived to be making for progress, but he sacrificed to that end even the free critical spirit that had previously inspired his activity. The best of him belongs to the past. As a storyteller he is a voice out of old Russia, exposing its evils, bespeaking its will to liberation, summoning attention to such humane excellence as shone in that darkness.

VI

Isaac Babel (1894-1941)–
An Odessa Maupassant?

S OME thirty years after Babel's death, about which we know only the date, much else that relates to the man and the writer remains, due to the blanks in our knowledge of his works and days, uncertain. What is certain is his mastery of language and, indeed, his genius, if genius is, as has been said, "perceiving in an unhabitual way." The immediate popularity of his work was in part due to its freshness. His stories were miniscule, where Russian fiction had generally been long-winded. More significantly, they had a new vigor and effulgence. They gave in the fewest words the essence of an experience. Babel might tend to romanticize whatever he touched (or, more truly, labored over with great pains), and yet the reality, spiritual or coarsely animal, tender or passionate, lovely or hideous, was there—only larger than life.

In an early sketch he threw out the suggestion that nowhere save in Odessa could "our own Maupassant" be born. Was he the man? It will be remembered that Maupassant was introduced into the literary world by Flaubert. Babel won his introduction from Maxim Gorky. This patron was as remote from Flaubert as the world, literary, political, economic, into which Babel entered was remote from that of Maupassant. The Norman locale that fed the imagination of the Frenchman was quite other than the Odessa ghetto and the Cossack battlefield which furnished Babel with much of his material. The obvious gulf between the two writers is enlarged by the fact that Maupassant, in addition to his many short stories, wrote plays and noteworthy novels, while Babel, although he scribbled scenarios for a living, even wrote two plays, and kept referring to one or another mysterious big work, practically confined himself to the short short story, examples of which his scrupulousness, probably combined with the difficulties of writing under the pressure of political control, limited strictly.

And yet? Was there not a kinship between Babel and Maupassant? Both men exalted style, and each forged one of great power and with unique timbre. Both produced work which, for all its compactness, is remarkably resonant. Finally, what Henry James (of whom Babel presumably had never heard) said of the French storyteller can indubitably be said of the Russian: that he "takes his stand on everything that solicits the sentient creature who lives in his senses; gives the impression of the active, independent observer who is ashamed of none of his faculties, describes what he sees, renders, with a rare reproduction of tone, what he hears, and is more anxious to see and to hear than to make sure, in advance, of propping up some particular theory of things . . . his drollery is a direct emanation from the facts. . . ." "In default of other convictions," our critic concludes, "the feat of keeping his talent fresh . . . may still, for the artist, be an adequate working faith. . . ." It was Babel's conviction. His inability, toward the end, so far as we know, to give it body, form, and pressure was not the least tragic feature of his life.

Born into a middle-class Jewish family, Isaac Babel opened his eyes on July 13, 1894 (N.S.) in Odessa, the great port on the Black Sea. The house was situated in the outlying section, known as Moldavanka, which was both the ghetto and the habitat of the underworld. Shortly after the boy's birth the family removed to Nikolayev, another seaport not far away. There they lived rather comfortably, the father owning a warehouse. Isaac learned his letters at his mother's knee and then was sent to a primary school. At home apparently both Yiddish and Russian were spoken. The boy may have owed familiarity with bits of Jewish folklore to his grandmother, who at one time lived with the family and who had no Russian. She seems to have been an ogress for whom no one and nothing existed save her son, her grandson, her pug, and her flowers. In all likelihood Isaac saw her, if not his mother, bless the candles on Sabbath eve. Some of the holy days were observed, certainly the two-day New Year, the Day of Atonement, and the eight days of Passover, that Babel would remember as the best of the festivals. In later days, when he lived by himself, he went out of his way to secure unleavened bread on Passover, and was glad to accept an invitation to a *seder*. On the Day of Atonement he would sometimes go to synagogue and say a memorial prayer addressed to what had long since become for him ex-God.

An autobiographic story of Babel's details the triumph of his admission to the first year of the Nikolaev *gimnazyia* (high school) and the delights of the first blissful weeks there, which ended with a pogrom. That was the historic year 1905, in which the last Romanov granted his subjects a parliamentary regime "wrapped up in pogroms." The Babels were spared physical injury, nor were their possessions plundered, but for Isaac, if the sequel to the above-mentioned story is to be credited, the anti-Jewish riot was a traumatic experience, which resulted in a temporary nervous ailment. The family, now including a little girl, backtracked to Odessa, where they rented a flat in a respectable neighborhood. All his life his birthplace, with its sun and sea, the large Jewish contingent in its heterogeneous population, had a special place in Babel's affections. The city was good, he claimed, for both his spirit and his body. Odessa, not Moscow, where he lived as a grown man, was his home, the dwelling place, he wrote, of his Muse.

The boy was entered in the Nicholas I Commercial School, which offered secondary education and was less exclusive than a *gimnaziya*. It was an institution weak on discipline and attended by polyglot boys, many of whom were teen-agers chiefly interested in billiards. At school Isaac conceived a passion for the language and literature of France. We have his word for it that at fifteen he began writing stories in French. For a while, like so many

Jewish boys, he took music lessons, but they proved a total loss. Until the age of sixteen he was given traditional instruction in Hebrew by a private tutor. In his last autobiographical story he remarks that in his childhood he was "nailed" to the Talmud. As a matter of fact, the Babels, like many Jewish families in the larger population centers, stressed secular learning in the Russian language, rather than the study of the Torah and the commentaries in the ancestral tongue. He wrote later that at home he was forced to study various subjects all day long. This was probably an exaggeration. He managed to indulge his appetite for fiction, reading Turgenev, Dumas, Balzac, and also Sholem Aleichem. Years afterward he will return to those Yiddish pages. They will convulse him with laughter and bring his young days back to him. Welcome relief from the demands of the schoolroom was afforded by idle hours at the harbor, with its many attractions, particularly the thrilling sight of foreign ships. "In Odessa," Babel was to write, "every unmarried young man wants to be a cabin boy on an ocean-going ship. The steamers calling at our port kindle in our Odessan hearts the yearning for new and unblemished lands. . . . The only trouble is that in Odessa we get married with extraordinary obstinacy."

There was a university in the city, but the youth's chances of being admitted to it were less than slim, since the number of Jewish students in the institutions of higher learning was strictly limited. As a result, on graduation from the Commercial School he entered the Business Institute in Kiev which was open to Jews. In that city he became close to the family of a well-to-do manufacturer of agricultural machinery (the elder Babel had an agency for it), and eventually married Zhenia (Yevgenia), the younger of the man's two daughters, a pretty girl with a shock of reddish-chestnut hair.

Exempted from military service, presumably as the only son, the young man graduated from the Institute in 1915 and therewith made his way to Leningrad (then Petrograd). The capital was barred to Jews except for several privileged groups, but Babel had a spurious residence permit and was not molested by the police. In fact, he managed to attend some lecture courses, though not at the university. He had escaped from the ghetto, painlessly, but while he rejected its restrictions, he knew that he was not free from the stamp of his origin. He was emotionally involved with the particularity of the Jewish experience, an attitude which did not attenuate his involvement with the life of mankind. While he may not have had at heart the preservation of Jewish distinctiveness, he did not repudiate the Jewish ethos. In this respect he differed sharply from his contemporary Osip Mandelshtam, another victim of Stalin's Terror. The poet had been forbidden to read secular books, his family, which belonged to the middle class, intending him for the rabbinate. Instead, this extraordinarily gifted writer became completely estranged from his "uterine world," regarding it as an alien, fearful chaos and associating all culture with Christianity.

Babel brought with him to Petrograd at least one sketch done while he was at the Institute: an unfinished childhood reminiscence bearing the patent mark of talent. In the capital he continued writing. After unsuccessfully peddling several short stories, "as brief as they were risqué," in his own phrase, he decided to take two manuscripts to the office of a monthly recently launched by Maxim Gorky. More than once he returned home before he reached his destination, finding something to change in the text. He kept filing and polishing it until he was nearly satisfied. (This was to become his usual method of writing.) Only then did he take the plunge and leave the pieces with the editor. When he returned a few days later, Gorky invited him into his study and dazzled him with the announcement that both stories had been accepted. Thereupon Gorky held forth on the cruel hardships and the glory of the literary calling, and consecrated the novice to it. This interview was the beginning of a lifelong friendship in which the older man played the part less of the mentor than of the protector.

The two stories, which were not reprinted during Babel's lifetime, are of considerable interest. One is about a Jewish drummer from Odessa who finds himself without a residence permit in a town barred to Jews. The police tell him to leave on the next train or be forcibly deported. But this may mean the loss of an order that he needs badly. He gets out of his predicament by spending the night with a prostitute. The following day he manages to evade the police and in the evening comes back with the makings of supper. As the two eat, they talk amicably, airing their respective troubles. Later on an atmosphere of domesticity prevails, the man writing business letters while the woman washes her hair. In the morning the prostitute comes running to the train on which her client is about to leave, and hands him a package of patties that she had baked. The sordid stratagem has resulted in a genuine human contact. The piece has all but one of the characteristics of Babel's mature work: his daring metaphors. The other narrative, too, a less successful performance, is equally frank. In fact, the author was brought to book for pornography. "The trial was set for March, 1917, but late in February the people, coming to my defense," he wisecracked, "burned the documents in the case and while they were at it also committed the Circuit Court to the flames."

II

No section of the empire's population could be more elated by the overthrow of the autocracy and the inauguration, in March, 1917, of a liberal regime, than the Jews. Overnight their age-old chains fell off. One of the first measures taken by the Provisional Government was the abolition of the entire complicated system of Jewish legal disabilities.

Babel volunteered for the army and saw action on the Rumanian front. By the time the Bolsheviks took power he was out of uniform and back in the capital. Like many Russian soldiers, he seems to have voted against the continuation of the war with his feet. Resuming his pen, he turned out several sketches, and heeding

Gorky's advice to "go among the people," he tried his hand at reporting. Less than wholeheartedly favoring the Bolshevik seizure of power, he contributed short notes on current events to Gorky's daily, which in 1918 was sharply critical both of Lenin and of the Party. This reporter did not overlook the seamy side of the new order. His viewpoint was that of a humanitarian. Thus, in commenting on the news that the wives of eight sailors and workmen were the first to be admitted to the Maternity Hospital, formerly an Institute for Well-Born Maidens, he rejoices in the fact that the building will not house confiscation and requisition offices and that constant talk of arrests will not be heard within those walls. "To shoulder a rifle and shoot at each other," he adds, "may sometimes be sensible, but that is not all that revolution comes to. Who knows, maybe that is not revolution at all. To make it possible for children to be born in decent surroundings—that, I know, is real revolution."

Recalling the months that shook the world, he wrote that he was then "a pink, pudgy, still fermenting mixture of a Tolstoyan and a Social Democrat." In fact, a 1918 issue of a Menshevik (Social Democrat) paper—such publications were still tolerated—carried a contribution by Babel. It was an adaptation of one of the facetious tales ascribed to a jester at a Hassidic "court." There was nothing political about this piece, except that it appeared in an organ of the opposition. Babel did not feel called upon, however, to attack the Bolsheviks, and the idea of expatriation was far from his mind. Moreover, he may not have remained untouched by the millennial hopes that the Revolution had raised.

If he failed to join the Communist Party, he was soon to work under its aegis. He accepted employment in the Commissariat of Education, and took part in food requisitioning expeditions and in defending the capital against the counter-revolutionary forces of General Yudenich. In an autobiographical note he stated that he also worked for the Cheka. He repeated this in conversation. A literary project of his lends color to the statement, and so does "The Road," published in 1932, which closes with the narrator's being hired, at the end of 1917, as a translator in the foreign department of the Cheka—the start of an "excellent life full of thought and joy." Babel's wife, however, denied the statement. He may have inserted it in order to improve his public image.

He continued to do writing of sorts. Thus, the June, 1920, issue of an obscure Odessa periodical carries a group of his miniatures based on excerpts from accounts by French army men of their war experiences. Entitled sarcastically "On the Field of Honor" and set down with the dryness of a police report, they underscore the brutalities of war. When these sketches appeared, Babel, married the previous year, was acquiring war experiences of his own. He had neither volunteered for nor been drafted into the Red Army. At his own request he was attached to the Cossack Cavalry Corps as a correspondent of the Southern Division of the Russian Telegraph Agency. The unit consisted of sixteen thousand men and was commanded by General Budyonny, a former sergeant of the Imperial Army. It was to win renown because of its part in the Soviet-Polish war, which broke out in the spring of 1920 and raged through the summer. Hostilities were opened by the Polish troops. Counting on the support of the partisan bands of Ukrainian separatists, they invaded the Ukraine, much of which was under Soviet rule. The plan was to promote the secession of that rich area from Russia and its transformation into a sovereign state friendly to Poland. The Poles made rapid strides, occupying Kiev early in May. Before long, however, under the pressure of the Cossack Corps, the offensive turned into a retreat, the Polish forces being pursued by Budyonny's men across southern Poland.

Sharing the vicissitudes of a campaign fought in defense of both Mother Russia and the Revolution, Babel gained intimate knowledge of that savage conflict and also glimpsed the horrors of the civil war, the fires of which were still smoldering. His principal duty was writing for and editing *The Red Trooper,* a propaganda sheet. In addition, he helped prepare war communiqués, keep a record of operations, and was drawn into some staff work. He was often on the move, accompanying units in action, chiefly as an observer. Of the letters that he must have written to his family and friends only a fragment of one, dated August 13, has been preserved. It is worth quoting in part:

I lived for two weeks in complete despair, because of the ferocious cruelty that does not abate here for a minute and because I clearly realized how unfit I am for the business of destruction. . . . I am recovering, but, well, some people will make the revolution, but I shall deal with what is on the side, deeper down. I feel that I shall be able to do it, that there will be a place and a time for it. . . . A hundred horsepower rage in my breast.

Babel also kept a diary during those months. A part of it has been preserved and recently published. It is a medley of random jottings—names of people and places, weather notes, landscapes, details of interiors, thumbnail sketches of picturesque figures, situations in barest outline, glimpses of battle scenes, observations on human nature (man's "ineradicable cruelty"), musings on the effects of war ("Will not some Cossack commanders turn into condottieri?"), reflections on Communism ("The Budyonny troops bring Communism—an old woman is crying"). There are also memoranda addressed to the diarist ("Describe rain in the woods." "Describe orderlies"). Much of all this is set down for future use. He will eventually arrange the details, modify an episode to heighten the dramatic effect, and in other ways manipulate his material inventively.

To return to the war, the northern sector of the front, too, was the scene of Soviet victories. As the summer wore on, Polish territory under occupation kept growing. Bolshevik propaganda pictured the offensive as directed not against the Polish masses but against their oppressors: the landed gentry and the bourgeoisie. Official Moscow was convinced that the war would bring about a Communist revolution in Poland. When in August the Red Army reached the outskirts of Warsaw, the men expected to be welcomed by the populace as liberators. Instead, the troops met with stiff resistance and were forced to retreat. Neither side achieved its objective, nor were the two countries in a position to stand the strain of a long war. Peace came in October.

Late that year Babel rejoined his wife and the rest of his family in Odessa, a freezing, starving city, which had barely begun to recover from the ravages of foreign intervention and civil war. He soon became the central figure in a small coterie of young people who had already broken into print or were about to do so. The work of some members of the group found its way into the columns of a new gazette called *Moryak (The Seaman)*. As no newsprint was to be had, the issues were run off on wrapping paper and on the blank verso of sheets left over from before the Revolution. In those days they had been cut in narrow strips and used as labels on packages of tea. Since the double-headed eagle was printed on the recto to give the labels an official look, the staff of the publication was nervous about using these sheets.

Babel was particularly close to the managing editor, Konstantin Paustovsky, who was to become popular with his romantic fiction and autobiographical tales. Paustovsky was to remember his friend as bespectacled, portly, stooped, with practically no neck, a wrinkled forehead and a duck's bill for a nose—a man who could be mistaken for a drummer or a broker, but only until he looked at you and opened his mouth. There was "persistent irony" in his voice and a piercing look in his small eyes—another literary friend described them as "sharp, calm, like two drops of molten pitch." A mime and a storyteller of genius, Babel was given to mystifying and baffling people, which earned him the reputation of a troublesome character.

In the summer of 1921 the two young men were inseparable. Generally sparing of words, Babel broke his reserve in talking with Paustovsky. He had much to say about the literary craft, although he was just beginning as a practitioner. The sentence, he said, indeed, the word, must be short (he was frank enough to account for this rule by his asthmatic shortness of breath). Adjectives should be few and chosen with great care—"only a genius can allow himself two adjectives with one noun." Participles are to be avoided. Metaphors must be precise and fresh, similes "as natural as the odor of dill." His first draft of a story, a wretched affair, was followed by a repeated "brutal" weeding out of verbal tares. This time-consuming, excruciating, exhausting labor, combining the drudgery of ditch-digging with the nervous tension of tightrope-walking, was at once his cross and what gave meaning to his existence. His fate was that of a craftsman possessed by the demon, or angel, of perfectionism. He was a galley slave who had "fallen in love with his oar."

He showed Paustovsky a bulky folder with twenty-two variants of a six-page story, adding that he was by no means satisfied with the final draft. "He stroked the manuscript gingerly," Paustovsky recalled, "as if it were a not wholly tamed wild beast." A short story reaches the acme of excellence, he said, not when no word can be added but when no word can be deleted without damaging the plot. Then it is a monolithic thing, holding together by the cohesion of its separate particles. Not even a bolt of lightning can shatter it. These words echo Henry James's observation that "innumerable repeated chemical reductions and condensations . . . tend to make of the very short story one of the costliest, even if, like the hard, shining sonnet, one of the most indestructible forms of composition. . . ."

Babel was not in a hurry to deal with his war experiences. He concentrated on stories about the city's Jewish underworld, which had thrived before the advent of the Soviet regime. To write on any subject, he told Paustovsky, he had to know the setting, down to the last detail. "Authenticity," he asserted, "is the motto engraved on my shield." He and his wife were staying with his parents, and during the hot season, moved with them to a seaside cottage, but in order to immerse himself in the life of the thieves and robbers that was his concern, he rented a room from an elderly couple in the very heart of Moldavanka. The old man, who looked the image of innocence, turned out to be a tipster who, for a cut, purveyed information to holdup men about promising jobs. One day he gave the same tip to two different gangs. Their chiefs arrived simultaneously at the cashier's window, ready for business. According to gangsterdom's unwritten law, this was a capital offense on the part of the informant. He was forthwith rubbed out, and the militia (the Soviet term for police) advised the tenant to give up the room, which he did.

Such is the story, not without doubtful elements, that Paustovsky claims to have been told by Babel, and that he recorded nearly forty years after the event in such detail as to seem suspicious. Be that as it may, a June, 1921, issue of *Moryak* carried a story by Babel entitled "The King." This is the nickname of Benya Krik, modeled on Misha Yaponchik, a semilegendary Odessa gangster. Benya rules his band of robbers, colorful specimens of their kind, with an iron hand. As resourceful as he is fearless, he invariably manages to make game of the police. He holds up a well-to-do dairy farmer, but captivated by the charms of the man's daughter, gives back the money he had extorted from him, asks for his daughter's hand, and marries her. Returning to town after the honeymoon, he arranges the marriage of his forty-year-old sister to a submissive youth, bought with the money of Benya's father-in-law. The end of this sumptuous wedding is marked by a fire which reduces the police station to ashes and obligingly prevents a raid on the underworld, set for that night by the new police chief.

Benya, now at the beginning of his fabulous career, is the hero of another story, which came out two years later. His first holdup is marred by a mishap. While he is robbing a moneybag who owns a chain of stores, the merchant's young clerk is fatally wounded by a tipsy member of the gang. Benya forces the merchant to hand over five grand to the innocent victim's mother, a poor woman who sells chickens in the marketplace, and give her a pension. Furthermore, he sees to it that the clerk has the grandest funeral Odessa has ever beheld. Near his grave is another for the body of the gangster who fired the fatal bullet. He is buried forthwith in an unpainted coffin, but not without the complete funeral service. Over the clerk's grave Benya makes a speech, in which he says, among other things, that the deceased has perished for the entire working class. Benya's behavior faintly resembles that of the romantic hero of the Robin Hood ballads who robs the rich to give some of the loot to the poor. Soviet commentators are prone to see the operations of the gangsters as an ill-chosen form of protest against the established order.

Although this story, too, was printed in an Odessa newspaper, since late in 1921 Babel had not lived in that city. His months with the Cossack Corps had aggravated his asthma, and he and his wife stayed two or three years in the Caucasus, hoping that the climate would benefit his health. They stopped in Batum, a port city, and in Tiflis (now Tbilisi), that "oriental Florence," in Paustovsky's phrase, which at the time was a center of modernistic poetry and painting, and over which the red flag had been flying since February. Much of the time the Babels seem to have spent in the rustic surroundings afforded by the easternmost section of Transcaucasia. It is not known to what extent his asthma improved, but it is certain that the enchanting land and people of the Caucasus made a lasting impression on him.

During this period Babel did a good deal of writing. He contributed several articles to a Tiflis journal. They reflect an attitude sympathetic to Bolshevism: the term "propaganda" is used without any disparaging connotation; the Mensheviks are described as "flabby woodlice"; references to failures in the tasks of reconstruction are balanced by a recital of successes.

With incomparably greater care he wrote two more Odessa tales, which were printed in a Moscow magazine in 1924. Benya Krik appears in one of them, but the central figure is a widowed, dutiful father, Froim Grach, an elderly trucker who is a holdup man on the side. He has on his hands the business of securing a husband for his two-hundred pound, stentorian-voiced daughter. He turns for help to the far from motherly Lyubka, foul-mouthed, two-fisted, nicknamed "the Cossack," a receiver of stolen goods, who owns an inn, a wine cellar, a store, a quarry, and a whorehouse. She suggests that Benya Krik, then unmarried, would be just the match for the girl. The father succeeds in persuading Benya to become his son-in-law after patiently waiting in Lyubka's brothel at the door of a room in which the young man is engaged, until he emerges, bashfully draping a sheet about himself. It is stipulated in the marriage contract that a certain opulent grocer, who had refused to marry his son to Froim's daughter, is to pay Benya two thousand rubles, which he undertakes to extort from the wretch. "God will help us," he says, "and we will punish all grocers." Lyubka is the key figure in the last of the four tall tales, forming an epic of Odessa's Jewish underworld. They are couched in the local vernacular, a variety of substandard Russian, which is used with side-splitting effect. Whether reprinted separately or with selections from Babel's other work, they are widely read.

There is one more story belonging to this group. Unlike the others, it is laid in the first year of the Soviet regime. Benya is no longer in the picture. The exploits of his men are masterminded by Froim Grach. They attack the rear guard of the White troops, slaughter the officers, and seize some of the equipment. By way of reward, they demand from the locial soviet freedom of the city for three days. Refused, they loot a number of shops and rob a bank. After a while the Cheka starts arresting and shooting the bandits. The rumor spreads that one of them has squealed. He is murdered. More gangsters are executed. Finally Froim calls on the head of the Cheka and says, "Master, you are killing eagles. You'll be left with garbage. Set my boys free, name your price." The Chekist orders him shot out of hand. So imposing is the death of the high-hearted old man that one of the executioners remarks upon it. There is a touch of admiration on the author's part for the towering underworld figure in this melancholy narrative, which puts finis to the saga of Odessa gangsterdom. The story was not published in the Soviet Union until 1964.

III

Work of an order totally different from the Odessa tales began to come out serially in 1923. It embodied Babel's experiences with the Cossack Cavalry Corps. These stories, as they appeared in periodicals, were avidly swallowed both by those who expected the millennium from the Revolution and those who had misgivings about it. A reviewer in *Pravda* hailed the author as "the rising star of our literature." On the other hand, the editor of the monthly that had published some of the pieces was castigated for having printed stuff that could have come from the pen of a counter-revolutionary. In 1925 half a dozen of the pieces were issued as a group and when, the following year, they were included in a much larger collection, still a slim volume, under the title *Konarmiya* (short for *Konnaya armiya* [Cavalry], eventually englished as *Red Cavalry*), Babel became the rage in Moscow, indeed, throughout literate Russia.

The book is made up of a sequence of thirty-five unconnected vignettes, sketches, mini-stories. Some characters appear in more than one piece. Many of the stories are first-person narratives, which reflect Babel's attitude to what he saw and heard during the turbulent months of his stay with the Corps, though he often lets the events speak for themselves. Each inclusion is an example of sensuous, severely pared prose. Here is work by an artist with a Flaubertian standard of craftsmanship, an untamed imagination, and withal a dedication to the factual which makes for brutal realism and, in Russian writing, unwonted eroticism. Elliptical, rapid, the style is richly figurative. The startling similes and metaphors serve to express as nearly as may be the author's idiosyncratic perception of actuality. There are also passages that achieve their effectiveness by directness and cool objectivity in presenting a shocking experience. Here is an instance:

(Babel is billeted in a house in a Ukrainian townlet.)
Right under my windows several Cossacks were executing an old Jew with a silver beard. The old man was screaming and struggling to get away. Then Kudrya of the machine gun section took his head and hid it in his armpit. The Jew quieted down and spread his legs apart. Kudrya pulled out his dagger with his right hand and carefully cut the old man's throat without splashing himself. Then he knocked at the

closed window. "Anyone interested," he said, "can take him away. Suit yourself."

Contrast being Babel's favorite device, orotund phrases are juxtaposed with colloquial, and sophisticated language is on neighborly terms with the homely dialect of the countryside, slightly tainted by propagandist rhetoric. Several pieces—Cossacks' monologues or epistolary efforts—are entirely in the vernacular, the weird usage providing comedy unintended by the speaker. Examples of the author's most telling work, they attest to one aspect of his genius: his unfailing ear for living speech.

Babel joined the Corps under a name which is obviously that of a Russian of unmixed stock. Yet the narrator rarely figures in the text as that character. The alias cannot have been intended to hide the author's Jewish identity, for he makes it unmistakable. *Red Cavalry* opens with a two-page piece about the brutal murder of an old Jew before the eyes of his pregnant daughter. The book ends with a description of the final moments of a young man who is the last prince of a famed Hassidic dynasty, and commander of a routed Red regiment. Babel had seen him several weeks earlier at a ceremonial meal, presided over by the young man's father. That experience is the subject of another story, entitled "The Rabbi."

There are glimpses of the ghettos of the Ukrainian and Polish towns that Babel's unit halts in or passes through. The contending armies and partisan bands have decimated these communities and the Revolution has wrecked their economy. The author is not at home in their moribund world. Yet a vague sense of personal involvement in the catastrophe attaches to the lines in which he briefly focuses on the "lifeless" Jewish townlets clinging to the outskirts of Polish estates or lost in the steppes of the Ukraine. Decrepit synagogues squat behind scattered hovels. Narrow-shouldered Galician Jews loiter mournfully about crossroads. How different they are from the comfortable Jews he had known in Odessa, "jovial, potbellied, bubbling like cheap wine," and from the hearty gangsters, the legends about whom he had retailed.

Babel perceives "bitter disdain in these long and bony backs, these tragic yellow beards. In their passionate, anguish-carved features there is no fat, no warm pulsating of blood. . . . The depth of their grief is full of somber grandeur."

History breaks into the present with a vignette of a scanty page devoted to the cemetery of a Volynian townlet. Under an oak shattered by lightning stands a crypt, "as shabby as a water-carrier's lodging." Under the terse epitaph "The Mouth of God" it holds the body of Rabbi Azrail, who was killed by Cossacks in the seventeenth century. A representative of each of three gener-ations of his descendants are buried with him.

The melancholy story entitled "Gedali" is lyrical with overt nostalgia for the traditional way of life that Babel had known in his early years. It is Friday evening and he is assailed by "thick sadness" as he recalls how his "grandmother in a lace cap used to hold her knotty fingers over the Sabbath candles in a blessing and sob sweetly. On these evenings the child's heart rocked like a little ship on enchanted waves." The place is a Ukrainian burg, which formerly had a large Jewish population, but is now a ghost town, the pavement of its marketplace "as clean as the bald spot of a corpse. . . . Killed is the fat soul of abundance." The narrator comes upon a curiosity shop hidden among the padlocked stalls. Its owner is a little old Jew by the name of Gedali. He and the stranger have a talk, sitting on empty beer barrels.

The episode is based on an actual experience of Babel's. An en-try in his diary thus sums up Gedali's philosophy: "All [Reds and Whites] say that they fight for justice, and all plunder. If at least some one government was kindly!" In the story he says aye to the Revolution, but asks, "Shall we say nay to the Sabbath?" And be-sides, the Revolution, in Gedali's quaint phrase, "sends forth only shooting." Babel's response is that the Revolution cannot avoid shooting. But he seems to sympathize with Gedali's longing for "a sweet revolution." When Gedali asks with what sauce the Inter-national is eaten, he replies, "It's eaten with gunpowder and sea-soned with the best blood." And upon that grim word—"lo! the young Sabbath ascended its throne, coming out of the blue darkness." Now it is Babel's turn to question Gedali. Where, he asks, can he get a Jewish cookie, a Jewish glass of tea, and in the glass a little of that God who has been retired. "Nowhere," answers Gedali, and goes off to the synagogue. Failing to accompany him, does not Babel feel, if temporarily, nowhere?

Gedali also figures in "The Rabbi," mentioned above. It appears that he is a pious Hassid. It is he who takes the narrator to the *tzadik's* quarters for a meal. A secular-minded skeptic, Babel is aware of the extent to which Hassidism has been corrupted. Yet he is curious about it, at the very least, and hospitable to its exuberance of spirit. The unbeliever harbors a kind of unadmitted religiosity, which draws him not only to the battered synagogues but also to the Catholic churches of the Poles. He describes with fervor a cathedral flooded with light and a kind of "cool gaiety," and invests it with canvases by a devout, if heretical, painter of genius —Babel's invention—whose model for St. Paul is a lame Jewish convert and whose Mary Magdalene is the town's Jewish whore. The cathedral also holds an amazing sculpture of Christ: "a curly-haired Jew with a tousled beard and a low wrinkled forehead—his mouth torn like a horse's lip."

IV

The impact of the war, the Revolution, the civil war, on the Jewish minority is a peripheral theme in *Red Cavalry*. The book concentrates on evoking the world of the Cossacks with whom the author shares the varying fortunes of a savage campaign. History had allotted to a section of this quondam privileged military class, which was deeply rooted in the native soil and had long been a prop of the monarchy, the role of soldiers of the Revolution and defenders of the Soviet fatherland. However they regarded themselves, they were not inclined to look favorably on a puny, bespectacled stranger, as Babel discovered on his first day with the Corps.

The divisional commander, a dazzling giant, sketched in with admiration and envy, laughingly greets the simpleton with specs on his nose as "a mangy runt." When he is introduced by the quartermaster to several men with whom he is to share temporary lodgings, they make it clear that they don't care for his company. One Cossack turns his behind to Babel and emits an obscene salvo. They accept him as a comrade only after he curses and shoves the old woman on whom they are billeted when she ignores his demand for grub, and then brutally kills her gander so that she may cook it for him. Brutality, however, even when directed at dumb creatures, even when exercised in self-defense, goes against the grain with him.

"I grieve for the bees," is the opening phrase of a vignette. In Volynia the men, short of food, invade what he mistakenly calls "the sacred *republic*" of the bees, digging out the honey with their sabres, ruining the hives and slaughtering the insects. "The chronicle of these everyday crimes," Babel confesses, "tirelessly afflicts me like heart disease." The trooper to whom he ventures to mention his feelings explains, "The bees have got to bear it. It is for them, too, that we are mucking about here."

Such matters as the perennial problem of the justification of present evils for the sake of good to come play almost no part in these pages. What they unflinchingly make present to us is extreme situations and the individuals who create or endure them. One story brings together briefly, as usual, a dying regimental commander, his woman, Sashka, who has been a camp-follower and also acts as a nurse, and his orderly, Lyovka. The commander, lying in a cart, mutters his last bequests to the orderly: what money there is goes to Sashka; all his clothes, his "Order for selfless hero-ism," the cottage, to his mother; and his horse to the regiment for prayers for his soul. The orderly violently extorts Sashka's promise to carry out the will. Then he tries to feed the dying man, but in vain, and starts to chew the food noisily himself. Having licked his lips, he drags Sashka into the tall grass, where they "warm each other" in the moonlight, while the commander looks on. Returning to him, the woman examines his wound and says, "By morning you'll be gone. Death is in your guts." All this happens while not far away a battle flames and thunders. When the commander dies, the orderly gives him the ritual last kiss and "the widow" mourns him, calling him "my Jesus Christ." "She's taking it hard," the orderly observes. "No one can say that they lived badly together. Now she'll have to take on the whole squadron again. Tough luck."

The next morning he sees "the widow" riding in the funeral procession. He overtakes her and bashes her face with his fist, to remind her that she must carry out faithfully the dead man's last will. Rejoining his squadron, Lyovka announces that he had given it to "the viper" good and proper, and that he will beat her again if it's necessary to refresh her memory. If this story is taken as representative, the Cossack is a man of primitive animalism, but not without concern for moral obligations.

In his diary Babel noted, among other Cossack traits, feral cruelty and proneness to looting. Both characteristics, combined with soldierly prowess, are exemplified in the story that follows. In defiance of regulations, and despite Babel's protests, a squadron commander kills two prisoners whom he suspects of being officers. (Killing prisoners was apparently discouraged only when they were likely to possess useful information.) Then he fires at one of his own men (missing him) and prevents him from getting away with loot, which includes the trousers he has pulled off one of the dying prisoners. Though himself bleeding badly, the commander remains at the antiaircraft gun and the would-be looter chooses to match his heroism. The two die gunning an American bomber. Just before he expires, the commander hands his new boots to a machine-gunner who is taking cover.

Of the several examples of Cossack vengeance sadistically wreaked, the one about a certain Red general is indelibly set down. Still intoxicated with the glorious Year Eighteen, he considers himself licensed by Lenin to take lives at his own discretion. A former swineherd, and still illiterate "to the bottom of my heart," as he puts it, he visits his former master to square accounts with that lecherous beast. Having decided that shooting the man would give him so easy a death as to amount to a pardon, he spends over an hour "trampling" him to death before the eyes of his insane wife. That is the treatment, the monologue concludes, he has given to more than one enemy. The troopers' appetite for wreaking vengeance on the enemy is satisfied in Poland when they loot and desecrate a cathedral. Babel, marginal Jew that he is, has sufficient regard for piety, even that of Catholics, to report the outrage.

There are among the men some few compassionate, gentle souls. A chum of Babel's who figures in two stories is Sashka, a syphilitic, nicknamed "the Christ" for his kindness. He had caught the disease from the beggar woman who on the same evening infected his stepfather. The old Cossack songs that he sings to the accompaniment of his harmonica go straight to the hearts of the troopers. One night, out of sheer goodness, he volunteers to show "attention" to an old woman in whose bare hovel he and Babel are billeted. She is in such a bad way, she complains, that she can't get any pleasure out of sinning. In the end she pushes to the wall the dumb misbegotten son of hers who is snoring in the big bed to make room for Sashka beside her.

It has been seen that on his very first day with the Corps, Babel discovered that, tough as they were, the troops were a comradely lot. The feeling of these centaurlike men for their horses was, if anything, more intense than that for their fellows. Several tales illustrate their devotion to their mounts. By the same token, they were profoundly contemptuous of mere footsloggers, and on one occasion took pleasure in playing a mean practical joke on an infantry unit.

A bullet pierced the neck of the horse of a platoon commander. Dismounting, he "scanned the shining horizon mournfully. 'Farewell, Stepan,' he said in wooden tones, stepping away from the dying animal, and bowed to it from the waist. 'How shall I return without you to the quiet village? What shall I do with the embroidered pillow under your saddle? Farewell, Stepan,' he repeated more loudly, choked, squeaked like a trapped mouse, and broke into a gasping howl like a hysterical woman seized with a fit in church." He solemnly promised the charger to butcher the Polish gentry more ruthlessly than ever. Laying his face against the horse's wound, he quieted down. A superior officer put the horse out of its misery and spoke gently to the bereaved man, bidding him collect the harness and go to his unit. The man was seen walking toward his squadron bent under the weight of Stepan's harness and "limitlessly alone."

With the Cossacks the passion for horses is bred in the bone. Vaska, the office boy in the Propaganda Department of the Corps, has Babel pen a letter to his mother at his dictation. He bids her write him about Styopka, whether he has been shod; asks if she has the right soap for the scabs on his forelegs; begs her to be sure to take good care of him, and then God will not forsake her. After a few words about the crops where he is stationed and the way hops are grown there, he coolly relates how Pop was done in by brother Semyon. The previous year Pop (to whom the boy regularly refers in the respectful third person plural), as a White Guard, had killed brother Fedya "for the sake of what is right." When Semyon caught up with him and performed his act of vengeance, he had sent Vaska out of the courtyard so that he would not witness it. Vaska goes on for a bit about the city where they have been stationed and his present job at the Front, and winds up with the original plea, bidding his Mom to look out for Styopka, again promising that God will then not forsake her.

A mount and the Communist Party are involved in a dramatic incident which is the subject of a seriocomic piece. A squadron commander has been arbitrarily deprived by a superior officer of his white stallion, to the nurture and training of whom he had wholly devoted himself and with whom he is in intimate rapport ("I can feel his wordless needs"). In exchange he has been given a black mare, for which he has no use. His complaints notwithstanding, the stallion has not been returned to him. He spends a day framing a statement addressed to the Party. This has been established, to his knowledge, "for joy and limitless justice, and it ought to have consideration for the little man, too." But since it cannot restore to him his "very own," all that is left him is to resign his membership, "with tears that do not befit a soldier, yet flow all the same and slash the heart."

"Revolutionary spirit" is another Cossack trait noted in Babel's diary. In the stories the morale of the men is high. It springs from patriotism, from the pluck of born warriors, and also from zeal for the Soviet republic, creature of the Communist Party. On the other hand, *Red Cavalry* leaves the impression that not a few of the troopers are more interested in loot or in squaring private accounts than in world revolution and in "striking the anvil of future ages with the hammer of history," to quote from a funeral oration delivered by a regimental commander for an officer fallen in battle. The new regime is still in a state of flux, the power of the state is weak, regimentation is resisted, there is room for the individual to assert his autonomy. The zealot does not hesitate to take the law into his own hands. He is likely to consider it his duty to ferret out and on his own authority summarily destroy counter-revolution, *treason*. This is the title of a piece, virtually untranslatable, about three wounded troopers, who on being hospitalized resent the doctor's order to remove their clothes and arms. One of them asks, "What infection can there be in a sharp Kuban saber except for the enemies of the Revolution?" Their adventures are retailed with comical effect in a letter to "Comrade Investigator" which concludes: "Treason is going about the house barefoot, treason has taken off his boots, so that the floorboards don't creak in the house that is being robbed."

A lynching is central to "Salt," one of Babel's best-known stories. It is in the form of a letter to an army newspaper, the writer adding to his signature the words, "Soldier of the Revolution." A train packed with troopers is being besieged by a mob of black-marketeers. Thanks to a kindly Cossack, a woman with a baby in her arms is pulled into the train. He persuades his fellows not to molest her. The next morning he discovers that the baby is a heavy bag of salt. He could forgive her for having cheated him, he tells her, but he cannot forgive the harm she has done to Russia. He throws her out while the train is moving. Unhurt, she insolently picks herself up and is on her way. He is so aggrieved that he wants to end either his life or hers. On the advice of his comrades he takes his rifle and "washes this shame from the face of the workers' land and the republic." In conclusion he assures the "comrade editor" that the men of the second platoon have sworn "to deal mercilessly with all traitors."

It is the men's mercilessness that repels Babel. The troopers, as has been seen, are not without moral and even religious resources. They have compassion for one another on occasion, and they lavish tenderness on their mounts. Some few are gentle souls. Yet most live by violence, which takes on diverse forms. It is in the fibers of their being. Pacifism is apt to be regarded as treason. Magnanimity toward the enemy, foreign or native, is unthinkable.

Babel's anti-Polish animus breaks forth now and then. Yet one night when, having urinated out of doors in the dark, he finds that the stinking fluid fell on a Polish corpse, he is at pains to wipe clean the skull of his "unknown brother." He uses the same word in speaking of the Red Army commander, the *tzadik*'s son whom he attended as the youth breathed his last. While not overtly, these stories do leave the reader with the sense that the author of *Red Cavalry* would have applauded Chekhov's insistence on a writer's being "humane to the tips of his fingers."

As for the troopers and their commanders, Babel is involved with them; he does make friends among them; yet they are seen through the eyes of a man who remains an outsider. This lends an objectivity faintly tinged with irony to his account, the testimony of a witness corrupted by nothing but his tempestuous imagination. The Cossacks are tough, mettlesome, teeming with vitality, traits that Babel admires and wishes were his own. He watches with obvious gusto squadrons in battle array riding "with majestic and cool insolence," or a newly appointed brigade commander after his first victorious engagement seated in his saddle with "the sovereign nonchalance of a Tartar khan." Babel feels the same way about the Cossacks' self-assurance, their lack of squeamishness, and the guts that enable a man to commit a mercy killing. He hasn't the heart to do it, and he shamefacedly begs Fate to grant him the simplest knowhow: the ability to kill a fellow man. One assumes that he meant it as an act of compassion. On the one hand, he shies away from these companions, repelled by their obedience to the instincts of "natural" man whose appetites and lusts, cruelty and coarseness are theirs. On the other hand, he is attracted by them, in the same way that he was attracted by the vigorous, sensual, daring Jewish gangsters of his native city. It is notable that he could write so evocatively about both the men of the under-world and Gedali, though it was with the latter that he tended to identify himself. Babel seems to have gravitated toward plenitude of spirit, especially as manifested by his fellow Jews. And equally he gravitated toward the Cossacks' physical exuberance. Not far from the surface of these stories there seems to be a covert longing for the fullness of a life that can encompass both. Certainly the author of *Red Cavalry* did not escape what Robert Penn Warren calls "the haunting duality of human experience."

The book belongs to the limited number of prose works of liter-ary quality produced before Stalin's death. As such it has found a secure place in Soviet writing. Not that this place was established without question. True, on its appearance a Soviet reviewer wrote that "Fragments of *Red Cavalry* will always remain a striking ex-ample of candid representation of the Revolution in literature." But there was also adverse comment on the book. Under pressure from the censor Babel toned down his frankness in dealing with sex, although not enough to satisfy his critics. When Gorky praised *Red Cavalry*, General Budyonny retorted that it was "crude, delib-erate, arrogant defamation of the Cossack Corps." He went on to declare that the author's ignorance of Marxist dialectics disqualified him as a portrayer of the Corps. Others attacked Babel on the grounds of having interpreted the Revolution as an elemental force of which he was afraid, rather than as the carrying-out of a planned program that it was. Above all, he was accused of having failed to stress "the organizing and educational role played by the Party in the civil war."

Babel did not yet realize the seriousness of these charges. For the time being he was not disturbed. In the twenties literary criticism was still the work of the intelligence, not the business of the intelligence bureau. His own status was that of a literary "fellow traveler," to use Trotsky's familiar phrase. By a resolution dated June 11, 1925, the Central Committee of the Party requested that Bolshevik critics treat such writers "considerately and tactfully," in the hope of winning them over. Babel must have known, what the reviewer first quoted recognized, what even those who cannot read him in the original feel, that he verily makes the reader breathe the acrid air of the early years of the Revolution.

V

As an author whose work was gaining a wide audience—*Red Cavalry* and his Odessa stories were already being translated into several languages—Babel had reason to be at ease. Yet his private circumstances were far from happy. According to his daughter, he had been having an affair with an actress and his wife was aware of it. Furthermore, she abhorred the Soviet regime. As a result, in the summer of 1925 Zhenia expatriated herself, settling in Paris. The marriage survived the shock. They wrote to each other, he took a lively interest in her, he considered himself responsible for her welfare. Earlier in the year his only sister had emigrated to Belgium to get married there. Before long the couple were joined by his mother, recently widowed, in Brussels, where she was to live with them for the rest of her days.

His numerous letters to the two women (those to his wife were seized by the Gestapo and have disappeared) were published several years ago in Italian and English, and are the chief source, which has to be handled warily, for a chronicle of Babel's life from this time on. They eloquently attest his extraordinary devotion to both his sister and his mother. Their freedom from anxiety, their ailments and the treatments that they receive, their domestic arrangements, pastimes, vacations, documents—their passports had to be renewed with a view to eventual repatriation—all are the objects of his constant solicitude. He clamors for letters, telegrams, snapshots. The dispersal of the family depresses him severely. He never stops planning to reunite it and, failing that, to visit his people as often as is possible for a Soviet citizen.

Meanwhile his interest in Soviet-Polish hostilities as a literary theme had grown lukewarm. Indeed, this happened even before *Red Cavalry* came off the press. He had planned more stories for the book, but years later added only two pieces to that cycle. Babel said that in his attack on *Red Cavalry,* Budyonny should have appealed for help to the author: he disliked the book. Turning away from the war, he started a group of narratives dealing with the experiences of a Jewish boy in pre-Revolutionary Russia. One of them shows, among other things, a ten-year-old boy in love with a voluptuous young woman. Autobiography is transmuted by a large measure of fiction. The writing is still eccentric, but to a lesser degree, and somewhat relaxed, allowing for plot development and some psychologizing.

At the same time—this was during 1925—Babel was busy composing movie scenarios. One of them was based on a novel by Sholem Aleichem; in another he attempted, unsuccessfully, to link the Odessa underworld with the Revolution. Babel found the cinema work "a hellish trade," but he had a knack for it, and it was lucrative. If, like countless others, he followed the line of least resistance, he loathed doing so. As soon as he carried out the commissions he had accepted, he wrote to his sister on New Year's Day, 1926, he would go to Paris and, his mind refreshed, return to "real work." The situation was to repeat itself intermittently to the end.

He did not cross the border at this time. During the summer, working with a speed unusual for him, he composed *Sunset,* a bleak drama. The protagonists figure in the Odessa tales, but while there the atmosphere is jovial and the gangsters and teamsters are

slightly romanticized and idealized, here, against a black por-
tentous background, greed, viciousness, depravity prevail. The plot
centers on a tragedy in the Krik family. Without saying a word to
his wife and children, old Mendel, under the influence of liquor,
is about to sell his large carting business and with the proceeds
leave home, in the company of a loose woman. In the climactic
scene his two sons, one of them Benya, thwart his plan by main
force. Mendel attacks his other son, and while the two are trying to
maim each other, Benya knocks out his father. In the end the old
man is undone, and Benya, now in the saddle, patches up a dismal
kind of peace.

The author, however he may have regarded the other faults of
the play, was certainly aware that it was "monstrously" out of
harmony with what was being done in the Soviet theater. Both in
Moscow and in the provinces the life of *Sunset* was short. Nor was
it a hit during the sixties when it was revived in foreign parts,
including New York, Off-Broadway. But the text of the play was
printed in a monthly, and that meant a fee. Part of Babel's earnings went to his dependents, but there was enough left for him
to plan a trip abroad. As his standing with the authorities was
good, he had no difficulty in obtaining a permit to leave the
country.

Early in July, 1927, he arrived in France. Of course, there was
a family reunion in Brussels, and during the summer, which he
spent in a North Sea resort not far from Ostend, he visited Mar-
seilles and was fascinated by the city: that was what Odessa should
become. For several enchanted weeks he lived as Gorky's guest in
the "patriarch's" house at Sorrento. Most of the time he stayed
with his wife in Paris. At first he found the city "triply foreign,"
but soon discovered its attractions: personal freedom, creature
comforts, the unique magic of its spring, which gave him "wings."
The couple's means, drained by the expenses of his trips, did not
permit them to take advantage of life in Paris. They managed to
make ends meet, what with some borrowing, royalties from
the German edition of *Red Cavalry,* and Babel's monthly stipend

from *The New World,* a Moscow magazine. This was an advance
on writing which he obligated himself to deliver exclusively to
that publication at fixed dates. But when the deadline was impending, all he could do was to beg his dear, martyred editor to be
patient with a man tortured by conscience.

During the next eight months he delivered no copy to *The New
World.* He still felt bound to give the magazine whatever he wrote,
but in spite of his "hideous pecuniary circumstances" he wrote the
editor that he would not change his way of working by a jot or
speed it up by an hour. As a matter of fact, during his stay abroad,
which lasted well over a year, the one short narrative that he attempted he chucked after six weeks' work on it. What absorbed
him was a literary project of a totally different sort. Commenting
on essays about his work, he said that they made him feel as though
they were written about a dead man, so remote from what he had
done previously was what he was doing now. He was aiming at
something "calm, serene," that demanded of him what he had not
demanded of himself before. This must have been the "accursed
book" in which he was "stuck," as he wrote to Gorky, the "Sisyphean labor" on which he was toiling slowly, painfully, fiercely,
all the while suspecting that he was unequal to the task. It could
scarcely have been the "big thing about the Cheka" that he had
spoken about to an acquaintance before the publication of *Red
Cavalry.* Nor was it likely to have been a long narrative about
rural collectivization which he also contemplated. All references
to the "Sisyphean labor" cease toward the end of the summer.

In Moscow his extended stay abroad gave rise to rumors that
he had applied for French citizenship. He was at pains to scotch
the gossip. In letters to friends he had explained that what was
keeping him in Paris was the hope of straightening out his
"messed-up private affairs" and of completing his work—presumably the "Sisyphean labor." He was eager to return to the land
where "we long for the wind of great thoughts and great passions"; his soul was pining for Russia's "planetary dimensions";
as soon as he carried out what he had planned, he would fly home

"with rapturous cackling." These protestations seem to have been sincere. Was the halo of the Revolution indeed still untarnished for him?

Early in October he was back in Moscow, alone and with empty hands. Zhenia had refused to leave Paris, and his mother remained in Brussels with his sister and her husband. A financially bleak prospect faced him. He had no book-length manuscript, no copy for *The New World*. Unabashed, he persuaded that publication to renew its contract with him. Six months later he was solemnly assuring the long-suffering editor that should the agreement be renewed with a larger advance, it would acquire a model contributor. He added, however, "You can flog me at 4 P.M. in your office, but I will not hand in a manuscript one day before I consider it ready." Nothing by him appeared in *The New World* before the issue for October, 1931, which contained two of his contributions. One was the opening chapter of *Velikya Krinitza,* a novel about collectivization in a Cossack village. The piece was never reprinted in the Soviet Union. Another section of the tale was first published in 1963 in a miscellany under a New York imprint. Politically the theme was safe only for an orthodox Communist like Sholokhov. To judge by its two sections, the work, if completed, would have been a major literary event.

A reprint of *Red Cavalry* may have helped to chase the wolf from the door. And then there were, of course, scenarios, though he still felt that it was "criminal to spend energy and time on this useless rubbish." At least the business enabled him to contribute to the support of his people abroad, as well as to travel in the south for the sake of his own health.

In July, 1929, while he was staying in Kiev, he received a telegram announcing that his wife had borne him a daughter. He had lived through an ordeal of waiting for that telegram. Knowing Zhenia's procrastination, he had decided that she must have taken eleven months to bring the child to birth. The baby was named Natasha (Natalie), though he would have preferred a

Biblical name. Separation from the family now weighed on him so heavily that it made work difficult.

VI

When he was not traveling, Babel lived in the country, renting a room in a shoemaker's hut, at one time acting as secretary to the village soviet, and paying visits to nearby Moscow, where he had a flat. In a letter to a friend he admitted that on occasion he would have a bad time in the village, what with a persistent headache, foul weather, and the daylong mooing of a cow who, having a frank disposition, stubbornly demanded three things: grass, the sun, and a husband. Writing to his family, he would dwell exclusively on the delights of his "village heaven." Thus, at haymaking time, leaving the house before dawn, he would be overwhelmed by the serene enchantment of the scene, though the thought that he could not share his good fortune with his people was a fly in the ointment. In winter he would make his way through snowdrifts to a neighboring stud farm, where he learned the wonderful art of exercising racehorses—he had caught the passion for horses from the Cossacks. He would spend the night at the home of a jockey in order to go to the stables with him early in the morning. Staying with horses, he found, gave him peace of mind and renewed his sense of human limitations. He frequented the track, not to play the horses but to feast his eyes on their beauty.

Occasionally his work on scenarios involved reference to archival materials, but mostly visits to government offices, factories, steel works, mines, building sites, and sojourns on collective and State farms. Here was a welcome opportunity to rub shoulders with people, to gain insight into their lives. But he valued his work on the scripts chiefly for the monetary return that they brought. This, he persuaded himself, gave him leisure that enabled him to devote his talent to "pure literature," labor obedient to the laws of art, "the devil who thirsts for my soul." The hack work, he insisted, did not infringe on his integrity as an artist. He worked at his fictions spasmodically, writing not page by page, but word by word, and redrafting endlessly. Under these circumstances his literary earnings could not but be an uncertain and subsidiary item in his budget. What he needed was a source of sure, steady income. The scenarios were such a source. Indeed, they were to be his bread and butter and jam for as long as he lived.

In the four years after his return from abroad Babel published half a dozen stories. Two of them completed the group of tales about a Jewish boyhood. A special interest attaches to "Awakening," the title referring to the Odessa child's introduction to the natural world from which the Jews were then still excluded. His kindly, self-appointed mentor sets him afire by announcing that "A man who doesn't live in nature, as a stone does or an animal, will never in his life write two worthwhile lines."

Odessa is the locale of a grim sketch of a poorhouse during the famine years, as well as of a *nouvelle* rich in humor. It deals with a lawsuit brought by a candidate for membership in the Party against his mother-in-law. The charge is that she stole his newborn son and had him circumcised without the parents' consent. Babel complained that the text had been "horribly distorted," presumably by censorship. Of a totally different order is "Guy de Maupassant," an account of an incident during the narrator's stay in wartime Petrograd: the penniless man is hired to correct a wretched translation of Maupassant into Russian made by a lawyer's seductive wife. The story is a fine specimen of Babel's sensuous prose. A characteristic maxim that the protagonist offers his pupil is: "No iron can enter the human heart as icily as a period set down at the right time." A postscript to the narrative briefly summarizes Maupassant's biography, concluding with the statement that he died at forty-two and was survived by his mother. As the writer pens this his heart contracts with foreboding. And rightly. Babel died in his forties and was survived by his mother.

These stories, together with those written before he went abroad and not included in *Red Cavalry*, formed a collection which was issued in 1932 under the title *Stories*. A miscellaneous group, it lacks the impact of his war book. At the time he was anxiously trying to get a permit for foreign travel. Alone in the company of the racehorses did he relax. When September came he finally found himself in France as a delegate to a conference of the International Organization of Revolutionary Writers. Again he stayed abroad about a year. For the first time he laid eyes on his daughter, now a three-year-old person who spoke French, had a large appetite, and was given to delightful mischief. He had a taste of the full family life that he had long missed, his mother and sister coming to Paris for a visit. He was apparently free from surveillance, and as a result, he did not shun contacts with Russian refugees, who were legion in Paris. One of them was the painter Yury Annenkov, of whom he saw a great deal.

In November, Babel was writing to him about being badgered by "dull receptions, demands to speak at meetings and write idiotic articles," presumably in connection with his duties as a delegate, and went on: "Today I have grown furious and decided to become a free citizen in the next two days." He did not clarify this, leaving it for the talk that he was "panting" to have with his *"très cher ami."* The talk did take place, and in his reminiscences Annekov set down the gist of Babel's part of the conversation. The painter was writing some thirty years after the event, and his memory may have played him false. He reports Babel to have said:

I have a family: wife and daughter. I love them and I must support them. But on no account do I want them to return to the land of the Soviets. They must live here where people are free. And I? To remain here and become a taxi driver, like heroic Gaita Gazdanov [an émigré fiction writer, one of whose novels has been done into English]? But he is childless. To return to our proletarian revolution? The revolution! Go whistle for it. The proletariat? The proletariat has shot its last bolt. Nowadays, brother, central committees with machine guns rule. . . . A cab driver here has more freedom than the president of a Soviet university. . . . Chauffeur or not, I will become a free citizen.

He had arrived in France firmly resolved to take back to Moscow his wife and daughter, if not the entire family. In fact, before leaving Moscow he had secured a flat there for at least the three of them. What Annenkov reported, if true, may have been said under the influence of a passing mood. While Babel was no doubt aware that the Revolution had gone sour, his being, his work, were too deeply rooted in Russia for him seriously to consider expatriation. He did not become a "free citizen." Instead, he cast his lot with the order born of the Revolution, though it is un- certain exactly when he decided to do so. In any event, he and his wife celebrated the New Year like any local petty-bourgeois cou- ple, taking in a movie that starred Marlene Dietrich, having supper on the Boulevard St. Michel, strolling past Les Halles, returning home in the small hours.

He was glad to accept a chance to do a scenario for a French studio on the fabulous career of Yevno Azef, the Russian Philby, who for years was an agent of the Imperial secret service and at the same time headed the terrorist arm of the Socialist-Revolu- tionary Party. In March, Babel interrupted his work to accept Gorky's invitation to Sorrento. Leaving his wife and child behind for want of funds, he spent most of the spring there. During those radiant weeks he had what he would have called a burst of crea- tivity, had he not hated that word. He wrote or put in final shape four stories. Gorky recommended them for publication in a mis- cellany, but the editors turned them down. Two appeared in periodicals the following year.

One is of the kind that could have been written, if not so con- cisely, by Maupassant. It is about a *crime passionel* in Paris: a used-car dealer whose sole concerns are his dinner and his women is neatly killed by one of them. The other story gives a sense of the atmosphere in which Soviet people carried on their bustling in- dustrial activities and made light of hampering conventions, though the evils of bureaucracy are not ignored. One of the re- maining two is the last tale, dealt with earlier, in the Odessa gang- ster series. Finally there is the story of a generous prostitute who gives object lessons to a youth posing as a pathic. The original text figures in a New York miscellany (1963). It never appeared under a Soviet imprint. In Sorrento, Babel also composed *Maria,* a play. This Gorky found disappointing and the author laid it aside for revision.

On his way back to France he stopped off in Rome and in Florence, but did not have enough money to get a glimpse of Venice. In Paris he faced a bleak situation. Zhenia had a monthly allowance from her brother, but the remittances failed to arrive, and to cover current expenses Babel went into debt. He now concentrated on the scenario that he had left unfinished when he went to Italy. In the end the script was turned down, and the lean weeks dragged on. He was really on his uppers.

Meanwhile, as on the occasion of his previous stay abroad, the rumor was spreading in Soviet literary circles that he did not intend to return. This time, as indicated above, the gossip was not wholly without substance. Late in August he was writing to Annenkov "about a strange summons from Moscow." He was "penniless and debt-ridden" but "glad to be returning." Annenkov never heard from him again. Once more he went back home alone.

VII

Before long he was given a mandate by *Pravda* for travel in the Caucasus and the Ukraine. He expected great things from the trip, perhaps the bonus of another chance to visit his family. The rest of the year he spent in the mountainous region, "a blessed land," where he did some hunting and fishing, but was mainly busy observing life on the collective farms. He met the new year (1934) in a town in the Donetz Basin, where he had himself lowered into a coal mine and watched the men digging. He found the miners and engineers an attractive breed. Babel told an intimate that he had gathered facts and impressions for an extensive narrative about a gangster like Benya Krik who abandons his evil ways and becomes first a collective farmer and later a coal miner. It was a theme in keeping with official policy, and it is possible that the Party newspaper granted him the assignment on those grounds.

In February he was back in Moscow. He was greatly in demand by the functionaries who presided over the Soviet film industry. Besides payment for scripts, there were royalties: *Red Cavalry* ran through eight large printings during the author's lifetime, and a new edition of *Stories* was in preparation. He was able to start paying off his debts and offer help to his people abroad. He had biting things to say about some of his needy relatives who had not emigrated, but he sent them remittances nevertheless.

In the letters that went off to Brussels and Paris he was at pains to picture his life as one of ease, privilege, *security*. He assured his "darling Mamasha" that he lived "in greater comfort and freedom" than she in Belgium and Zhenia in Paris. He was, no doubt, trying to keep his family from worrying about him. But he went further. He indulged in effusive glorification of his native country. Natasha, he wrote, like the rest of the family, belonged in the Soviet Union, where she would get a better education than in Paris. No one now doubted that the country would catch up with and surpass the West. His encomia must have been intended for eyes other than those of the addressees. In the fall he and another "bachelor," an Austrian business agent, share a small two-story house in Moscow, the services of two domestics, and an electric samovar constantly on the boil. Babel can afford to entertain guests in the best restaurant and take a cure in a Caucasian resort. What he needs is a place in the country as his "summer residence." What he needs above all else is to have his family with him, at least Natasha and Zhenia.

Scenarios were not all that occupied him. He revised the play that he had written in Sorrento. By way of trying it on an audience, he read it at a literary evening. Thereupon both the Vakhtanagov Theater and the Moscow Jewish troupe accepted *Maria,* and in fact paid the author a considerable sum for it. The scene is laid in Petrograd during the first years of the Soviet regime and the characters are mostly victims of the war and the Revolution who operate in the black market. In addition to a speculator who battens on goods smuggled by war invalids, there are a kindly, studious ex-general and an ex-prince. The latter entertains long-shoremen by playing the cello, and frequents a monk, with whom he discusses the nature of happiness. One of the former general's daughters, who gives the play its title and who from the Bolshevik viewpoint is the only "positive" character, never appears on the stage.

Small wonder that, printed in a 1935 issue of a periodical, *Maria* had a hostile press. The dialogue was praised, but the play was condemned for letting the victims of the Revolution have the floor, while its beneficiaries are mute, as well as for other ideological blunders, and for overemphasis on sex. Its staging was forbidden. Babel refused to be discouraged. He had conceived *Maria* as the first play in a trilogy, and he was already at work on a sequel. For a time he was haunted by the idea that drama, not fiction, was his true medium. Some thirty years after its publication *Maria* was produced in Florence, in Olomonc (Czechoslovakia), and in London.

The disaster of *Maria* did not surprise Babel. He knew that the play was not in line with what the theater, like the other media, was required to offer the public. Since the early thirties Party control over the arts had been growing more oppressive. The Party arrogated to itself the roles of both legislator and judge. Nothing could be less congenial to a man like Babel, who regarded writing as a sovereign art.

He did try to conform. At the first Congress of Soviet Writers in August, 1934, which promulgated the "method" of "socialist realism," he delivered an address that met with applause. The victory of the Revolution, he declared, was "final," the scaffolding had come down from the edifice of socialism and its "beauty" was disclosed to all eyes; the struggle that was taking place in their country would spread throughout the world. The speaker mentioned Marx honorifically and even contributed to the cult of personality with a pæan to Stalin's style. Obviously Babel was flattering himself when, several months later, he wrote to his "distant relatives" that he was incapable of compromise. It is hard to believe that his tongue was not in his cheek when he stressed the unique consensus of Soviet citizenry (he had seen something of the civil war and was not unaware of the peasants' ferocious resistance to collectivization), or when he contrasted the capitalist publishers' want of deference to the workers' selfhood with the esteem for "unusual and slow" methods of work in the Soviet Union. Babel concluded by quoting a fellow writer's words to the effect that "everything is given to us by the Party and the Government and only one thing is taken away—the right to write badly." He added that it was "an important right and what has been taken from us is no small thing. It was a privilege of which we took ample advantage. So, comrades, let us give up this privilege, and may God help us. As there is no God, let us help ourselves." It can only be hoped that the *double entendre* of this peroration was not lost on his audience: it was at once an indirect acceptance of political tutelage over literature and a warning of the consequences.

In the latter part of the speech Babel is able to voice his own feelings without offending the authorities. He may have given an orthodox cast to his condemnation of "fabricated, vulgar words, officialese" by declaring "vulgarity is counter-revolution," but the sentiment is an honest one, dictated by his concern for the quality of language. The readers must be given bread, but that does not mean a standardized product. Rather is it well to bowl them over with the unexpectedness of art. Clearly, Babel is here preaching for his own saint.

He went on to describe himself as a past master of what he called the "genre of silence." He was hinting at the fact that between 1925 and 1931 he had made no contributions to *belles-lettres* and that since the publication of *Stories* only two new vignettes of his had appeared, neither longer than "a sparrow's beak." Slackness on the part of so gifted a writer puzzled the public. It was mentioned in the press, alluded to at writers' meetings, frowned upon in high places. He was unhappy about his delinquency, but joked that awe of his prospective readers, grown so exacting, had silenced him. Earlier in the year he had offered in a serious vein an explanation of the paucity of his appearances in print. "I kept trying to overcome my natural bent," he told a group of literary novices, "and to learn to write long things. It was an ambitious but mistaken enterprise."

It was partly his own fault that his unflagging labors for the movies were ignored. He persisted in regarding the scripts as a trivial diversion from his real work. His first two scenarios were printed in book form, the others he refused to publish. Not that he failed to recognize that cinematography as practiced by a man of genius like his close friend Eisenstein had the potentialities of an art.

Apparently the people in control did not disregard the fact that while most of Babel's stories were apolitical, and, by the same token, open to criticism, a few were unexceptionable from the Bolshevik viewpoint. One sketch celebrates the workers' solidarity and offers a glimpse of the mourning for Lenin in Odessa. Another piece is a civil war episode, ending with a tribute to the Cheka. A third sketch, incomparably wrought, has to do with a trade union's transformation of an ancient monastery into a housing development for textile workers. In little more than two pages Babel performs the miracle of conjuring up at once the beauty that flowers out of the suffering and evil of the past and that which blooms in the coarse, healthy self-assertion of the future.

In any event, Babel was in good odor with the authorities. Indeed, he was included in the Soviet delegation to the anti-Fascist Congress which met in Paris in June, 1935. He traveled to France in the company of Boris Pasternak, another delegate. Again there was a family reunion in Brussels, but first a children's party in Paris to mark Natasha's sixth birthday. The father was ruffled to find that her Russian left much to be desired, what with Zhenia's insistence on speaking French to her. Greatly to his satisfaction, she entered Natasha on her Soviet passport, thus giving the little girl the status of a Soviet citizen. The weeks flew by as he strolled through the streets of Paris, avidly gathering impressions, not all of them to the credit of the City of Light. Happily, he did not know that this was to be his last stay with his family.

VIII

At the end of August he was back in the Soviet Union. He visited a collective farm near Kiev and as always was fretted by the absence of letters from his people abroad. The fall he spent in Odessa, doing some work for the local film studio, and luxuriating in the delights of that city, where even newspaper vendors and street cleaners greeted him. In the winter he settled in Moscow, and by spring he had carried out his movie assignments and paid off most of his debts. After years of painful search, he wrote to his "enchanting Mama," he had discovered his true road. He was at work on his "own stuff" with ease and zest such as he had not known for a long time. His writing had definitely improved. If only he could live in Odessa instead of in Moscow! It is useful to have a *pied-à-terre* in the capital, but the place for "pure work" was his native city, the local habitation of his Muse.

What his painful search had been is disclosed in a talk that he gave before a gathering of Moscow writers that March. He cast a backward look at his literary career, without even glancing at his work for the cinema and the theater. Shortly after the publication of *Red Cavalry,* he said, he grew dissatisfied with the short-story medium that he had cultivated (Turgenev and, briefly, Chekhov had known that feeling). He decided to try his hand at a spacious tale, composed with "classical coolness and composure." He carried out his plan by dint of assiduous and wearisome labor, but the effort was a total loss. When he reread the opus, after it had remained on ice for some time, he discovered that it was flabby and boring. Presumably the reference was to the mysterious "Sisyphean labor" which had absorbed him during his first stay abroad. The *Wanderjahre* that followed, the speaker went on, added much to his knowledge of Soviet life. It occurred to him that since unprecedented events of world importance were taking place here, and a new breed of men was born, a factual account of these things was bound to be more thrilling than an imaginative piece in his customary style. He did produce such an account, but it, too, turned out to be a failure. There is no clue to what this composition was or when it was set down.

The two disasters, the speaker continued, were an eye-opener for him: he had chosen a format, a dispassionate objectivity, which, being alien to his nature, proved fatal to his efforts. A work of literature should reflect the author's feelings, propensities, desires, resound with his own voice, wholly embody his self. Only a heterogeneous fellowship of writers, each a strong-minded, passionate character, a law unto himself, can produce a healthy literature, and, he added by way of sugaring his individualistic pill, create a new, socialist culture.

Babel emerged from his difficulties apparently resolved to return to the way of writing that had resulted in triumphs for him, such as *Red Cavalry*. He had misgivings, however, about his predilections for eccentric imagery. When a fellow author urged him to give up his figurative style, he promised to try, adding, "It is possible, of course, that I shall throw out the baby with the bath." He warned a group of literary tyros against the idea that talent consists in devising unexpected similes and metaphors. Yet in the same breath he honored this precept in the breach by remarking that he used to be guilty of that error, "and even now I crush metaphors in my writing, just as a none too fastidious individual crushes insects on his body." Was he trying half-heartedly to accommodate himself to that aspect of "socialist realism" which demanded a pedestrian style accessible to the most sluggish mind?

The evening before Babel departed for the Anti-Fascist Congress he had told a close friend that should his wife refuse to return with him to the Soviet Union, he would try to provide himself with another family. We have this on the authority of Babel's daughter, writing many years later. In the letter to his sister of January 28, 1936, he declared that his wife and daughter must come and live with him, for from so far away he could not keep an eye on Natasha, who mattered most to him. Yet he was then living with Antonina Nikolaevna Pirozhkova. In none of his letters is there any allusion to this union or to the fact that in January, 1937, she bore him a daughter.

A native of Siberia and an engineer by training, Antonina Nikolaevna was an attractive blonde, young and slender. In spite of her unfeminine profession, she had an inordinate interest in clothes and was in the habit of delighting Babel with the gossip that she picked up on her frequent visits to her dressmaker. That is how she appears in the diary of Babel's friend Ervin Sinkó, a Hungarian writer of Jewish birth. It is part of a detailed account of his two years (1935–37) in Moscow, which was published in 1962.

In his youth Sinkó had been active in an abortive attempt to establish a Communist regime in his native country, and became a refugee. With his wife, a physician, he arrived in Moscow for the purpose of placing his novel about the Hungarian fiasco with a Soviet publishing house. Early in 1936 the Sinkós moved into the flat on the street floor of the little house tenanted by Babel and his second wife. The two couples got on splendidly together, forming a common household, which included a cook and a maid. Both men were night workers, and Babel would go downstairs in the small hours to invite Sinkó for a heart-to-heart talk (he had mastered Russian) in the kitchen over a snack.

The diary entry dated February 9, 1936, records one such nocturnal talk, conducted in whispers so as not to be overheard by the cook, who slept near the kitchen. Babel is in a bad humor but not visibly troubled. Himself a writer whose work is unwanted, Sinkó congratulates his friend on being greatly in demand by editors and publishers—indeed, these vied with the moviemakers in besetting Babel with requests for manuscripts. Babel assures him that he misunderstands the situation, and proceeds to clarify it. True, people pursue him with pleas for copy, and he has a hard time shaking them off. Now so long as he fails to publish, he is merely accused of being a loafer. On the other hand, were he to appear in print, a veritable avalanche of serious, indeed, dangerous, charges would descend on his head. His work would be condemned as setting an example of defiance. Putting his finger to his lips, he explains: among those who beseech him to break his silence there are many who do it in the hope that his publications will furnish them with enough ammunition to unleash a devastating attack on him. He bursts into wry laughter and makes a gesture as if to wave a last farewell.

The conversation left no doubt in Sinkó's mind that his friend lived in a constant state of anguish. Babel was a man of resilient, cheerful disposition, given to joking and laughing "with his whole body," as Sinkó put it. He firmly believed in the power of humor as a weapon of self-defense. His optimism was *"inébranlable,"* and he declared that *joie de vivre* never deserted him. In the light shed by Sinkó's diary, Babel's joviality appears to have become a mask intended to deceive himself as well as others.

Before the year 1936 was over the Hungarian couple lived through a harrowing experience which showed them how intense and morally crushing Babel's anxiety was. In May, Comrade Sokolovskaya, deputy head of the Moscow Film Studio, commissioned Sinkó to write a scenario. As Babel was a consultant of the Studio who read scripts, revised them, and supplied dialogue for others, she suggested to Sinkó that he turn to his housemate for advice. This he did, the two spending hours together over the script. In July he handed it in and his friend called up the Studio to commend the work. During August the Sinkós spent a few delightful days in Odessa with Babel, who assured the man that the scenario needed no changes. Back in Moscow, Sinkó tried to get in touch with the Studio—he had received only half of the fee agreed upon (20,000 rubles, equivalent to 2000 present rubles)—but week after week he was given the runaround. Finally, at the end of October a Studio official brusquely told Sinkó that his script had been rejected and that the concern would have nothing further to do with him. Now it was stipulated in the contract signed by Sokovlovskaya that the work was considered accepted unless within twenty days after delivery of the manuscript the author was informed in writing that it had to be changed or was rejected.

Distressed, outraged, Sinkó retailed his dealings with the Studio in a letter to an editor of *Pravda* whom he knew. He wound up by saying that he held it to be his duty to bring to account functionaries behaving in a manner "both unsocialist and uncivilized." And he actually sued the Studio. The quixotic fellow, for whom Communism was an ethical ideal of the highest order, had not the slightest doubt that Babel, who was still in Odessa, would applaud his steps. When, on the last day of November, Babel walked into the Sinkós' flat, after the first hearty greetings he listened with sympathetic interest to his friend's sorry story and the account of the measures that he had taken against the Studio. But when Sinkó said that in his letter to *Pravda* he had mentioned Babel's involvement in the affair, the man visibly panicked. He clutched his head, and moments later dashed upstairs to his room, waving Sinkó away.

The next day he behaved as though nothing had happened, but the intimate nocturnal meetings in the kitchen had come to an end. One night, however, he came into the Sinkó flat and, after some persiflage, went on to say that he had persuaded *Pravda* not to print the letter, as this would merely have made more enemies for its author. Oddly enough, he encouraged Sinkó to go on with the lawsuit. Moreover, when told that he would be summoned as a witness for the plaintiff, he welcomed the opportunity and spoke confidently of the happy outcome.

He appeared in court punctually, but took Sinkó aback by failing to greet him by as much as a glance. Called to testify, Babel resolutely denied the plaintiff's every allegation: he was not the person whom Comrade Sokolovskaya had advised the plaintiff to consult; he had never had anything to do with the scenario with which the case was concerned; he could say nothing about its quality, but did not question the judgment of the Studio staff. Asked by Sinkó if he recalled the conversation about the scenario that they had had in Odessa, he calmly answered in the negative.

His replies to the questions addressed to him by the judge were equally damaging to the plaintiff's case. The lawyer who represented Sinkó must have decided that his client was out of his mind to have named Babel as a witness. The complaint was forthwith dismissed, although the representative of the Studio had not opened his mouth once to claim that the organization had abided by its contract.

Outside the courtroom Babel was waiting in a window recess for Sinkó, who was going to pass by without a look at him, but Babel seized his arm and mumbled some words to the effect that he would explain everything. Sinkó shrank away from him. He never obtained from Babel an explanation of his shocking behavior. The couple failed to get an extension of their residence permit and left the country in April, 1937, bereft of the illusions that they had had about what they held to be the first proletarian state in history. During the three or four months that they continued to live under the same roof with Babel their contacts with him were confined to a few conventional phrases. On the afternoon when the Sinkós carried out their luggage to put it into a taxi, Babel loitered near them in the street, looking embarrassed. In the house strangers were already quarreling over the right to occupy the vacated flat.

How is one to account for Babel's shamelessly perjuring himself, especially when he knew his friend's situation to be so difficult? If he did not want to antagonize the Moscow Film Studio, his main employer, he could have urged Sinkó to give up the lawsuit, instead of encouraging him to go on with it. Fear of something incomparably worse than loss of income must have motivated him. By 1936 the purges unleashed after the assassination of a leading Leningrad Bolshevik two years previously were gathering momentum. The Terror was intended to destroy all opposition to Stalin's dictatorship. In addition to public trials of prominent Bolsheviks charged with trumped-up crimes, mostly high treason, and often condemned to capital punishment, innumerable arrests, followed by prison terms, deportation to forced labor camps, execution, took place behind an impenetrable wall of secrecy. According to a recent study,* by January, 1937, five million were in prison or in concentration camps, and within the next two years, that is, by December, 1938, seven million more had been arrested; of these, one million were executed, some without trial or investigation, and two million died in the camps. These staggering figures were arrived at by careful study of what evidence was available. As the security forces were intent on ferreting out nonexistent conspiracies, a person would be caught in the police net because of the shadow of a connection with a suspected Trotskyite or other dissenter. Acquaintances of those arrested were invariably suspect. Under torture some people denounced others.

Babel was in a better position than many to know what was going on. He told Sinkó that he had "an intimate friend" in the wife of N. I. Yezhov, the infamous head of the Secret Service (whose low stature earned him the nickname of "the Bloodthirsty Dwarf"), appointed in September, 1936. He had known her before her marriage—she was reputedly Jewish. He may have told her of his predicament; he certainly looked in on her just before appearing in court. Indeed, he was driven to the courthouse in her car. Perhaps she was able to tell him what had become of "Comrade Sokolovskaya," who had vanished from the Film Studio in October. If she had been arrested, it was dangerous for Babel to admit any association with her. Closeness to Sinkó was possibly also compromising. This stranger was not a welcome sojourner in the Soviet Union. He was not permitted to take part in a purely literary discussion at the Union of Soviet Writers, and was given the cold shoulder, to put it mildly, by the editors and publishers whom he approached in trying to place a translation of his writings.

One is inclined to agree with the conclusion that Sinkó reached after brooding on the enigma of his former friend's conduct, in an effort to find some extenuating circumstances for it. The Terror isolated individuals and gave them the feeling of being at the

* Robert Conquest, *The Great Terror*, London, 1968.

mercy of an invincible and implacable power, as irrational as it was evil. Few people in a vulnerable position could resist the dehumanizing, demoralizing effect of existence in such a nightmarish, Kafkaesque atmosphere. Hence the possibility of a sad defection from rectitude by a man like Babel. He was in a particularly insecure position. The death of Maxim Gorky in June, 1936, had deprived him of a powerful protector. In that year and the preceding one he had published nothing. Non-performance by an author with such a background and with his history was apt to be interpreted as a sign of disaffection.

IX

In 1937 Babel broke his silence with two pieces. One, which is apolitical, illustrates the proposition that "in the frenzy of noble passion there is more justice and hope than in the joyless rules of the world." The other belongs to the *Red Cavalry* series: a glimpse of a romantic incident, faintly Chekhovian in tone and plot, and with a pro-Soviet passage. Babel also published a brief eulogy of Gorky as "the man in whom the world proletriat found its writer," as well as a matter-of-fact account, without a hint of squeamishness, of a killing by the Cheka. Furthermore, he contributed to the organ of the League of School-Age Communists a summary of his impressions of France that could have been written by a staunch Bolshevik who paradoxically harbored an appreciation of France as a land "laid out with care, love, and taste" and of its capital as a city "fashioned like a work of art."

In 1938 Babel's name appeared over a two-page narrative tracing the post-Revolutionary career of an elderly former lieutenant-colonel, the scion of a noble family. He emigrates with Baron Wrangel to Yugoslavia, becomes a police officer, absconds to avoid arrest for larceny, turns up in Paris, where he becomes a gigolo in the service of a dowager rentière, steals her securities and her jewelry, and gets a ten-year prison term. It is gratifying to know that Babel's last appearance in the Soviet press during his lifetime was not with that malicious vignette but with a wish for the new year, namely that the bookstores be stocked with the works of Tolstoy in low-priced editions. "With the passing years," wrote the man who in his youth had been something of a Tolstoyan, "my admiration for the beauty and truth of those books has grown irresistibly."

Some time after Babel's return from the Anti-Fascist Congress he was given to understand that if he resumed publishing he would be enabled to revisit his family abroad. He may have hoped that his "output" in 1937–38 would bring about that result. (It did not.) He had betrayed a friend, presumably owing to the morally traumatic effect of the Terror, but he remained steadfast in his attachment to his kinfolk. Naturally, there is no hint in his letters at anything that could arouse their apprehension. The only thing that troubles him, he insists, is his separation from the family, and absence of news from Paris and Brussels makes him despondent. His health is excellent, he knows no fatigue, in his veins flows the blood of his ancestors who stood behind a counter eighteen hours a day. He feels so young and Natasha looks so grown-up in her photograph that when she is a bit taller, the two of them will seem to be of the same age.

Babel had long been painting his existence in glowing colors. In the fall of 1936 he and Eisenstein were occupying "palatial" rooms in Yalta, where they were collaborating on a film.* Next year in Kiev, while working on a scenario, Babel was living in "unbelievable" comfort. In the winter his Moscow flat was cheerful and warm, what with logs blazing in the fireplaces. On a May day in 1938 he takes possession of a "villa" situated in the woods of

---

* The motion picture director seems to have recovered from the shock that he had experienced in May, when the film about collectivization on which he had been at work for two years was charged with formalism, nationalism, mysticism, as well as with slandering the Russian peasantry, and was ordered destroyed by a committee that included Molotov and Mikoyan, while he himself was threatened with having ugly rumors spread about him if he raised objections. At the time Eisenstein, beside himself, came to Babel, in the hope that he might induce Maxim Gorky to help save the movie—Babel had the highest opinion of it—but the "patriarch" was on his deathbed, and nothing could be done.

Peredelkino, the celebrated suburb of Moscow. It is an admirably
built two-story house, provided with every convenience, except—
deliberately—a telephone, and isolated from neighbors, mostly
writers and artists, by acres of land. The *dacha* includes a kitchen
garden, a chicken coop, a dovecote with pigeons—the master's
childhood dream come true—on the roof of a cowshed, as well as
separate quarters for the caretakers: a peasant couple, who have a
little daughter. Aside from the fact that the villa is not located
on the Odessa seashore, it is an ideal retreat for meditation and
work. He wallows in its peace and creature comforts. On an autumn evening, seated at an open fire, he reads Sholem Aleichem
"in our highly original tongue" (he has been appointed editor of
a Russian translation of that author), or on a wintry moonlit night
watches from his windows a fairy-tale scene. He regales his corre-
spondents abroad with such news as the arrival of five hens and a
rooster and the addition of four pigeons to the population of the
dovecote.

Of course, now and then he absents himself from the splendors
of the villa to visit Moscow for such pleasures as telephoning to
Brussels, going to the races, seeing his friend, the actor Michoels
in the stage version of *Tevya, the Milkman,* but chiefly on business.
In addition to his work on motion pictures there are now his duties
as Deputy Chairman of the Editorial Board of the State Literary
Publishing House. The confession that he has a very hard time
both physically and morally he entrusts to a letter, dated November 30, 1938, and addressed to an old friend, the lady from whom
he had rented a room when he first arrived in Petrograd.

It turns out that the cottage is not as solid an edifice as he had
made it out to be. When winter comes he discovers that it is in
need of a thorough overhauling. By the end of April, 1939, however, the paint having dried, the parquet having been polished, a
supply of ice packed in the cellar, he is again settled in his country
place, but now he has a house, he writes, that will last half a
century. With a villa like that he could omit going south in the

summer, but he is determined to have plenty of sea bathing in Odessa.

Since he shared his Moscow flat with Antonina Pirozhkova and their baby daughter, it may be assumed that they lived with him on his Peredelkino "estate" as well. Yet he continues to regard himself as Zhenia's dutiful husband. They write to each other, though she is a laggard correspondent. His "Parisians" worry him beyond words. Hearing of inflation in France, he frets: is she able to make ends meet? He is excited by the sound of Zhenia's and Natasha's voices over the telephone. He finds "spiritual nourishment" in learning Natasha's report card by heart. Embittered though he is by her distance from him, she remains the apple of his eye. He clings to the hope that at least the two of them will rejoin him. He is deeply saddened, he writes on April 3, 1939, by the suspicion that Zhenia, in her procrastinating way, has failed to renew her Soviet passport, thus forfeiting her Soviet citizenship. (As a matter of fact, she held on to it until she became convinced that her husband was no longer among the living; she died in 1957, a French citizen, like her daughter.) Reflecting on Babel's sustained attachment to his family abroad, one wonders whether his extramarital liaison helped to stabilize the marriage of this uxorious male.

The moral corruption brought about by panic did not weaken Babel's concern for the welfare of his family. It also left his integrity as an artist largely intact. He was never free from the impulse to give up hack work and live "an honest life" devoted to what he called "pure literature," or some such phrase. During his stay in Odessa in the summer of 1936 Babel had started what he called "a little book dear to my heart." He decided to remain there until he had finished it. In November he wrote to his sister that it would be ready for publication in two or three months. By the end of the month he was back in Moscow, where he was making steady progress toward the completion of the book. In order to concentrate on it he broke a contract for a scenario. But from a letter of January 2, 1937, it appears that the work done on "the little book" resulted in only a preliminary and unfinished draft, and furthermore that when it was completed he would stow it away for a time, so as to write the final version with a clear head. Nothing more is heard of the matter. At the time the Terror was at its peak. Did this discourage him from completing the book or from attempting to publish it?

Later in the year he let fall a word about an arcane literary project of his: an effort to sum up the results of years of meditation. All that he disclosed about it was that instead of tomes he had, as usual, only a miniature to show. Its fate is shrouded in darkness. During the summer he declined jobs offered by his "customers" so as to devote himself to "pure literature." He produced three stories, which have been mentioned, and they were printed without delay. This contradicts what he had told Ervin Sinkó about his avoiding appearance in print, but consistency was not his most notable virtue—if it is a virtue.

The following winter, after slaving over a script based on a novel not suitable for filming, he is looking forward joyfully to the time when he can turn to his "own, true writing." He hopes that by the middle of April he will be able to busy himself with it "exclusively." The letters from Peredelkino for the second half of 1938 stress the fact that he is engaged in writing, presumably his "own stuff," at least in part. Scenarios occupy him, however, the following year, both in Moscow and Leningrad, where he turns out a script in twenty days. In a letter from Peredelkino dated May 10, 1939, he informs his people in Brussels that he is hale and hearty, that he has mailed some books for Natasha, and that he is finishing a script for a film about Maxim Gorky. As soon as he is through with that order, he declares, he will put the last touches to his "true work," which he expects to deliver to his publishers in the autumn. He was not given the opportunity to carry out this plan.

That was Babel's last letter. Five days after it went off he was arrested at Peredelkino and taken to the Lubyanka prison in Moscow. According to his daughter, people who saw him there reported that he had not lost his cheerful appearance. And so he vanished.

While he did not lack friends in high places, his enemies, whom he had mentioned to Sinkó, proved dangerous, what with the sycophancy that thrived in the climate of the Terror. It was a time that Ilya Ehrenburg describes in his memoirs as one in which a man's fate is not, as in a game of chess, a matter of skill, but a matter of chance, as in a lottery. Luck was against Babel, crushed, like millions of his fellow countrymen, by the Stalinist Juggernaut. He was not a Party member, for whatever that was worth, he was a Jew, some of his work had had a hostile press, his next of kin, with whom he was in constant contact, were expatriates. The Secret Service had a special file for those who had any contacts abroad. Finally, there was something evasive and enigmatic about him that may have helped to make him suspect. An official certificate delivered to the family shortly after Stalin's death gave March 17, 1941, as the date of Babel's death, but mentioned neither its cause nor where it had occurred.

The crime or crimes with which he was charged are not known. One story has it that he rashly made a joke about Stalin. In 1947 at a reception in Zagreb, Ervin Sinkó, who had settled in Yugoslavia, ran into Konstantin Simonov, the prominent Soviet author. In response to an inquiry about Babel, the then staunch supporter of the Party line in literature muttered something to the effect that the man had spied for Japan and had been deported. "Babel was executed as a Japanese spy," was the reply given by other Russian writers on a visit to Yugoslavia to the same question of Sinkó's. The charge of espionage was a standard way of getting rid of people. What makes the report cited by Sinkó plausible is the fact that Babel was tried by the Military College (Department) of the Supreme Court of the U.S.S.R., which hears cases of high treason. In a statement dated December 23, 1954, this department declared that the sentence it had pronounced in the trial of I. E. Babel on January 24, 1940, had been revoked because of newly discovered circumstances and the case was terminated in the absence of the corpus delicti. Moreover, by way of further rehabilitation, Babel's collected works (in one volume) appeared in 1957 under a Moscow imprint. A somewhat expanded edition, provided, like the previous book, with an appreciative preface, was issued in 1966. Excluded from these collections are the two published scenarios, the journalistic items, some pieces deemed too insignificant or dealing with sex in a way that the authorities held would offend a prudish public.

On arresting Babel, the police seized his papers. He is said to have been inordinately careful of his manuscripts. They were safeguarded from strangers' eyes in a chest. The story goes that from time to time he would take out a yellowed sheet, change a phrase or a word in the text, and then replace the paper. He preserved even some of his juvenilia, along with the jottings that formed the diary he had kept while attached to the Cossack Army Corps, and his notes for *Red Cavalry*. As stated above, after the publication of that collection he was at work on half a dozen large literary undertakings, the nature of which remains a mystery, from the "Sisyphean labor" of 1928–29 to the "true work" that he hoped to turn over to the publishers in the fall of 1939. Nor is there any trace of the collection called *New Stories,* which, according to his second wife, he was to have handed over to the publishers shortly before his arrest. No vestige of the papers relating to these projects has come to light. Their fate is but one of the enigmas in Babel's story.

VII

Russian Poetry—A Survey

Russia's Middle Ages may be said to have lasted until the end of the seventeenth century. During that period Church Slavic, formed on a South Slav tongue, was the literary medium. It was first used in a translation of the Bible and of liturgical texts made by two Greek missionaries to Moravia in the ninth century. On Russian soil this language was modified under the influence of the vernacular. Both translations and original writings took their rise shortly after the Christianization of the country toward the close of the first millennium. The works produced during the next seven centuries were for the most part of a devotional or edifying nature. Bookmen, mostly monks, also composed chronicles and made versions of Byzantine secular compilations, such as histories, cosmographics, a bestiary.

A single work of a high literary order relieves the aridity of the scene: *The Lay of Igor's Campaign*. A short epic couched in rhythmic prose, it is an account by an unknown bard of a disastrous campaign led by several Russian princes against hostile nomads. Descriptions of valor in battle are followed by passages of patriotic oratory and there is also a moving lament for the captured Prince Igor; the tale ends on a note of rejoicing at Igor's escape from captivity. There may well have been other such gests, set down for the entertainment and exhortation of the princes and their retinues, but if there were any, none has survived. Thus, to the haunting quality of the *Lay*, its uniqueness adds a touch of mystery. Certainly there was a large body of tales and songs, as well as ballads that mingled fantasy and traces of myth with faint echoes of history. The language of all that was told or sung was close to folk speech. Passed on by word of mouth from generation to generation, this material was not recorded until recent times.

The modern era, inaugurated in the reign of Peter the Great (1689–1725), meant an abrupt break with the past. For the land of the Czars, which knew nothing in the nature of a Renaissance or an Age of Enlightenment, the eighteenth century was a period of apprenticeship to Western masters, in literature as in other skills. The meager medieval heritage had pitifully little to offer by way of form or substance. Russians translated, and imitated, the authors of classical antiquity and the French neoclassicists as well. Verse evolved before prose, though this was eventually to become the country's chief glory. The unbroken tradition of modern Russian literature, specifically poetry, goes back no farther than the middle years of the century.

There had been versifiers before that time, but no poets, and they used an imported prosody unsuited to the native speech. It prescribed a set number of syllables in the line, with no fixed pattern of stresses, although accent is so prominent a feature of Russian as to make this desirable. There was no swing to the poetasters' productions: heavy-handed, often crudely didactic pieces, abounding in archaisms. In spite of the obligatory feminine rhyme, they were indistinguishable from lame prose. By mid-century, syllabic versification was abandoned in favor of another system based on the regular alternation of stressed and unstressed syllables. This accentual-syllabic prosody, also apparently taken from the West, became the mold in which Russian verse was to be cast. Succeeding generations were merely to refine upon it, until in our own time it found rivals in freer arrangements.

The prosodic reform was launched by Mikhail Lomonosov. Perhaps again taking a hint from foreigners, who since the days of the Elizabethans had emphasized literary decorum, he sought to bring order into the prevailing stylistic chaos by formulating standards. Works of a "high" rank, i.e., dealing with serious or solemn matters, demanded, he taught, a style abounding in elements derived from the language of the Church books and a syntax patterned on that of Latin periods. In other works he permitted an admixture of the vernacular. In addition to being a preceptor regarding style, Lomonosov was a practitioner of verse. He wrote chiefly odes, often to order, on court occasions (two of these compositions were dedicated to Emperor Ivan VI, age one, who was deposed after "reigning" for thirteen months). The demand for panegyrics was also met by several of Lomonosov's contemporaries and immediate successors. Other classical genres—such as epistle, satire, song, and fable—were also cultivated in accordance with definite rules. These works, though not without literary merit, are chiefly of historic interest.

A genuine, though intermittent, poet, indeed perhaps the first to whom Russia may lay claim, was Lomonosov's follower, Gavriil Derzhavin. This courtier of Catherine II possessed great verve and a keen eye for movement and color, to judge from some of his descriptions, be it of a waterfall or a festive board, unfortunately too lengthy to be anthologized. He dealt with the commonplaces of poetry such as nature, God, death, in personal if stiff accents. Sometimes he made bold to deviate from conventional metrics and from other canons of classical rhetoric as set forth by Lomonosov. The prolix poems in which, tempering flattery with mild irony, he celebrates the virtues of his empress or the triumphs of her armies, or, again, attacks injustice in high places, contain passages of unusual effectiveness. The old sybarite's Anacreontic pieces occasionally achieve a homely charm, when he avoids didactic emphasis, the blight of the age. That verse with an explicit moral can, however, be delightful is proved by the shrewd and racy fables of Ivan Krylov (1769–1844), the Russian La Fontaine.

Derzhavin lived to witness Russia's victory over Napoleon. The venerable poet bequeathed what he called his "outworn lyre" to Vasily Zhukovsky. It was a generous gesture on the part of a writer who, if he had sometimes disregarded Lomonosov's precepts, was nevertheless a pillar of classicism. Young Zhukovsky, on the other hand, was one of the writers who preached, and practiced, "the new style." This faction, which originated at the turn of the century and was violently opposed by the diehards, championed a medium close to the speech of the educated gentry, a language purged of uncouth archaisms, modernized, simplified, emulating the elegance and precision of French and the mellifluousness of Italian.

Zhukovsky himself steered clear of heroics, solemnity, grandiloquence, indulging rather in reverie and lachrymose sentiment and speaking for the claims of the heart. There was little in the Russian temperament and the Russian scene to favor this early variety of romanticism, tender-minded and pietistic. The trend was short-lived and sterile. In any event, Zhukovsky—the author of elegies and ballads—was less a poet in his own right than a translator, sometimes at second-hand, of verse, ancient and modern, from both East and West. As such, he performed a signal service to the native culture. Literally speaking, Russia had long been a debtor nation, and it is notable that virtually every poet applied himself to making foreign verse accessible to his compatriots. Whatever defects Russian poetry may have, they are not the fault of inbreeding.

Not Zhukovsky but a younger and incomparably more gifted writer was responsible for the emergence of Russian literature from the awkward age. Alexander Pushkin's adolescence coincided with the second decade of the new century. Those were exhilarating years. The victory of 1812 enhanced national self-consciousnes; fresh winds were blowing from widened horizons, liberal influences were in the air. The time was ripe for the rise of a literature rooted in native soil and nourished by what had been absorbed from the West. Pushkin was foremost in shaping that literature and, by the same token, modern literary Russian. He completed the work of the promoters of the "new style" by drawing on all the resources of the language, including the speech of the untutored folk that Krylov, for one, had used earlier. The very indigenous quality of his work gave Russian letters for the first time a more than local significance and allowed them to transcend the national boundaries.

Pushkin's genius was manifold, but he was above all a poet, by the consensus of his compatriots an unequaled master of the language. He never lost the taste for classic sobriety and for what he called "the charm of naked simplicity," which made Mérimée declare him "an Athenian among the Scythians." His passionate nature knew the discipline of a keen intelligence, of a capacity for detachment, of a sense of measure. The Anacreontic strain in his youthful verse, which did not stop at blasphemy and cheerful ribaldry, was of brief duration, as was the Byronic unrest that marks the long narrative poems of his early manhood. The writings of his maturity, notably *Eugene Onegin,* which gives the fullest measure of his powers, have an objective, realistic quality that implies an acceptance of life on its own terms. Not that he remained unaware of the tragic predicaments inherent in the human condition. Although he hated bigotry, sycophancy, oppression, injustice, he was no rebel against either Church or State. A man of the world, he lived to the full in his works and days alike. Those who must depend on translation may agree with Flaubert that the Russian master is "flat." To the native, sensible not only of Pushkin's sanity and balance but of his generous humanity and, above all, the unobtrusive felicity, the superb artistry of his style (which, for Tchaikovsky, had the effect of music), his verse is a source of pure joy. The Revolution, which has caused so many revaluations, has only enhanced his luster. Ranked with the greatest figures in literature, he is the object and to some degree the victim of mountainous exegesis and of a veneration that in the Soviet era has acquired a quasi-official tinge.

There were a number of lyricists among Pushkin's contemporaries, some younger, some older men. They admired him, without paying him the tribute of imitation, each having a character of his own. Their work, while of a minor order, is that of skilled, style-conscious craftsmen who took their vocation seriously. It wants the tone of self-assured serenity that poetry had in Derzhavin's age. There is no lack of light and witty pieces, such, for example, as those of Prince Vyazemsky, but the elegiac mood prevails. Melancholy is characteristic of the melodious verse of Konstantin Batyushkov (1787–1855), the last half of whose life was darkened by insanity. Baratynsky's verse, often falteringly cerebral, is marked by a persistently gloomy outlook. In one of his poems he projects an apocalyptic vision of mankind passing from a brilliant era of industrial progress to one of complete prostration and ending with extinction, whereupon "imperial Nature," rid of the human species, returns to its primeval majesty.

While the language of the poetry of the age abounds in classical clichés like the Muses, the Graces, nymphs and naiads, traces of realism and even of naturalism are discernible in the verse. Thus, Baron Delvig (1790–1831), Pushkin's schoolmate and lifelong friend, invites his Muse to don now the chiton and now the sarafan. In some of the pieces by his fellows patriotism goes hand in hand with conservatism; elsewhere, notably in the clumsy performance of Kondraty Ryleyev, it has a radical orientation. Alexey Koltsov, a man of the people, who found congenial the style of the folk song, does not belong to this group of writers, all of them scions of the privileged class.

Tyutchev was another contemporary of Pushkin, surviving him by many years. Of the men, aside from the masters, who made the first four decades of the nineteenth century an age of poetry, Tyutchev is perhaps the most likely to elicit a sympathetic response from today's reader. His diction has a slightly archaic complexion, his sensibility and mentality are poles removed from those of the eighteenth century. He is indebted to German Romanticism, with its hunger for the transcendental and the ineffable, yet his verse is remarkably limpid. It is distinguished by a fine economy and by a masterful use of metaphor and allusion. He can evoke a mood of serene contemplation, notably in confronting the natural scene, but his most characteristic lyrics are the product of a mind bent over itself "on the threshold of double being." The ordered world upon which falls the light of common day is for him but appearance. True reality is "the hundred-eyed beast" that night is, "ancient chaos," which is ready to engulf man, his petty works and pitiful longings. Tyutchev does not turn away from the black abyss. Rather he lives in constant awareness of it, vainly seeking the resolution of the tragic duality either in passionate love or in Christian faith, two leading themes in his poetry.

Pushkin's mantle fell not upon Tyutchev, who wrote for posterity (recognition came long after his death), but upon Mikhail Lermontov. This brilliant, egotistical youth was a lyricist of rare gifts. His verse follows patterns different from Pushkin's, but the effect of music and magic is as strong. His poetry is of an essentially romantic cast, expressive of a longing for the unattainable and inexpressible. The growing civic bias of the mid-century made it possible to put a social interpretation on the disquietude that pervades his work and that sometimes breaks out in vitriolic satire, although he revolted less against the Tsar of All the Russias than against the God of heaven and earth. His imagination was haunted by the somber figure of a rebel angel vainly seeking regeneration through the love of a maiden. He had, however, moods of serenity and piety, and his verse, as indeed that of other Russian Romantics, could be sober and earthy. A realistic strain runs deep in the grain of the Russian temperament.

As he was approaching maturity, Lermontov, like Pushkin, tried his hand at prose, producing a remarkable novel, *The Hero of Our Time,* which was published in 1840. On a May morning two years later Gogol's *Dead Souls* appeared in the bookshops. The day of prose had dawned. The period, one of the most fruitful in literary history, lasted about half a century, coinciding with the better part of the Victorian age. In the course of it fiction held the center of the stage, the taste for poetry undergoing progressive deterioration.

There was one poet, however, who rivaled in popularity, if not in importance, the contemporary novelists: Turgenev, Dostoevsky, Tolstoy. This was Nikolay Nekrasov. He made articulate the consciousness—and the conscience—of the period of reform and in-

choate revolt which had set in with the death, in 1855, of Nicholas
I. His was, he said truly, "the Muse of grief and vengeance." His
troubled, uneven verse dwells upon the miseries of the oppressed
and plundered masses, particularly the peasants. It voiced the
aspirations of the democratic intelligentsia, as well as the *peccavi*
of the gentry, painfully sensible of their debt to the people. At its
best, his verse powerfully conveys profound self-scorn and bitter
compassion for the victims of injustice. In denouncing social evils,
he threw untransmuted into his poems—occasionally satirical,
some of them parodies—the raw stuff of *feuilleton* and pamphlet.
With great skill he reproduced the diction and swing of the folk
song by using trisyllabic feet and dactylic rhymes.

Nekrasov set the fashion for the middle decades of the century.
A socially indifferent poetry became anathema. In radical circles
the utilitarian view of literature as a vehicle of enlightenment
prevailed, and versemaking was rather looked down upon. In the
serious sixties an iconoclastic "Nihilist" critic advocated the abolition of all art and laid impious hands on the laurels of Pushkin
himself.

In this unfriendly atmosphere several authors continued to carry
on the tradition of pure poetry. Maikov achieved a small excellence in his genre pictures of the native scene and in his imitations
of the ancients. Alexey Tolstoy had among his various gifts a
talent for neat and graceful lyrics. Fet's work was furthest removed
from the concept of utilitarian art. His poems have the insubstantial quality of reverie. It has been said of this etherealist that
he could have paraphrased the familiar dictum thus: I dream,
therefore I am. So absorbed is he in the mood of the moment, that
time abdicates for him. Indeed, some of his most successful pieces
are verbless. He does not state but adumbrates, suggests. He employs a delicate imagery in an effort to reach out toward the super-
sensuous and to present nature as the cosmic context of human
life.

These poets professed allegiance to the principle of art for art's
sake. Nevertheless, with the exception of Fet, they all wrote some

political verse, as did also Tyutchev, preaching a pietistic and reactionary variety of nationalism. The performance of both the
civic-minded realists and the aloof esthetes reached its nadir during
the eighties and the better part of the nineties, and so did the taste
of the public. Those were years of bloodless, pretty, slovenly verse
of plaints and platitudes, twitterings and stammerings.

As the century moved to its close a change made itself felt in the
cultural atmosphere. When the Yellow Book was brightening
London bookstalls, a new literary trend began to develop in Petersburg (Leningrad) and Moscow. It went by the name of Modernism. The term was soon supplanted by Symbolism, while those who
disliked the movement were apt to refer to it as Decadence, thus
singling out its strain of mingled aestheticism, eroticism, and
morbidity. Although clearly the response to a stimulus from abroad
—its detractors branded it a warmed-over French dish—it was also
a reaction against native provincialism, lack of craftsmanship, and
devotion to the Social Muse. Modernism was both a fresh beginning and a revival, at first not without puerile affectations intended to confound the Philistine.

Its advent was preceded by a flourish of hortatory writing: articles inveighing against the subservience of literature to the cause
of social betterment, advocating individualism in Nietzschean
accents, and exalting art over life. An early apostle of Modernism
was Dmitry Merezhkovsky. In a muddle-headed essay published in
1893 the young author called for a poetry marked by heightened
sensory perceptiveness but also by idealism and mysticism, an art
engaged with absolutes and ultimates. Further, he urged using the
language of symbols, without clearly defining the term. Indeed, he
gave the title *Symbols* to a sheaf of poems issued at about the same
time and echoing Poe and Baudelaire. But verse was not to be his
vehicle.

Others dominated the movement for which Merezhkovsky had
spoken. The oldest of them was Fyodor Sologub. He came closest
to being a Decadent of Baudelaire's stripe. There is something

eerily obsessive, if not perverse, about his poems. They are weighted down with *tædium vitae* and with the sense that life, when it is not a dismal menagerie, is what Dostoevsky called "the Devil's vaudeville." From his "tormenting fatherland" Sologub escapes into "a valley of dreams," an enchanted world of his own imagining. Thence the sick and humorless phantast emerges only to utter threats to the sun, prayers to Satan, hymns to Death the Deliverer. True, he knows moods when earthly existence presents itself as a rung of "an endless ladder of perfection." But his hosannahs are far less compelling than his curses.

If there is a strong strain of morbidity in the small body of verse left by Innokenty Annensky, it is qualified by grim humor, by courageous confrontation of invalidism and the thought of death waiting on the doorstep. Evening and autumn are his favored death symbols, but winter and even spring serve the same purpose, the poet hearing "the call of death in the Easter hymn." Though free of self-pity, his lyrics dwell on waning, ailing, dying: his habitual cast of mind is one of anguish and hopelessness. Sometimes he is drawn to what he fears. He plays variations on such themes as loneliness, insomnia, dreams (chiefly nightmares). As might be expected of a Modernist who translated some of the French Symbolists, Annensky readily turns to music and moonlight and flowers (withering ones). Beauty redeems existence for him but, alas, life holds little of it, and that little is fragile. Poetry, like music, can adumbrate it faintly. Yet words are so inadequate that the making of verse is a torment, mitigated by the exhilaration of attempting a well-nigh impossible task. Although he occasionally touches upon the ideal world and his poems sometimes have an esoteric quality, there is nothing mystical about them. He wanted poetry to be concrete, dealing with three-dimensional objects and avoiding riddles, but he did not always practice what he preached.

A leading poet of the new school was Konstantin Balmont. His claim to being a Symbolist is founded largely on those lyrics in which he seeks to capture elusive moods. Furthermore, he grandiloquently celebrates the individual exulting in his own freedom.

"My only fatherland," he declares, "is my desert soul." One of his early collections bears the title *Let Us Be Like the Sun.* A spontaneous, exuberant, all too facile, all too prolific poet, he composed hymns to the elements, a series of poems about colors, verses for children, retold exotic myths, and adapted spells and folk songs in many tongues. Not for nothing did he develop, in a turgid essay published in 1915, the thesis that poetry is in essence magic. He also turned out a vast body of translations, chiefly verse. Unfortunately, his skill with rhyme, rhythm, and tone color saves little of his work from vacuity.

Shortly after the publication of Merezhkovsky's *Symbols,* three fascicules of a miscellany entitled *Russian Symbolists* appeared under a Moscow imprint. It was virtually an anthology of French verse. The translations and imitations were for the most part from the pen of a university student named Valery Bryusov. At twenty-two he bestowed upon eternity, to use his own words, the first collection of his poems, modestly entitled *Chefs d'Oeuvre.* Like Balmont, the young man was "a Narcissus of the ink bottle." In an early lyric he advised the poet to sympathize with no one, to love himself "boundlessly," and to worship art alone. For him life was but material for the fashioning of verbal patterns that would endure by virtue of their formal excellence. He continued to protest his allegiance to "Beauty," but with time his verse took on a degree of concreteness. Further, he became aware of contending social forces, and he responded to such public crises as the abortive revolution of 1905–06 and the World War. Like Emile Verhaeren, a friend and master, whom he translated—Bryusov was a prolific translator—but with far less success he sought to bring the modern city into his verse. He had early scandalized and amused the critics and the public, not only by his self-vaunting but also by parading an unprecedented eroticism. But by 1905 he was a prominent literary figure, the acknowledged *maître* of the Moscow Symbolists.

In an essay entitled "The Keys to Mysteries" he restated the thesis of the French Symbolists that poetry should use language to suggest the transcendent meaning of what the senses apprehend, should seek to glimpse eternity behind the fleeting moment and to penetrate to the secret heart of things. Yet he rarely adopted the vatic pose. He was not a visionary but a conscientious if uninspired craftsman, deeply concerned with verse technique. He likened his labors as a poet to the toil of an ox urged on by the plowman's heavy whip. The range of his subject matter is enormous. Russia is, of course, an inevitable theme. And having no allegiance to any one faith, he was able to declare: "Pantheon, the temple dedicated to all gods, has always been my dream." In accordance with the Symbolist canon, his style is metaphorical and allusive. Yet the language of some of his poems about the World War is so archaic that they struck a contemporary as the product of a gray-haired witness of the Crusades. Too much of his work is flawed by rhetoric and a weakness for such abstractions as Man, Time, Pride, Madness. Nevertheless, during the first decade of the century Bryusov's verse had a considerable vogue.

From the first, as has been noted, the advocates of the new poetry were drawn toward a religiosity tinged with mysticism. This was evident in the work of Merezhkovsky, but he was a devotee of a factitious faith that he called "the religion of the Third Testament," a synthesis of Christianity and paganism. Bryusov, too, employed religious imagery—as did Balmont—but for him Symbolism was distinct alike from science and from religion. As for Sologub, he was inclined toward the inverted religiosity that takes the form of satanism. It is the work of Vyacheslav Ivanov that has the private and ecstatic character associated with genuine mysticism. The word, he wrote, is "the cryptogram of the ineffable." If the other Modernists were influenced by French poetry, he was indebted to German Romanticism, the Christian stance of Dostoevsky and the thinking of Vladimir Solovyov. The latter was a visionary of an apocalyptic temper who made a major contribution to theology and also wrote a number of rather tenuous lyrics of soaring spirituality. Their main theme is the worship of the Feminine Principle, which he called Sophia—Divine Wisdom—and which, he taught, generates and governs all life. He devoutly looked forward to its incarnation at the imminent Second Coming, when the body politic would become a theocracy. In sum, this theologian held that his role as a poet was both priestly and prophetic, and so, too, did his disciple, Ivanov. Unlike his fellow Symbolists, Ivanov called in question the adoration of beauty and rejected the other cult that had inspired the Modernist revolt—that of the ego. Indeed, he regarded his verse as the crystal chalice of collective consciousness.

The pontiff of Russian Symbolism, Ivanov was the master of a monumental, quasi-ecclesiastical style. Some of his poems are marked by Byzantine pomp and ornateness. Others are cast in the Grecian and Latin mold (he was an accomplished classical scholar, at home in the antique world). They are apt to suffer from abstruse erudition. Yet there is a clear loveliness about certain of his lyrics, and a few, vibrant with his faith, burn with a pure flame.

Vyacheslav the Magnificent, as he was nicknamed, was the most notable figure in the Symbolist circles of the capital. Every Wednesday, from 1907 to 1912, he presided over night-long gatherings in his sixth-floor flat, known as the Tower (one thinks of Yeats and Mallarmé). The air at these assemblies must have been charged with portents, and words like "mystery," "eternity," "abyss" were as cheap as turnips. Among those who frequented these symposia on religion and poetry was Maximilian Voloshin. Since his middle twenties he had been contributing verse to Modernist periodicals. Like his host, he was drawn toward the sacred and the mystical, and shared the former's affection for, if not his knowledge of, classical antiquity, calling the Mediterranean "the fatherland of my spirit." As a poet he owed much to the French, but to the Parnassians rather than the Symbolists. His lines have something of the intense color and plasticity of Hérédia, from whom he claimed to have learned the art of verse. Like Hérédia, he was an expert sonneteer. It is noteworthy that he was a painter in a small way, limiting himself to watercolors. His most evocative poems bear witness to the vigor of his visual imagination. His

Crimean landscapes have a rare splendor. He also made verbal engravings, as it were, of figures from the past, and transposed into verse such works of art as the stained-glass windows of the Rouen cathedral. Neither the events of 1905–06 nor the World War dislodged him from his ivory tower.

Holding that symbols reveal the parallelism of the phenomenal and the noumenal worlds, Ivanov accorded reality to both. For Andrey Belyi, on the other hand, the physical world was a realm of shadows and echoes of the supersensual, which alone was real and which the poet could glimpse at the moment of inspiration. He regarded Symbolism as "a system of mystical experiences," and he was an ardent disciple of Vladimir Solovyov. Small wonder, then, that his first book of verse, like the prose poems that preceded it, celebrates Sophia, envisioning the glory of her imminent advent. *Gold in Azure,* the title of the book, describes his palette. Within a few years he was to lose his faith, and harsh realism was to invade his anguished verse. Cries of adoration gave way to laments and to curses upon Russia's material and moral wretchedness. A man of unstable temperament, he swung between euphoric anticipations and presentiments of doom. His style is frenetic, abounding in synesthetic, explosive imagery and enlivened by neologisms. His poems show sharp attention to tone color, and indeed his imagination seems to have been largely auditory. None of the other members of the group took so much to heart the conviction that poetry is allied to music, since that art comes closest to voicing the inexpressible. Belyi began by writing "symphonies": sequences of pieces in cadenced prose, elaborated in the manner of musical compositions. At the same time he was writing conventional verse. In his late twenties he bade farewell to youth, and gave up his former medium for prose, of which he made remarkable uses, returning to verse briefly after the Revolution. All he had ever written, he declared in a foreword to one of his late books—he was an incorrigible preface writer—formed a whole, the tenor of which was "a quest for truth." It was a quest that he conducted in terms too abstract and cryptic to promote the enterprise.

Linked to Andrey Belyi by a stormy friendship was a major poet who was prominent in the Symbolist movement, Alexander Blok. In his youth he, too, had belonged to Solovyov's following. The lyrics collected in *Poems About the Lady Beautiful,* Blok's first book (1904), have a singular unity of mood and tone. The prevailing attitude is one of worship, the atmosphere that of a vigil, a tense waiting upon mystic illumination, the miracle of contact with the ideal world. The Lady Beautiful, the object of the young poet's passion, is, of course, an alias for "Sophia" and is almost pure spirit, not visualized but wistfully foreknown. The sensuality that colors Blok's adoration is highly rarefied. At the time, like several mystically oriented friends, he actually believed in the imminent dawn of a new era under the aegis of Divine Wisdom: "Sophia." Before long, however, this belief was shattered, presumably under the impact of a crisis in his marriage and the failure of the quasi-revolution of 1905, when he had been sufficiently committed to head a demonstration, carrying a red flag. A poem of that year announced the Lady's departure "forever." As a matter of fact, some of the earlier lyrics he had addressed to his discarnate mistress suggest doubt and distrust, forebodings of fatal estrangement.

The poet now descends from the empyrean and finds himself in the physical world inhabited by creatures of flesh and blood. He takes increasing cognizance of his surroundings, his times, his civic responsibilities. The city with its fogs and fevers looms up in his pages. The object of his youthful adoration has undergone a degrading metamorphosis. Without ceasing to be beautiful, she has become a creature of evil, a deceiver, a prostitute, seen through the haze of intoxication. Again, she appears in the guise of a plain-featured girl, a snow woman, a cardboard doll. Is she consubstantial with Russia? His country inspires the poet with a profound emotion, of mixed love and loathing. And is not Russia's martyrdom strangely identified with his own, indeed with Christ's? Blok sees himself actually crucified, or else as a fallen angel scorched by hellfire. (This does not prevent him from describing himself in a later poem as "the child of kindness and light.") Prayer is supplanted by irony, ecstasy by despondency, even despair. The reader often finds himself in a confessional, overhearing an anguished sinner's avowals. Blok can write a lyric breathing a childlike faith or he can turn out a piece of light verse, but for the most part his poems record disillusionment, self-pity, self-disgust, horror. He gave a sequence of lyrics the title "The Terrible World."

Blok's verse is not centered solely on his private distresses. Now and then, as indicated above, the note of social concern is sounded. Furthermore, like Belyi and to a lesser extent Bryusov, he was troubled by forebodings of public disaster, of a catastrophe that would lay waste civilization. As mankind moved closer to the World War, his sense of doom grew keener. Perhaps this was an echo of Solovyov's eschatological ideas, or the sentiment may have been fed by his half-conscious sense that the generation to which he belonged was under sentence. Faith in the Russian people alone sustained the poet. With this went a strong anti-bourgeois animus. Nevertheless, with characteristic inconsistency, he hopefully anticipated the industrialization of Russia, its transformation into "a new America."

As Blok approached maturity he conceived a distate for whatever smacked of mysticism. "We need reality," he jotted in his notebook, and he did not mean the reality *behind* appearance, but that of the actual world. He gave up making poems out of the "astral dreams" of his youth and found more substantial material in the raw stuff of ordinary experience. Yet there is something spectral about many of his realistic poems—they form the bulk of his *oeuvre*—and they gain depth from undertones of the mysterious and enigmatic. This is enhanced by the rich texture of his verse. He hoped against hope for a miracle that would make the poet a whole man. But to the end of his life he remained a divided soul, a late devotee of realism who seems to have longed for the realm from which he had exiled himself, and who believed his finest poems to be transcripts of silent music coming from "other worlds."

The Symbolists' claims for their art were extravagant, and their performance, though ample and varied, leaves something to be desired. Yet they did quicken poetry and enrich it. An enhanced sense of the mystery and ambiguity of life deepened their work. Allusion and implication supplanted flat statement, sentimental or sententious. They made more effective use than had been made hitherto of the resources of the language. Subject matter expanded in scope and complexity. By translation, too, they widened poetic horizons. Imagery was relieved of outworn tropes and similes and enlivened by color. Preoccupation with structure and style made for a higher standard of craftsmanship. The Symbolists experimented with a stanza composed in varying meters, employed triple rhythm and stress prosody, which had seldom been used by their predecessors, and wrote free verse as well. The practice of Bryusov and Blok legitimized the off-rhyme, previously tolerated as a poetic license. Indeed, varieties of off-rhyme have become an established feature of Russian versification. The monotony and rigidity of much nineteenth-century verse was happily reduced by these innovations.

The best talents gravitated toward Symbolism. Ivan Bunin was one of those who definitely did not. When as a young man he first came upon the Modernists, he described them as "sick boys with complete chaos in their heads." He was himself a traditionalist in an age of innovation, a realist in a neoromantic generation, a sober man among the God-intoxicated. Religious feeling may enter into his poems without blurring their firm outlines. His lyrics offer landscapes and neat genre pictures that evoke the melancholy charm of vanished things and are touched with a longing for the distant. A strong exotic strain fills some of his work with Oriental color, fragrance, heat. Yet his poems can be examples of economy and precision.

Shortly before the World War a reaction against Symbolism began to declare itself. Early in 1913 two essays appeared which amounted to the manifesto of a new literary trend, Adamism, better known as Acmeism. Its adherents had for some time been banded together in a short-lived association that they called The Guild of Poets, to underscore their workmanlike concern with their craft. Though they emphasized their antipathy to Symbolism, they inherited some of its strategies. Yet they preferred a visible, tangible, solid world to the insubstantial shadow of a higher reality. Furthermore, while not lacking in piety toward the ineffable and the unknowable, they wanted to keep poetry separate from the mysteries of faith. Confrontation of the external world, not the exploration of arcane regions; detachment, not ecstasy; the precise word, the graphic image, not the hazy allusion; a balance of the elements of poetry, rather than the primacy of music; not Germanic obfuscation, but Mediterranean light that separates objects, bringing them into focus. Such were the main precepts of Acmeism; they were not always followed. All this indicated a penchant for the classical, akin to that of the French Parnassians, as against the neoromanticism of the Symbolists.

The new trend was represented by several gifted poets. The *maître* was Nikolay Gumilyov, the Russian Chénier. A loyal subject of the Czar and a faithful son of the Church, he was an imperialist with a Nietzschean streak who was drawn to the exotic, for all his classicism. His poems exalt the explorer and the conquistador—the dedicated and the daring. He set himself the task of rescuing Russian poetry from the effete state to which, he believed, Symbolism had reduced it.

Another prominent member of the group was his wife, known as Anna Akhmatova, who wrote intimately personal, chamber poetry. She endeared herself to the public by her finely wrought, limpid, fastidious lyrics which combine indirection with an admirable economy. They center on what Henry James called "the great constringent relation between man and woman." When the World War broke out, she voiced an intense patriotism colored, like Gumilyov's, by religious faith.

Mikhail Kuzmin, though usually grouped with Symbolists of the Decadent stripe, was close to the Acmeists in that he preached "beautiful clarity" and practiced poetry not as a sacred ritual but as a "gay métier." An esthete and a hedonist, to whom nightmares and beatific visions were alien, his elegant lyrics have a piquant charm, some of them discreetly celebrating love, both hetero- and homosexual. One of the few Russian poets to write free verse, he delighted in assuming the masks of varied stylization.

A professed Acmeist was that greatly gifted poet, Osip Mandelshtam. His first book, made up of verse that dates from the years 1908 to 1915, bears the title *Stone,* which suggests a Parnassian predilection for working with hard, heavy, durable materials. Curiously enough, the volume opens with poems that, far from exhibiting this preference, are notable for a gossamer, weightless quality. They move on a timeless level and have the veiled, nebulous character associated with Symbolism. The abundance of negatives is striking. The themes are loneliness, sadness, silence, emptiness. "Can it be that I am real?" the poet asks. In "Silentium" he urges Aphrodite to remain foam and the word to return to music. His tendency is to attain what Gumilyov called "the periphery of consciousness."

On the other hand, some of the later poems in *Stone* have substantiality, density, gravity, an almost lapidarian stamp. The poet's eye is focused on works of architecture: the Petersburg Admiralty, "this chastely builded ark," Russian cathedrals, Hagia Sophia, Notre Dame. The lines on the last-named conclude with the presage that some day he, too, will create beauty out of "hostile ponderousness." In keeping with the Acmeist canon is devotion to classical antiquity. This is amply evidenced in *Stone.* Several poems have to do with the city of the Caesars and the Popes, a symbol of the perdurable might of State and Church. It is an imagined Rome (Mandelshtam, it appears, was never in Italy), conjured up by means of expressive, parsimoniously chosen, concrete details. Russia's northern capital, which had been Mandelshtam's home for years and which had a powerful hold on him, is evoked with equal economy and an unparalleled freshness of vision. There are also chiseled stanzas on such diverse themes as an ice-cream vendor, a Lutheran funeral, an American female tourist, the organ music of Bach, "the irate interlocutor," and a reflection on the change of Europe's "mysterious map," dated 1914.

Almost simultaneously with Acmeism, another post-Symbolist, distinctly *avant-garde* development arose. This was Futurism. Both the Symbolists and the Acmeists spurned certain of their predecessors, but they appreciated the masters of many ages and countries. The Futurists, on the contrary, repudiated the cultural heritage lock, stock, and barrel, though their animus was directed chiefly against the nineteenth century. They had nothing but abuse for their contemporaries, and when in 1914 Marinetti visited Russia, at least some of them denounced the master of the school to which they owed their name (if little else). It was formally adopted in 1913, though occasionally it had been used earlier. The first manifesto of these frantic iconoclasts, entitled *A Slap in the Face of Public Taste,* appeared in a pamphlet issued under a Moscow imprint in 1912. "We are the face of our time," it announced, going on to say that "Academia and Pushkin are less intelligible than hieroglyphs" and that Pushkin, together with "Dostoevsky, Tolstoy, etc.," must be thrown overboard from "the steamship of modernity," an image that dates. The Futurists were "new people of the new life." Their hatred of the "stifling" past extended to the language itself. They declared war on Russian spelling, punctuation, syntax.

The opuscule that opened with the manifesto was the second collection of Futurist verse. Others followed. They were brought out by feuding splinter groups, into which the movement had promptly broken up and which made doctrinal confusion worse confounded. The eccentric titles, the weird metaphors, the grotesque juxtaposition of words—all were meant to bewilder and shock the Philistines. Neologisms were an outstanding feature of the verse written by this harum-scarum *avant garde.* The Symbolists and Acmeists occasionally produced coinages; the Futurists "ordered" the public "to respect the poet's right to expand the vocabulary with arbitrary and newly coined words."

Indefatigable in minting them was Velimir Khlebnikov, a signatory of *A Slap in the Face of Public Taste,* and one of the most improbable figures in literary annals. He made up thousands of words, derived from Slavic roots—when it came to vocables of foreign stock he behaved like a fanatical xenophobe. Alas, not one of his inventions has passed into the language. Since a newly coined word is imprecise, its semantic mold not having hardened, so to speak, its use is in keeping with his doctrine of *samovitoe slovo* (word as thing in itself), which subordinates meaning to the purely physical features of the vocable. This principle is, indeed, the heart of Futurist poetics. Khlebnikov also originated the idea of what he called the "metalogical, alias transmental, tongue" (*zaum*), a potentially universal language composed of separate phonemes, each denoting a cluster of related variants of a concept, expressed in geometric terms. Some of his fellow poets not surprisingly misinterpreted this delightful invention, and produced "metalogical" verse by stringing together "freely made" words, mostly monosyllabic, devoid of meaning, in short, a kind of jabberwocky.

For a man who died young (at the same age as Pushkin), and who devoted a large part of his energy to pursuits other than literary, Khlebnikov left behind a substantial body of writing. Some of his work is lost (during one of his stays in the country, peasant boys stole a sackful of his manuscripts "for cigarettes"); much consists of fragments, rough drafts, unfinished pieces. Coinages, sometimes incomprehensible, are numerous in his early efforts and are never absent from his pages. A relatively simple example of an almost wholly neologistic text is "Incantation by Laughter." For the most part he uses ordinary vocables, of the kind he called "day, or sun words," conventional names of objects, in contradistinction to "night, or star words," which denote what he felt to be the essences of things and which would seem to be somehow related to the "metalogical tongue." Now and then elements of it, in the form of enigmatic single capital letters, figure in his texts, as do numbers that had a private significance for him. He is quite ready to treat words in the dictatorial fashion of Humpty Dumpty. The surrealistic incongruities and idiosyncrasies of his style are prominent alike in his shorter poems and in the dozen lengthy verse narratives that he wrote before the Revolution. These are marked by helpless formlessness and sometimes have the absurd illogic of dreams. His innovations include what he called "supertales," each a kind of collage made up of pieces on diverse themes, written in verse or prose, at diverse times. His last work was such a supertale, entitled *Zangezi,* the name of the hero, who is the author's double.

In addition to producing a quantity of unconventional verse and prose, he was occupied with more than one madly fantastic project. He held that both past and future events were subject to numerical laws, and he was busy working them out. During the First World War he founded "The Society of Presidents of the Globe," also called "The Society of 317"—the number had an arcane meaning for him. Its members were to come from the planet's elite, including himself and some of his friends. Presumably the expectation was that they would take the place of heads of existing governments. One of the Presidents of the Globe resigned in protest against Khlebnikov's readiness to admit "practically everybody, even Kerensky and Woodrow Wilson."

Khlebnikov was attached to the Red Army unit which in 1921 was sent to Persia to incite a Communist insurrection. Back in Moscow the next year he fell ill, due to chronic malnutrition. A friend was taking him to a country place to recuperate, but he died on the way. His coffin bore the inscription: "President of the Globe." Most of his writings were published posthumously in Leningrad (4 volumes, 1928–33).

Insofar as he avidly experimented with language in an attempt to shape a new vehicle for poetry, he belonged in the camp of the Futurists. In certain basic ways, however, his attitude was at variance with theirs. One finds in his work a strong note of nostalgia for the primitive world, and he was hostile to industrialism and all it entails. Besides, being something of a recluse, he was inclined to stay away from the gatherings of the coterie and shun the discussions. Nevertheless, he was looked up to even by the most outstanding member of the group, another signatory of *A Slap in the Face of Public Taste,* Vladimir Mayakovsky. The Futurists gave frequent public readings (at which Khlebnikov rarely appeared). To scandalize their audiences more thoroughly, they affected such eccentricities as boutonnières of wooden spoons, while Mayakovsky, anticipating the Flower People, is said to have painted roses on his cheeks.

This young man's poems—five collections of them, with such titles as *A Cloud in Pants,* appeared between 1913 and 1917— were beginning to attract attention. There was a vitality in his riotous, cacophonous lines, with their bold imagery, broken rhythms, clever off-rhymes, their mixture of the colloquial and the neologistic. For all the persiflage and saucy exhibitionism in his work, it carries overtones of sharp social satire and asserts humane values with Bohemian exuberance and far from Bohemian earnestness.

On the fringe of the group moved an author named Boris Pasternak, then in his twenties. He was the son of a painter and an accomplished pianist. He started out not as a maker of verse, but, influenced by his parents' friend Scriabin, as a composer, and then turned to philosophy, studying at the University of Moscow and that of Marburg, Germany. His passion for literature developed during the First World War. He was repelled by the brashness and self-vaunting of the Futurists, yet he found congenial their free way with language. His first two books of verse, which appeared during the World War, revealed an authentic and original talent. He was to develop into one of the major poets of our time.

With the outbreak of the war Futurism went into a decline. It would probably have shared the fate of an ephemeral fashion, had it not been for the Revolution.

       ❖   ❖   ❖

The establishment of the Soviet regime in October,* 1917, forms the great divide in the history of Russian poetry, as in that of every phase of Russian art and life. Verse did manage to reach the public either in printed form or through recitals at literary gatherings, but the publication of fiction practically ceased in the general disruption. As a matter of fact, the misery and bloodshed that marked the stormy dawn of the new era, the breakdown of the routine of living, the giant hopes and fears, the apocalyptic visions —all this created an atmosphere rather favorable to poetry. True, there were those among the older poets who, seeing their world crumble about them, were paralyzed by despair, or who, abhorring the objectives and methods of Bolshevism, felt called upon to oppose it. Shortly after the outbreak of the Revolution some escaped abroad, there to eat the bitter bread of exile. Such was the case of Merezhkovsky, Balmont, Bunin. As the work of the expatriates was proscribed, it was effectually excluded from their country's literature. Others became exiles at home and continued to write without making any concessions to the radically changed intellectual climate. Kuzmin, after issuing a book of poems in his usual vein in 1923, published nothing more. A year earlier Sologub had brought out a little collection of frivolous *bergerettes,* a gesture of such complete disdain for the *Zeitgeist* as to be audacious. This was his last appearance in print.

The Revolution put an end to Voloshin's aloofness from public issues. In 1919 he published a sequence of poems which was a survey of Russia's past from the vantage point of a retrograde and mystical nationalism. As for the Revolution, he envisaged it as a "fiery furnace" in which the country was being tempered to "a diamond hardness." He also contributed to the émigré press some pieces depicting the horrors of the upheaval with brutally objective images. A Soviet critic described these as "counter-revolutionary," but instead of siding with the Whites, Voloshin called for reconciliation of the two camps. He continued to live in the

* November, according to the Gregorian calendar, which the Soviet Government adopted in 1918.

Crimea, where he was practically unmolested by officialdom. But he was not heard from for years before he withdrew into the final silence.

Believing that the Revolution had religious roots, Vyacheslav Ivanov welcomed it. For some time, in fact, he occupied the post of Vice-Commissar of Education in the Azerbaijan Soviet Republic. His cycle of "Winter Sonnets," which appeared in 1920, belongs to his finest work. These poems realize the physical privations that made living so hard at this period. Yet they are buoyant with faith in the integrity of the poet's "true self," while their patent genuineness, their simplicity and directness help to make them the moving lyrics that they are. As time went by, Ivanov found existence under Communism increasingly distressing, and in 1924 he expatriated himself, settling in Italy.

Bryusov, on the other hand, resolutely threw in his lot with the Bolsheviks. Back in the troubled year 1905, when reproached for writing poems without social significance, he had stammered an absurdly helpless reply in verse. The same year he composed a piece in which he told the revolutionaries: "Destroy with you I will, build—no!" Now he underwent a complete change of heart. He made a pathetic effort to pour the new wine into old bottles. In his critical essays he took to using Marxist terminology; he versified on scientific themes in the vein of dialectical materialism, hymned Lenin in an erudite hyperbolic style, and apostrophized Soviet Russia and its emblem in manic metaphors.

Not unnaturally, Andrey Belyi's political stance was an equivocal one. He hailed the new era with his customary exultation and in the field of culture collaborated with the Bolsheviks. Although in 1909 he had concluded a lyric thus: "Go, vanish, Russia, my Russia, / Vanish away into space!," in 1917 he ended another lyric: "Oh, Russia, my Russia, Messiah of the days to come!" The next year he published a lyrical sequence, "Christ Is Risen," which the public took to be a stuttering hallelujah to the Revolution. In later years he was to insist that it dealt with "very intimate personal experiences, independent of country, party and astronomical time."

This work was followed in 1921 by a remarkable semi-autobiographical verse narrative, having to do with his early life. Thereupon he expatriated himself, but after two years in exile he returned to Russia. In the decade left him he made a further effort to move toward acceptance of Bolshevism, but without success. He had by then abandoned verse for prose.

Alexander Blok greeted the Revolution with enthusiastic acclaim. He had long since come to loathe official Russia, both Church and State, and the middle-class civilization of the West repelled him equally. It has been noted that he was haunted by forebodings of impending catastrophe. The prospect of the collapse of the world in which his own being was rooted did not appall him. He accepted the violence and destruction of revolution in the belief that it had the power to replenish the deepest sources of the people's vitality. For him, as apparently for Andrey Belyi, too, here was something other than a change of government or the adoption of a new system of economy. Rather was it the prelude to the creation of a new heaven and a new earth, where life would be "just, clean, gay, beautiful."

It was in this mood that early in 1918, hot upon the heels of the epochal events, Blok wrote a long poem, "The Twelve." Its full meaning was not clear to the poet himself, but it was not, he was certain, a political piece—he had a profound contempt for politics. It held, he wrote, no more than "a drop of politics." We have his word for it that while he was composing "The Twelve," and for some days afterward, he perceived with his "physical ear a great, composite noise, probably the noise of the old world crashing." The poem reverberates with that harsh music. Among the writings spawned by the Revolution, "The Twelve" stands out, a monument to the days that shook the world. Couched partly in a coarse ballad style, new to the delicate and sophisticated lyricist, it harmonizes its heterogeneous elements and maintains a mood of revolutionary fervor, closing with a religious apotheosis, which, recognizing its mawkishness, he came to dislike, but never changed.

"The Twelve" was promptly followed by "The Scythians," a

rhetorical, confused piece, in which the poet assumes the unaccustomed role of one who speaks in the name of his people, and which was a response to the threat of foreign intervention. In his last three years he said nothing further in verse. His mentality was wholly at variance with that which was beginning to assert itself in Soviet Russia. A few months before his death (on August 7, 1921) he made this entry in his diary: "The louse has conquered the whole world, that's already an accomplished fact." He foresaw changes, but all in the wrong direction, and he was well aware of the dangers to literature that lurked in the new regime. In his last public address, delivered in February, 1921, on the anniversary of Pushkin's death, he sounded a prophetic warning against the bureaucrats who were "preparing to direct poetry into channels of their own, attempting upon its secret freedom and preventing it from accomplishing its mysterious purpose." Nevertheless, Blok's works are reprinted and accorded praise as one of the glories of Soviet letters.

Two weeks after Blok's death Gumilyov, at the age of thirty-five, was executed for alleged participation in a conspiracy against the Government. The verse of his last years, which belongs to his best work, was, as before, remote from the life of the day. His collected works, in the original, were published in a scholarly edition under a Washington, D.C. imprint (4 volumes, 1962–68). Anna Akhmatova, her powers heightened, clung to her sensitive, intimate, backward-looking art. After 1924 her name vanished from the public prints, reappearing in 1940, when the verse she had written during the previous sixteen years came out between covers. Mikhail Zenkevich, a member of the quondam Guild of Poets, accepted the Revolution as an elemental force and continued to compose tight, colorful lyrics on subjects of no topical interest. The poems of Nikolay Tikhonov were marked by exaltation of virile action and a predilection for the exotic, which allied them to Gumilyov's verse. But the young Red Army volunteer, who was to become a pillar of the Establishment, had had no personal contact with the Acmeists.

The last representative of the trend that a Soviet critic dismissed as "a Petersburg disease" was Mandelshtam. Few writers were by temperament so sharply antagonistic to Bolshevik totalitarianism. He remained in Russia, however, and continued to write. If he hailed Kerensky in a poem, at first he was inclined to accept the Soviet order. Yet as his "Twilight of Liberty" suggests, he recognized that he was paying a high price for acquiescence: "ten heavens for the earth." Concern with what he called "my age, my beast" was now not totally excluded from his work. As time passed, the beastly nature of the age became increasingly present to him. His defiance of the official ideology took the form of withdrawal. By and large his verse was apolitical. Classical antiquity continued to exert a spell over him. His second book of poems (1923) is entitled *Tristia,* with a bow to Ovid. A wag nicknamed him "Gaius Julius Osip Mandelshtam." Furthermore, his style was completely at variance with that to which a proper Soviet writer was expected to adhere. The idiosyncrasy from which his early work was not free had grown with the years. Imagery, syntax, sequential development—all are affected. The language is often extremely private. One peculiarity of the diction adds to the difficulty of deciphering some pieces which are, after all, communications: on the fascinating theory that in the union between the word and what it signifies, the former is the master and that it is free to choose its denotation, the poet ascribes an arbitrary and arcane meaning to ordinary vocables, like "swallow," "salt." In reading the later Mandelshtam, the utmost acumen is on occasion futile. He wrote jokingly in a late letter that he was "becoming intelligible to positively everyone," adding, "This is horrible." As a measure of defense against the ubiquitous censor, the poet may have half consciously intensified the obscurity of an elliptical style natural to an exceedingly eccentric mind. This applies particularly to the verse that he wrote in his last years, when he lived as a deportee under police surveillance in a provincial city lost in the steppes. (He had been arrested in 1934 and four years later died in prison.) One hears in these remarkable pieces, published posthumously abroad, a strangled outcry, a farewell to the culture of the West, in which he was at home, the moan of one longing to flee a place intolerable to him, as when he asks for "an inch of blue sea, just enough to fill a needle's eye."

There are those of Mandelshtam's poems that are models of cryptic utterance, outdoing the surrealim of Khlebnikov, to whom he was, in fact, indebted. They have, however, what Khlebnikov lacks: emotional impact, and the verbal magic, the enchantment that the *avant-garde* poet today is content to miss. For Mandelshtam is an esoteric poet possessed of an extraordinary mastery of language. A friend of his recalled that, hearing him recite his verse, he felt "a kind of chill, fear, shudder, as if in the presence of the supernatural. Never in my life," he wrote, "have I witnessed such a manifestation of the unalloyed essence of poetry as in this reading and in this man." Even in cold print some of his lines can make the skin prickle. Of late he has become the subject and to a degree the victim of a cult, both at home, where his unpublished verse is circulated clandestinely in manuscript, and in the Russian diaspora.

As a group the Acmeists appear not to have survived Gumilyov. By the time he died other trends were developing. The early years of the Soviet era witnessed a proliferation of coteries—Russian writers had long been a gregarious lot—which kept forming and reforming their ranks and fighting among themselves. Some of them were offshoots of Futurism. Before 1924 there existed, among others, expressionists, luminists, fuists, forme-librists, biocomists (they issued their program from a *creatorium*), nothingists (*nichevoki*), even rubbishists (*yerundisty*). Each splinter group claimed to speak for the poetry of the age. Most of them had a shadowy existence on the lunatic fringe of literature and produced little beyond their pretentious and often unintelligible manifestoes.

There were also Constructivists and Imagists. The latter may have taken their name from the Anglo-American group, but the Russians did not appreciate its sophisticated approach or adopt its poetic techniques. The Moscow coterie originated in 1919, when it published its first manifesto, signed by six versifiers, headed by Sergey Yesenin. The declaration repudiated both Symbolism and Futurism and affirmed that "the only law of art, its sole and incomparable method, is to make life manifest by means of the image and the rhythm [*sic*] of images." One of the signers of the document advanced the proposition that a poem should be no more than a catalogue of images, and that it should be so written that it could be read from end to beginning as well as from beginning to end. For him the individual image *per se* was of greater importance than the poem as a whole. The poet's task, he announced, was to rediscover the image (often "eaten" by the meaning) at the base of the word. This comes close to the precept of T. E. Hulme, a chief influence on the Anglo-American group, to the effect that one should see each word "with an image sticking to it, never as a flat word passed over a board like a counter." Other members of the group did not go so far in emphasizing the predominant role of the image.

It was characteristic of them that they should be apolitical. Their Muse was aloof from the civil war that was still raging. While the Imagists looked down on the Futurists, they tried to outdo the latter in their search for striking metaphors. Furthermore, they too sought to flabbergast the commonalty by outlandishly formal attire that contrasted oddly with their bohemianism. At one point their behavior brought down on them the wrath of Lunacharsky, the Commissar of Education, who denounced them as "charlatans." They responded by demanding that he stop vilifying them or else banish them. They were left alone.

Their rejection of Symbolism apparently did not include a distaste for aestheticism. *A Hostelry for the Travelers in the Beautiful* was the title of their organ, which came out irregularly from 1922 to 1924, when the association broke up.

The group included several minor versemakers, notably Marienhof, and a poet of consequence: Yesenin. This peasant lad had a fresh and authentic, if fragile, lyric gift, but did not fulfill the rich promise of his youth. His work is rooted in the rustic landscape, as also the peasant's faith and way of life. In a class-conscious society he and several other writers were lumped together as peasant poets. They were by no means simple tillers of the soil who composed their songs as they followed the plow, but their sensibility and mentality were molded by village customs and habits, by immemorial folklore and by the Church books that had long been the sole reading matter of the masses. Yesenin had been writing delightful imagist poems, chiefly about the fields and forests of his native Ryazan province, before the Imagist group came into existence. He had nothing to learn from it. He joined it because he harbored the ambition of captaining a new poetic movement, befitting the new age. As a matter of fact, he looked askance at his colleagues' exaltation of the image. "I've never forgotten," he wrote, "that it is only one side of the thing, that it is only the exterior. Most important is the poetic feeling for the world." Like Klyuyev, another peasant poet, he had hailed the Revolution in ecstatic verse. Ignorant of its actualities, he took it to be a mammoth *jacquerie,* an apocalyptic conflagration, and he hoped that out of the ashes a peasant paradise on earth would arise. Disillusionment was inevitable. The Proletkults—about which a word later—and the worship of Marxism disgusted him. He developed an animus against the new regime, with its march toward industrialization and urbanization, which doomed his world.

Yesenin attempted unsuccessfully a dramatic poem on the Pugachov Rebellion, dwelling on the tragic end of that peasant insurrection. More in character was a fine lyric of an incident that he had witnessed during a journey by train, when a colt took it into its head to race the locomotive, and, of course, was defeated. The poem bleakly symbolizes the coming triumph of the mechanical over the organic that was dear to his heart. He decided that he was "the last poet of the village." Goaded to madness by a set of circumstances in which frustration and a sense of failure must have played a part, he committed suicide in 1925 at the age of thirty. His collected works appeared shortly after his death, but were not reprinted until Stalin had been dead for some three years. Selections from his verse, which are very popular, have been published, and some of his poems have been translated into several languages.

The Constructivists began by repudiating all art as passive and consequently unsuitable to a society in process of drastic transformation. Eventually they reconciled themselves to the idea of producing literature—that is, chiefly verse. They sought to ground it on science and technology, to saturate it with the here and now, to make it a genuine factor in the building of a socialist culture. They have to their credit the introduction of so-called Time Prosody. In this system the lines are of approximately equal duration, the number of syllables varying and having no set pattern of stresses. It was meant not to replace but to supplement the traditional modes of versification, thus making for greater rhythmic freedom and flexibility. A number of Soviet poets have used this prosody. The moving spirit of the Constructivist group was a poet of considerable inventiveness, Ilya Selvinsky. His talent, which was not without a vein of humor, thrived in the atmosphere of experimentation and of seemingly unlimited possibilities that prevailed when the Revolution was young.

By 1930 the Constructivist group was no more. At one time it had included Eduard Bagritzky, a conscientious if uneven poet of unusual originality and power. His intimate lyrics gave place to verse inspired by fervor for the Communist cause. When the civil war reached his native southwest, he turned from pieces influenced by Futurist works and Gumilyov's exotic lyrics to Soviet propaganda. Though matters of public interest were not his sole themes, to the end of his short life he remained a poet of the Revolution. Nevertheless, he clung to his private vision of the world, and his tense, full-blooded poetry is not seldom obscure.

In addition to the groups enumerated above, the Futurists were still on the scene, and prominently so. They had embraced the revolutionary cause from the first. While others were hostile or hung back, these young bohemians leaped to the support of the new regime. They, too, were for a complete break with the past, were they not? Obviously they could provide an appropriate literature for the victorious proletariat. Not without some misgivings, the Bolsheviks welcomed this ally. Because the term Futurism trailed unsavory associations, it was rejected in 1923 in favor of LEF (Left Front of the Arts). Marxist critics had much to object to in LEF's theory and practice, but they gave their unqualified approval to the work of its leader, Vladimir Mayakovsky.

He was becoming a towering figure. Under the new dispensation he stopped clowning, curbed his weakness for the bizarre and the extravagant, without, however, giving up all his odd ways with words, and stepped, as he put it, on the throat of his song. He made himself the megaphone of Bolshevism, the loudspeaker, in more senses than one, of the Revolution. He hymned it, he composed marching songs for it, he eulogized Lenin and the Party: "the million-fingered hand clenched in a crushing fist"; he vociferated against the enemies of the Soviets. In numerous pieces, some written to order, he exhorted, explained, jeered, boasted, threatened—all on behalf of Soviet policy. There was no task too mean for him. He wrote poems urging his fellow citizens to brush their teeth and, also for the sake of hygiene, to avoid handshaking; to visit the new Moscow planetarium, patronize communal restaurants, observe fire regulations, refrain from celebrating Easter. He wrote advertisements for the department stores and denounced the mills for the poor quality of the socks they turned out. By his own account he produced six thousand rhymed slogans, which appeared on posters, three thousand of them painted by himself, or which were used in other ways—on candy wrappers, for example. "I am not a poet," he wrote in 1927, "but first of all a man who has put his pen at the service—mind you—the service of the present hour, the immediate actuality and its builders: the Soviet Government and the Party." Yet if he subordinated to the political requirements of the hour the poet's concern for craftsmanship, he still retained it. His skill with off-rhymes was extraordinary. He paid attention to typographical effects. He spurned traditional meters, branding iambics and trochaics as White Guardist, himself using stress prosody. Some of his poems combine what is virtually prose with lines in that prosody and in disguised conventional meters. He wielded his powerful pen now as a weapon, now as a tool, always in fulfillment of what LEF theoreticians called "a social assignment." His verse, with its posteresque crudities, its oratorical exuberance, its raucousness and didacticism, was a complete denial of the lyrical graces, the subtleties, the intimacies belonging to the poetry of the age that lay behind him.

Khlebnikov, too, ranged himself on the side of the Soviet regime. The Revolution and the civil war figure in the verse narratives that he wrote in his last four years and that were, for the most part, published posthumously. In one of them Lenin, not named, is described as "your new image, Time," and the White soldiers as "sons of deceit." In another long piece, capitalism is destroyed by "divine explosions." He projected a socialist utopia of his own, in which songs and smiles are used instead of money; nutriment is introduced into lakes so that the water, on boiling, becomes *shchee* *; whales are employed as draught animals. These and other such innovations are retailed in iambic pentameter without any suggestion that the poet is out to emulate Baron Münchhausen. His new order is ruled by Futurists. On the other hand, in one of his last short poems this self-appointed President of the Globe announces that he will "never, no, never, become a ruler." Attitudes at variance with Bolshevism are discernible in his writings. He did try his hand at propaganda but partisanship was alien to him. "Night Search" (1921), a dramatic sketch which deals with a brutal episode of the Red Terror, involving a crew of "holy murderers," is a politically ambiguous piece, faintly echoing Blok's "The Twelve." It stands out among Khlebnikov's writings as a psychologically sophisticated, nearly finished product. The other compositions are in his usual outlandish vein. One of them is a narrative poem subtitled "An Incantation by the Double Flow

* Cabbage soup.

of Speech, Double Convex Speech." Each of its 408 lines is a palindrome.

It could not have been such a tedious *tour de force* as this that led Mayakovsky to declare Khlebnikov "the Columbus of new poetic continents." The lands he discovered in his fantastic voyagings have not remained wholly unexplored or uncultivated. His wild vagaries and idiosyncrasies notwithstanding, his work, together with that of other Futurists, has been influential in encouraging the use of synesthetic, eccentric imagery and in enhancing concern for verbal texture and word play. As for the recent upsurge of regard for Khlebnikov (his body was lately transferred to Moscow), it may be a manifestation of the violent reaction against the blinkers and shackles of "socialist realism."

It has been stressed that Mayakovsky became "the big-mouthed agitator" that he called himself. He was also a vitriolic satirist. His thrusts at bureaucrats, pedants, parasites—not only in his poems but especially in his two plays, *The Bedbug* and *The Bathhouse*—earned him powerful enemies. It is not impossible that he would have become another victim of the bloody purges of the thirties, had he not killed himself. Exactly what drove him to take his own life when he was at the height of his powers is a matter for conjecture. Five years earlier he had publicly condemned Yesenin for committing suicide. Posthumously he was enshrined as the poet laureate of the regime. A Moscow square in which his statue stands was named for him. Most of the comment on his writing was in the nature of homilies on a text supplied, in 1935, by Stalin himself: "Mayakovsky was and remains the most talented poet of the Soviet epoch, and an indifferent attitude toward his memory and his works is a crime." Many years later Boris Pasternak was to write that Mayakovsky was being forced on the public. He added, "That was his second death."

The work of the two poets offers striking contrasts. Pasternak, too, accepted the Revolution. The poems that he wrote in 1917—they belong to his best—give expression, he declared, to "everything unprecedented and elusive that can be learned about revolution." In his verse the political upheaval is symbolized by atmospheric turbulence, such as downpours, thunderstorms, blizzards. "Lieutenant Schmidt" (1926–27) is a long poem about an officer who led the naval mutiny at Sevastopol during the abortive revolution of 1905 and was executed when the mutiny was crushed. In the last four stanzas of "Lofty Melody" (1923–28), another long poem, Lenin is glorified as a thinker:

> He ruled the flow of thought,
> And that is why he ruled the land.

Yet Pasternak as a poet did not feel called upon to celebrate the new faith or take part in the building of the new order. In a day and a generation demanding from the arts participation and even partisanship, he managed to remain virtually above the battle. He clung to an idealistic aestheticism in a society that has bestowed official status on the materialistic outlook. He went further: he hinted that poetry, with its concern for what is unique in the individual, is incompatible with collectivism.

Endowed with an extraordinarily alert sensibility, Pasternak on more than one occasion defined poetry as a sponge, commanding it thus:

> Grow sumptuous frills, fabulous hoopskirts, swell,
> And suck in clouds, roulades, ravines, until
> Night comes; then, poetry, I'll squeeze you out
> And let the thirsty paper drink its fill.

He went far beyond the limits that this seems to imply. He conferred on the fleeting impressions that his poems absorbed the quality of eternal essences. In fact, in his youth he defined art as "impressionism of the eternal." In his last years, without giving up the formula "poetry as a sponge," he emphasized it as the moral act of self-surrender.

His verse deals with a narrow range of ordinary events and not unusual situations: a summer rain, a sunrise, a mountain landscape, a thaw, an incident in an intimate personal relationship. Yet it is poles removed from conventional discourse. It is a kind of short-hand, which not infrequently defies transcription. Pasternak made no attempt to coin words, and his rhythmic patterns are by no means new. His innovations did not extend to metrics or stanzaic forms. Nor is his virtuosity with tone color or his ingenious elaboration of off-rhyme unique. What gives his verse individuality is the juxtaposition of words establishing connections and, often, paradoxical similarities, between the most heterogeneous objects and concepts. His work thus illustrates Wallace Stevens' definition of poetry as "a satisfying of the desire for resemblance." Here is a highly studied, personal style, dense and opaque, the vehicle of saltatory, idiosyncratic thinking. Following it entails strain but is also exhilarating. To find analagous work in English one must turn to the performance of such poets as Gerard Manley Hopkins or Dylan Thomas. Pasternak's metaphors and metonymies are as bold, subtle, and complex. Sometimes delightfully homely, more often they tax the imagination, demanding a difficult traffic in abstractions and violently dislocating habitual associations. His style is marked by an uninhibited and most effective indulgence in what Ruskin denounced as the pathetic fallacy. Thus in the first two stanzas of "Dawn Frosts," the spectator is being viewed by the landscape. The lines, in literal translation, read:

> On a cold morning the dim sun
> Stands like a pillar of fire in smoke.
> I, too, as in a wretched snapshot,
> Simply can't be made out by it.
>
> Until it comes out of the haze,
> Flashing on the meadow beyond the pond,
> The trees can't see me clearly
> On the far bank.

Sometimes Pasternak reverses the pathetic fallacy, translating the behavior of sentient beings into terms taken from the nonhuman sphere. Thus a stanza in one of the Zhivago lyrics is this apostrophe to the poet's beloved:

> You throw off your clothes
> As a grove sheds its leaves, . . .

The practice is founded on the tacit but firm assumption that the world of man and the world of nature are at one. The total effect of exposure to his work is to remove us from the daily commonplace and at the same time to intensify our sense of reality.

In the spring of 1922 Pasternak came upon a little book of verse from the pen of Marina Tsvetaeva and was struck by what he felt to be the close affinity between this young woman's work and his own. She had just accepted the bitter lot of the *dépaysé* writer by expatriating herself, and she was to die a tragic death some two decades later. Speaking of her poems shortly before his own end, Pasternak ranked them with the purest and most vigorous achievements of the Russian Symbolists. According to him, much of her work had remained unknown and, if ever published, would be "a great triumph and a great discovery." A fairly generous selection from her poems appeared in 1961 under a Moscow imprint. Unless it is wholly unrepresentative, one must conclude that Pasternak had been overly enthusiastic. Tsvetaeva was intensely emotional and intransigent, a born extremist, "a rebel in head and guts," as she phrased it. Her published writings include several plays and a number of perceptive essays. Hers is the work of an obfuscating poet, a virtuoso of compactness, using a breathless, hysterical idiom, exclamatory, incantatory, and stubbornly resisting translation. She saw the Revolution as an eruption of the forces of evil. A sequence of her lyrics laments the defeated White troops, but in one poem she writes of the fallen soldiers of both camps lying indistinguishable one from another: the Whites reddened by blood, the Reds whitened by death. The bulk of her verse has to do with her private drama.

There was yet another school that enlivened the literary scene and for years dominated it: the proletarian writers. Poems and stories on working-class themes written by working-class people from a working-class viewpoint had found their way into print before the Revolution. Fifty volumes of "proletarian" verse were published between 1908 and 1915. Under the new regime this sort of writing blossomed out fully in the sun of public encouragement. From the first, proletarian writers, the majority of them versifiers, were nursed along by "Proletarian Cultural-Educational Organizations" (Proletcults), which had originated shortly before the October Revolution. They issued books and magazines, and set up classes, seminars, and studios where poetry and the other arts were taught and practiced and which attracted not only beginners but people whose work had already seen publication.

The number of Proletcults kept growing and their prospects seemed bright, but their heyday was brief. Their leaders argued that since there was an unbreakable nexus between art and the class struggle, the literature of the new age could be created only by writers who were flesh of the flesh and bone of the bone of the revolutionary vanguard, the industrial workers. Here was a thesis in line with Marxism. But these ideologists had the temerity to claim for the organizations immunity from Party control. The Party rejected this claim, at Lenin's instigation. He, for one, preferred the development along socialist lines of the best elements in bourgeois culture. Other influential Communists, notably Trotsky, denied on theoretical grounds the very possibility of a proletarian culture. In December, 1920, the Proletcults were placed under the Commissariat of Education and made subject to the directives of the Central Committee of the Party. This was the start of their decline, and by 1922 they were definitely on the way out.

Long before their activities ceased, associations of proletarian writers had sprung up outside those organizations. The Smithy was formed in 1920 in Moscow, where another group, called October—the month sacred to the Revolution—which included secessionists from The Smithy, came into being two years later. Similar associations arose in Petrograd and in the provinces. They warred with each other and issued rival manifestoes, much like their despised nonproletarian *confrères*. Nevertheless, in 1925 these bodies managed to set up an All-Russian Association of Proletarian Writers. By that time they had given up any claim to immunity from Party control.

Early proletarian verse exultantly celebrated the might and glory of the working class, the joy of collective labor freed from exploitation, Russia as "the mother of Soviets" rocking "the cradle of beautiful centuries." Steel, concrete, electricity were glorified in hyperbolic rhetoric, and so was the machine, "the iron Messiah." With the millennium seemingly at the door and man about to move mountains and command the stars, why should not a poet urge revolution on a global, indeed on a cosmic scale? Several Leningrad proletarian versifiers banded together as Cosmists. One poem urged the erection of a "Palace of World Freedom" beside the canals of Mars.

The retreat from socialism signalized by the New Economic Policy, inaugurated at the end of the civil war, had a sobering effect. At least one versifier suggested that NEP was a betrayal of the Revolution. But such kill-joys were few and far between. As reconstruction got under way, the scene was increasingly dominated by poets, many of them proletarian in name only, who did not question the wisdom of the Party and took every occasion to proclaim their devotion to Communism. Mostly sanguine young people who had become articulate since the Revolution, they employed a realistic style and were engrossed in such matters as production costs and the state of the currency. Distrustful of lyricism, they were developing a penchant for rhymed narratives. While recently Balmond and Bryusov, as well as Verhaeren and Walt Whitman, had been the poets' models, now it was Mayakovsky, though some preferred more conventional meters than his. Straightforward propaganda, like that turned out for the dailies by the indefatigable Demyan Bednyi, gains in comparison with the more ambitious, if uninspired, performance of most of his fellows.

When the first Five-Year Plan was launched in 1928, the poets, like other soldiers of the pen, applied themselves dutifully to the task of promoting industrialization and rural collectivization. Alexander Tvardovsky, a gifted newcomer, glorified collective farming in long narrative poems written in a style echoing Nekrasov's and that of the native folk tales. Verse, however, was by this time quite overshadowed by fiction and semifictional reportage. Most of the literary schools that had added to the stir and excitement of the early twenties now folded up and the factional fury abated. The distinction between proletarian and nonproletarian (fellow traveler) writing lost its meaning, and in 1932 the Party abolished the Association of Proletarian Writers on the ground that all the authors had achieved an ideological homogeneity which made that organization unnecessary. It was replaced by a single all-embracing Union of Soviet Writers, which is still functioning. According to its statutes, its basic aim is "the creation of works of high artistic significance, permeated by the heroic struggle of the international proletariat and by exultation over the victory of socialism, and reflecting the great wisdom and heroism of the Communist Party." The statutes also impose upon writers a uniform way of treating their material, declaring that "the cardinal method" of Soviet literature is "socialist realism." This nebulous formula, attributed to Stalin, bolsters the doctrine that the proper task of the literary art as a handmaiden of the Party-State is to assist in the building of "socialism."

The trend now was toward simple, accessible, obvious verse, innocent of irony and paradox, eschewing eccentricities of style and all experimentation. In addition to conventional lyrics and variations on the inexhaustible theme of the civil war, many poems were written in connection with and furtherance of specific Soviet policies. There were pieces that carried a patriotic message and extolled stubborn strength and readiness to bear the brunt of battle; that paid homage to the heroism of the pilot Chkalov, and the labors of Michurin, the Russian Burbank; there were encomiums of Lenin and more particularly of Stalin. Writing assumed a made-to-order look. Few of the poets who had lent luster to the first dozen years of the Soviet period had survived. The newcomers were of lesser stature.

The thin sheaf of poems, under the promising title *Second Birth,* brought out by Pasternak in 1932, failed to justify the hope in authoritative quarters that he would fall into line with his colleagues. His work continued to defy the Party directives on literature. For the next ten years he published practically no original verse. A man of independent spirit in an atmosphere of abject conformism, he maintained his integrity as a writer by withdrawing into silence. Now and then critics held him up to scorn, and on one occasion he had to make a public apology for some of his lines. Yet, oddly enough, he was unscathed by the witch-hunt and terror of the thirties. He occupied himself chiefly with turning English, French, and German poetry, and—at second hand— Georgian verse, into Russian. Among his translations are *Faust* and much of Shakespeare. His fellow writers, notably Tikhonov, translated verse from the many languages spoken in the Union. As in the past, translation was an important function of the poet, but now its purpose was less to make world masterpieces accessible to Russian readers than to strengthen the bond holding together the various Soviet nationalities.

"The arming of the souls of our fellow citizens with flaming love of our country and searing hatred of the enemy," the Union of Soviet Writers, anticipating victory, declared in a message to Stalin in February, 1944, "has become the content of all our work in the days of the Great Fatherland War." * The versemakers' contribution to this effort bulked large. Intended to stiffen the morale of both soldiers and civilians, the war poetry addressed itself to the more elementary emotions in simple, direct language. Much of it was what Louis MacNeice called "slogan poetry." A novel note was the acknowledgment of man's spiritual resources and even an appeal to religious feeling. Practically every established poet was moved to utterance by the conflict, and a number of novices—the versatile Konstantin Simonov, for one—found their subject matter

* It is thus that the share of the Soviet Union in the Second World War is officially styled.

there. Tvardovsky, who virtually chronicled the war in prose and verse, achieved immense popularity with a poem on an epic scale, the hero of which, affectionately delineated in his usual style, is the Russian equivalent of G.I. Joe. Vasily Tyorkin is the typical *muzhik* in uniform, a descendant of Tolstoy's Platon Karatayev. A companion piece to this is a verse narrative exulting the indomitable courage and endurance of a peasant woman, a soldier's wife. Even Pasternak composed a number of war poems, quite different from his previous work in their simplicity and directness. Selvinsky took the same road. Anna Akhmatova's name reappeared under a few lyrics, one of them a noble call for valor in the national emergency. Some of the finest and most sustained war poems were written by women.

Control of literature was somewhat relaxed during the war, but when hostilities ended the reins were tightened again. The old injunctions were reiterated with a new urgency and intransigence: the writer's duty is to serve the people and the Party; he must produce ideologically impeccable works that meet the specifications of "socialist realism" and whose intention is to inspire action in furtherance of official policy; he must extol the heroism of the citizenry in battle and in peaceful labor exploits. Whatever was susceptible of being interpreted as showing the influence of—let alone sympathy with—the West was excoriated by umbrageous critics as a sure sign of bourgeois corruption, and so was any trace of "formalist," that is, apolitical and stylistically sophisticated writing. And adverse criticism implied a threat to more than prestige. Where imaginative writing is held to be a political instrument, an author's alleged fault verges on a political offense.

By way of intimidating the profession, an example was made of Mikhail Zoschenko, a popular writer of humorous short stories, and of Anna Akhmatova. In August, 1946, the Central Committee of the Party discontinued the publication of a Leningrad monthly because, in addition to other "faulty works," it had printed her verse. This, permeated as it was with "the spirit of pessimism and decadence," was pronounced harmful to the young and so "not to be tolerated in Soviet literature." Forthwith, in a speech that was given the widest publicity, a high Party official vilified her as a despicable purveyor of mysticism and eroticism, whereupon she was expelled from the Writer's Union. Pasternak, though not proscribed, was denounced as out of tune with Soviet literature, and laxity in combating the popularity of his work was deplored in a resolution of the Presidium of the Union.

The verse produced in the stifling atmosphere of the first half dozen postwar years affects a facile, commonplace style and moves in traditional prosodic patterns. Nevertheless, the inexact rhyme is widely used, and one finds, if less frequently, the steplike arrangement of lines that Mayakovsky often employed. There is an abundance of occasional pieces called forth by an anniversary, an "election," an event such as the revaluation of the ruble, a speech of Stalin's. The late Generalissimo had been adulated so long, so persistently, so variously, that each new paean is a real tribute— to the versifier's inventiveness. The Party gets a generous measure of fulsome praise. There are variations on such themes as "Our flag is the world's noblest," "There are no people on the planet stronger and happier than we." War reminiscences, particularly deeds of Soviet heroism and experiences of Red Army men abroad, are a favorite subject. Nor does the Soviet Muse fail to do her bit in the cold war: versemakers swell the chorus of anti-British and especially anti-American propaganda. They also celebrate the labor of the farmer, the miner, the steelworker, the road builder, driving home the moral that the construction front, though bloodless, is still a battlefront, demanding the utmost straining of every nerve and muscle. Promotion of the Government's forestation program is the sole purpose of a verse narrative printed in 1952. Another such work details the fortunes of a collective farm, concluding with a procession of trucks carrying a rich harvest. The last lines read: "The people are intoxicated with happiness and drink a toast to Stalin."

There are, however, during this period a number of nonpolitical poems. These lyrics deal, some of them felicitously, with such stock themes as love and nature. But irony, skepticism, bitterness are, of course, generally absent, and the verse is expressive of the high spirits and noble sentiments believed to produce the bracing and uplifting effect mandatory for all literature.

The death of Stalin (in March, 1953), while leaving the foundations of the system intact, brought about a significant shift in policies and in the methods of carrying them out. The new regime clings to the prerogative of directing all cultural activities, but it has been less coercive. To use a metaphor popularized by the title of a novel by Ilya Ehrenburg published in 1954 under a Moscow imprint, a "thaw" has been under way, intermittently and precariously, ever since the beginning of the post-Stalinist era.

The first signs of the new times were of a hortatory character. Pleas were heard for personal emotion in poetry, for sincerity and unvarnished truth in all literature, for replacing stereotypes with human beings. Protests against the regimentation of artists and the crudely mechanistic conception of the creative process were allowed to reach the public. Fiction and drama frankly suggesting that something was rotten in the state of the Soviets were not slow to appear. The unorthodox authors were sharply reproved by the watchdogs of the Party line, but no such punitive measures as imprisonment or deportation were taken against the culprits. Furthermore the posthumous rehabilitation of victims of the purges went on, and proscribed writers continued to emerge from oblivion. At the Twentieth Congress of the Party, Khrushchev, who was soon to emerge the victor in the struggle of the top leaders for supremacy, made a speech that dealt a crushing blow to the cult of the dead demi-god. In the months that followed the Congress the feeling spread that the time had arrived for a critical revaluation of received ideas, and that a long dark night was coming to an end.

The mood of the moment had its poets, among them Leonid Martynov, who envisaged the carting away of the "garbage" of "mistaken notions and false axioms" and, looking forward, ex-claimed:

> What bonds will be broken,
> What knots cut!

The October issue of a Moscow monthly carried a candid verse narrative, "Zima Junction," by a member of the Communist Youth League, Yevgeny Yevtushenko, of whom more later. It offers revealing glimpses of life in a Siberian town—among them alcoholism, intellectual stagnation, official corruption. Furthermore, there are thinly veiled allusions to the shattering effect of the denunciation of Stalin. The young author is deeply troubled. He has a visiting Moscow journalist admit that "there have been changes" and that people talk about matters not mentioned yes-terday, but add that

> behind the speeches
> some dark game is being played.

The poet invites his readers to "think about things great and little"; he reflects on the genesis of lies, and ends by declaring that "without truth there is no happiness."

The turbulence that Khrushchev's anti-Stalin speech caused far and wide, the unrest in Poland, and the Hungarian insurrection late in the year, checked the concessive mood that had prevailed in high places. The authorities proceeded to suppress the stirrings of discontent and encouraged virulent attacks in the press on writers who went too far in stressing the seamy side of Soviet life. In an address to Moscow literati in the spring of 1957 Khrushchev referred to the role played by writers in the Hungarian uprising and is said to have added that he would not hesitate to use bullets to silence the more recalcitrant members of the writing profession at home. Two months later he delivered himself of another "tough" speech in defense of the political control of literature and the dogma of "socialist realism." There was some beating of breasts and there were protestations of devotion to the Party line.

It looked as though the frosts had returned, but there were spells of more genial weather. Within the last fifteen years plays and works of fiction have appeared in which the characters behave like plausible, complex human beings, and Soviet life is presented more or less candidly. In 1962 the taboo was removed from revealing the nightmarish conditions in the Soviet concentration camps—until then the very existence of that institution could only be hinted at. Gradually polarization was taking place in the intellectual sphere. A liberal wing and a reactionary one, each with its own organs, came into being. The replacement of Khrushchev by collective leadership enabled both camps to further their interests. During 1965 the liberals were smiled upon by the Party. The newly appointed editor of *Pravda,* in an article which appeared on February 21, allowed that "genuine creativity . . . does not tolerate finical control and regimentation. . . . It is possible only in a setting of inquiry, experimentation, free expression, and the clash of opinions." Paying lip-service to some dogmas of official ideology, he declared that the sole criterion of literature was "the free, many-sided development of the personality of each member of society." A few days later *Pravda* printed another article on the subject in which "socialist realism" was not even mentioned. *Izvestia,* on the other hand, sided with the reactionaries and upbraided the young writers. This period of relaxation was short-lived. Yet even when harsh tactics were resumed, they were not as severe as formerly. The Soviet writer may not overtly question, let alone attack, the basic purposes and policies of the existing order, including the Party's tutelage over the arts, but the obligatory formula has occasionally been less stringently interpreted. Furthermore, Soviet culture is to some degree losing its parochial character. There has been more travel *in partibus infidelium,* greater access to foreign writings in the original as well as in translation, an organized attempt to promote personal contacts between Soviet intellectuals and their opposite numbers abroad.

In the less oppressive air, literature began to recover from the debilitating, corrupting effect of the political pressure to which it had been exposed since the Party-State laid rough hands on it. As might be expected, poetry showed new vitality. To be sure, much verse is of the tiresome, unregenerate variety. The message, to use the words of a Soviet critic, "sticks out like a spring in an old sofa." Encomiums of the Party, "lighthouse of the planet," are numerous. One rhymester avers that there is no happier man on earth than a delegate to the Twenty-Second Party Congress. Avowals of undying devotion to the Fatherland, "the world's conscience," abound. A female versifier declares that one heart is not enough to hold her love for her native land. Hosannas to Stalin have been replaced by panegyrics to Lenin. "Ilyich" is like the sun: "his warmth is felt by all." His mausoleum "is flying into eternity." There is no lack of self-congratulation even on occasions other than the Soviet penetration of outer space. If less prominently than before, the lyre is part of the cold war arsenal.

Even during the Draconian years, however, poems that failed to meet the quasi-official specifications of partisanship, social charge, wholesomeness, cheer, sometimes managed to get into print. The body of post-Stalinist verse—its bulk is staggering—includes a large proportion of such work. It is contributed by the younger lyricists who speak for a generation in revolt. A special place among them is occupied by Josif Brodsky, the victim of a trial conducted by a bigoted, stupid judge in an atmosphere of anti-Jewish bias. In 1964, at the age of twenty-four, he was sentenced by a Leningrad court to five years of forced labor in a remote region. The verdict was that, since the defendant had systematically evaded the duty of a Soviet national to produce material wealth, he was subject to the punishment provided by the decree on *tuneyadstvo* (idling, parasitism). As a matter of fact, far from being an idler, from the beginning of his adolescence Brodsky had been engaged in hard and fruitful intellectual work. Having had only elementary schooling, he studied assiduously by himself, becoming a master of his native tongue and achieving enough proficiency in other languages to turn out fine translations of English and Spanish verse. And writing poetry was his tireless occupation. Only half a dozen poems came out clandestinely in the Soviet Union, but a volume in the original and one in translation were published in the United States and in England, respectively. The work exhibits considerable technical skill in the service of a poet's eye and ear. If his style shows any influence, it is that of Khlebnikov. He can sustain a long piece, but his eccentric imagination is most effective in shorter ones. His art has a deep inwardness, yet he dwells on the concrete particulars of the external world. Abysmal loneliness, ghostly isolation are haunting themes. Brodsky is obsessed by darkness, but in "A Definition of Poetry," dedicated to the memory of Federico García Lorca, he enjoins poets to remember how the sun rises. Not a political, he is anti-Soviet only in the sense that literature is inherently hostile to totalitarian power.

After his trial Brodsky became an unperson * and was deported to the district of Archangel in the Far North, where he is said to have been working on a collective farm, carting manure. It can only be hoped that he will cease to be a proscribed author and go on making his anguished, difficult poems for the public that he deserves.

A few older poets who have managed to preserve their artistic integrity have also been producing after Stalin's death. An eminent figure in this group was Anna Akhmatova. Signal distinction attaches to those of her poems that appeared since Stalin's death. She returned to the theme of her early lyrics: love as a woman knows it. In dealing with it, the septuagenarian showed the familiar intensity of feeling, touched sometimes by acrimony, but now the crystal clarity of her verse might be clouded by a breath from arcane regions. Some of her poems, such as those from the cycle "Secrets of the Trade," are esoteric pieces in the manner of poetry as practiced in the West. In 1963 her compatriots were first al-

---

* The late Anna Akhmatova, who had a high regard for the young man, dedicated one of her last poems to him. It was reprinted in a Soviet edition of her collected poems without the dedication.

lowed to read her "Epic Without a Hero," a phantasmal "triptych" enveloped in an impenetrably misty, Hoffmannesque atmosphere. The poem, composed during the Second World War, is a farewell to the friends and lovers of her youth. Still inaccessible to the Soviet public is "Requiem," a sequence of lyrics written during the Terror of the thirties and commemorating its victims, among them her husband and her son.

In June, 1965, Anna Akhmatova received the honorary degree of Doctor of Letters from the University of Oxford. In March of the following year she died in Moscow at the age of seventy-seven. The first volume of the two-volume edition of her collected works in the original appeared in 1967 under an American imprint.

No less nonconformist is the poetry of the late Nikolay Zabolotzky, a stammerer among the glib. Although on occasion he protested against the poet who, "playing charades, puts on a sorcerer's cap," he was incapable of writing for the mass mind. Zabolotzky's work is the product of a pantheistic imagination that transfigures the lower forms of life—birds, insects, plants. His lyrics vibrate with feeling, keen awareness of evil, pain and death. His bold, sometimes grotesque, imagery and elliptical style suggest the influence of the Futurists and of Pasternak.

Since, as every newspaper reader knows, the publication of *Doctor Zhivago* abroad in 1957 and Pasternak's acceptance of the Nobel Prize in the fall of 1958 made him a proscribed author, the verse that he composed in his last years came out in the original abroad without appearing at home. Appended to the novel is a cycle of twenty-five poems, printed as "The Poems of Yury Zhivago." Seven of them are not included in the scholarly Moscow edition of Pasternak's collected verse, provided with an admirable introductory essay by Andrey Sinyavsky and dated 1965. The reason is that these lyrics are religious poems on themes from the Gospels. They do, of course, belong in the body of his verse. Though born of Jewish parents, Pasternak was baptized in his infancy and, what is more significant, "Christian thought"—he wrote to a friend shortly before his death—was a decisive influence in his formative years. The other poems attributed to Zhivago appear in the 1965 edition under the heading "Poems from a Novel, 1946–1955." As *Doctor Zhivago* has not been published in the Soviet Union, its title is taboo. Thematically these pieces have great variety and their language is relatively simple and lucid in syntax and imagery, quite unlike the difficult, esoteric writing, both verse and prose, of the author's early manhood. The stylistic change occurred during the Second World War. In 1958 Pasternak was writing to a friend: "When I now reread the poems I wrote in my youth I have the feeling that they are something entirely alien to me, even a caricature, a parody, as it were, of my own verse. Now my writing is entirely different. This has been going on since the early forties."

Pasternak began as a poet and he ended as a poet. In the five years that were left him after he completed *Doctor Zhivago* in 1955, he wrote some two score poems, forming a group entitled *When the Skies Clear*. They are written in the same lucid, transparent style as the Zhivago verse. The first lines of the piece with which the cycle opens read:

> In everything I want to reach
> The real essence.

They strike a note characteristic of the entire collection. *When the Skies Clear* is largely concerned with the essential nature of ordinary objects, with ultimates. The poems deal with timeless values and remain corporeal, concrete, yet still rich in metaphor. Over the years Pasternak's writing altered, but not his sharp sense of the unity of various modes of being, his conviction of the measureless worth of human life and its sacramental meaning.

Unlike such poets as Zabolotzky and Pasternak, Alexander Tvardovsky is a master of the homely, limpid style. A staunch member of the Party, he seems to hold that basic freedoms, including freedom of the press, are compatible with Communism. In fact, he is the leader of an informal group of liberal writers who are at war with the neo-Stalinist diehards. His position is manifested in two remarkable verse narratives recently published. The first, completed in 1960, is a personal, semiautobiographical work, of the sort frowned upon in the black years, when the poet's duty was to be "the speaking trumpet of the times." In one passage Tvardovsky suggests that the fraudulence of Soviet fiction is due to the timidity of writers still living in the fearful past. In another, the author encounters a childhood friend on his way from a concentration camp, where he had spent seventeen years as an innocent victim of a purge. The second verse narrative relates the further adventures, this time "in the other world," of Vasily Tyorkin, the hero of Tvardovsky's wartime epic. A delightful blend of fantasy and humor, couched in time-honored trochaics managed with great skill, it is also a satire on the Soviet regime so biting that for two years "Tyorkin in the Other World" circulated secretly in manuscript. It was published in 1963 in the Moscow monthly edited by its author, only after it had been printed abroad earlier that year.

Other poets of the older generation, though none of them is of the first rank, are publishing work that is respectable or better. The fantastic and the whimsical have their part in it. The subject matter is apt to be private, and even when public themes are touched upon, the approach is indirect, while the tone is not aggressive and may even be quietly ironical. The poetry produced is definitely not of the kind that, in Keats's phrase, has "a palpable design upon the reader." One finds an attractive obliquity here. There is also a stronger feeling for economy, as in the work of Stepan Shchipachev, a maker of miniatures that give off fragrance and freshness. Further, some of these writers have technical competence as well as a gift for unhackneyed imagery. Though sophistication is rare, their simplicity has its engaging aspect.

A poet who is on the sunny side of middle age and who stands out from his contemporaries is Yevgeny Vinokurov. Like so many of them, he was schooled by the war. If his wartime experiences made him respect blunt, forceful ingenuousness that will not be deflected from its goal, he was to repudiate this lesson. "There is nothing in this world / More terrible than simplicity," he was to write. His is a skeptical, questing intelligence, feuding with the obvious. The war, he says, robbed him of his youth, and perhaps for this reason he prizes that period of life above maturity. In any event, he has written lyrics instinct with the dynamism, the animal faith that belong to youth. But he is aware of the ubiquitousness of pain, "the tragic basis of the world," and with sobriety and wit he keeps returning to the mysteries of infinity and eternity. His reflective verse is suffused with human warmth. He longs to speak out about the horrors that he had lived through, the abysses that he had plumbed. The word has supreme potency for him. He is impatient with vacuous words ("barren bean pods") and he recognizes that "suffering is mute. Music is mute."

The range of his subject matter is wide. He vividly recalls adolescence, evokes the effect of music ("It removes the hard crust of rationality from people, the way a knife barks a birch"); he muses on the enigma of woman's beauty, on "the great and complex art of wonderment," the unpredictability of the ways of the mind as against the regularity of Nature's; he sets down an episode of the war; he speaks of his craving for truth, "as a patient craves something sour." Regardless of theme, the stance is candid, the language plain, the tone conversational, intimate. By his own account, technical matters do not interest him much. The genesis of a poem, he ventures, is like the birth of a child, adding, "The organic is dear to me." He generally uses conventional meters and regular rhyme. Expressiveness is achieved by piling up separate, concrete, humdrum, evocative details—leaving something unsaid. Here is poetry distilled from life's prose.

Vinokurov's work is clearly in line with the verse produced by the more gifted members of the post-Stalinist generation. The performance of these young poets is most adequately represented by the writing of two friends, both born in 1933: Yevgeny Yevtushenko and Andrey Voznesensky. For all their difference, they share certain characteristics which appeal to their contemporaries: nonconformism, active self-definition, an inquiring mind, a passion for freedom of expression. A youth of vivid, striking personality, Yevtushenko has already been mentioned as the author of "Zima Junction," one of the landmarks of the "thaw." This verse narrative was followed by numerous lyrics. They have brashness and verve, are alive with a lust for action, for experience, a "greed for people." His pages are dominated by the "I," so long in hiding, and are not free from posturing, concern for his public image. Now he dwells on his failings, such as proneness to compromise, thereby endearing himself to his audience, now speaks with unabashed pride of his endurance, gift of his Siberian origin and upbringing. He will have nothing by halves. Declaring that mediocrity is unnatural, he demands that everyone be "great." He writes, too, about grief, tenderness, and, of course, love. In one poem he has it that when love entered his life, "everything vanished, and it alone was in the world"—a sentiment scarcely befitting a Communist. And he commits a breach of Soviet proprieties, as does Vinokurov, by admitting sex into his lyrics.

For all his self-assertion, Yevtushenko is a poet much of whose work is in the nature of civic verse. He believes that he has the mandate to proclaim the truth to the people. In pieces that combine the topical with the personal, he denounces Soviet society's deficiencies, seen as Stalin's bequest: mendacity, toadying, widespread official corruption, bureaucratic abuse of power, the arrogance of the new upper class. Possessed of a combustive temperament, he pleads for change, warns against a return of Stalinism, the dead hand of the past. It is largely this verse that has won Yevtushenko an immense and ardent following, made him the idol of discontented youth, and has spread his renown far beyond the confines of the Soviet Union. What may be effective as platform poetry, in cold print sometimes gives the impression of versified editorials. Such is the case of "Babiy Yar," commemorating the massacre of thirty-four thousand Jews by the Germans in a ravine near Kiev, "unmarked by any memorial." As an impassioned outcry against Soviet anti-Semitism, it was a courageous act which has justly had ample resonance; as a poem, it is wanting. Yevtushenko can be heavy-handed in driving home his message, and his spontaneity and improvisation are apt to result in slovenliness.

There is nothing in his writing that implies disloyalty to the regime or deviation from the fundamentals of ideological orthodoxy. A prophet within the law, what he inveighs against is not Communism but the betrayal of that ideal in all its pristine purity. His versified account of a journey, composed in 1958, is the work of a patriot deeply attached to his native region and enraptured by the might of his country, for which he envisages a revolutionary mission in the world. He and his contemporaries, he declares, will match the exploits of their fathers without jeering at their (unspecified) errors, but without committing them, either. He adds:

> We enter life angrily and bravely
> As befits the young.
> We want not half-truths, or untruths,
> But the whole truth.

In another poem, however, he is at pains to dissociate his generation from the angry young men of the West. They have no faith in anything, he argues, and despise even themselves, but he, for one, believes in "Lenin's truth." More recently he has explicitly affirmed his devotion to Communism and was one of the writers who signed a statement to the effect that all Soviet poets, regardless of age, are fighting for Lenin's cause.

In the spring of 1965 Yevtushenko published an opus, on which he had been at work for years, running to nearly five thousand rhymed lines. The foreword states the theme: two philosophies, one of unbelief, the other of faith, are at war in the world. They are symbolized respectively by the Egyptian Pyramid and the glory of Soviet industrialization: the mammoth Hydro-Electric Station at Bratsk, Siberia, which gives its title to the *poema* (epic). The choice of the grand monument of ancient Egypt as the image of skepticism is peculiar, to put it gently. The pyramid, of course, represents a culture that lacked anything but faith. This is, however, a minor flaw. As the text of the epic makes clear, what the poet means is that a struggle rages between a doctrine that is brutal, cynical, bleak, and one that is humane, idealistic, hopeful of man's bright future. Announcing his readiness "for death or victory," he opens surprisingly with a prayer. "Quietly" he gets down on his knees to Russia's major poets, from Pushkin to Mayakovsky, to help him accomplish his great task. Alas, the orison proved ineffectual. His most ambitious literary enterprise is his greatest failure. Sprawling, tedious, cliché-ridden, *The Bratsk Hydro-Electric Station* is a monumental example of ineptitude.

The first section of the *poema* is a description of the drive eastward that took the poet and his wife across the vastness of Russia. As long as he engages in no pretentious philosophizing but simply sets down what he sees, hears, feels on the way, the lines make pleasant, anodyne reading. The trouble is that the author, to quote Andrey Sinyavsky's admirable essay * on the work in question, "has the knack of meditating on everything in the world and not speaking to the point on anything." In an access of self-deprecation, Yevtushenko writes:

> Having looked over all my verse,
> I see that I have squandered my energy
> on soiling paper with so much trash,
> and there's no burning the stuff: it is scattered
> all over the world.

Therewith he serenely proceeds to add thousands of lines to the trash. About the section in which he disposes of the Pyramid's theory and practice, the less said the better. The long "Mono-

---

* The last from his pen before he was arrested and sentenced to seven years' imprisonment. The article was turned down by the leading Moscow monthly, *Novyi mir (The New World)*, but included, under the title "In Defense of the Pyramid" in a typed underground Moscow miscellany, printed in the original in an anti-Soviet periodical issued in West Germany, and reprinted, in an English version, in *Encounter* (London, April, 1967).

logue" of the royal tomb, "The Song of the Overseers," "The Song of the Slaves," can only be described as puerile.

The bulk of the epic is devoted to celebrating the Power Station, which, in the author's words, is turning Siberia, formerly a gigantic, thousand-year-old prison, into a source of light for the country. In the main, the performance accords with the spirit of "socialist realism." The builders are most of them heroes of labor, possessed of undying faith in Communism and devotion to the Party. The author's own conception of the Party membership is indicated in these lines:

> Only he is worthy of the Party card
> for whom to the end of his days
> the Party card is his second heart,
> well, and his heart is the second Party card.

The construction of the mighty Power Station, the poet holds, was but the culmination of the great feats, industrial and cultural, achieved by Russians in the past. Furthermore, he believes, the best of the native literature, as well as works of European art, helped the builders to endure the trials that they courageously faced.

These indomitable, dedicated men and women are also cultivated people. The author is at pains to parade their (and perhaps his own) *kultura,* a favorite Russian term, not without unintended comic effects. Thus a fitter says:

> I know there are better writers,
> but *I* love Saint-Exupéry.

A work superintendent declares that he does not waste his leisure drinking vodka, and proceeds:

> The times in my opinion are grim—
> I love serious music.
> As soon as I return from work in the evening
> and take off my dirty shirt,
> I rush to Schubert and Bach,
> I make a bee line for Scriabin and Moussorgsky.

> I lie down and the records turn,
> while at the door, grown rigid,
> like puppies, work-shoes listen,
> plastered with clay and cement.

A woman mechanic observes:

> I have a kind of treasure:
> the slim Skira booklets.
> I see in the forest Gauguin's gardens,
> and Cézanne's dove-colored hayricks,
> and through the spray of autogenic welding
> Degas's blue girls.
> Forgive me the fantasy,
> but when the snowstorm whistles
> Rodin's Thinker, snowed under,
> sits on the edge of the dam.

And now the workingmen speak collectively:

> Sharing all our hardships with us,
> Tolstoy walked in the raging snow,
> Dostoevsky, tossing about, was tormented,
> Gorky toiled along with a child in his arms.*

The poem is nothing if not inclusive. Indeed, it defies summarizing. Taking advantage of the new permissiveness, the poet more than once mentions Soviet concentration camps. He says nothing about the conditions that prevailed in them, as revealed by Alexander Solzhenitsyn. The sore subject is touched upon chiefly in order to drive home the fact that the innocent victims of Stalin's Terror did not give up their commitment to Communism. On the contrary, they diligently toiled for it and, when the war came, they fought and died for it. As for the war itself, it was Russian bodies, Yevtushenko imperturbably claims, that protected the planet from fascism and saved Paris and New York from slavery.

It is the thesis of the Pyramid that man is by nature a slave and

---

* The allusion is to the story in which Maxim Gorky, after acting as a midwife, carries the newborn infant in his arms.

will always be one. A perpetually recurrent refrain is "A Communist will never be a slave." Also, by way of rebutting the Pyramid's proposition, the poet runs on about "the alphabet of revolution" and "the cement of socialism." Furthermore, he introduces a series of sketches forming a chronicle of Russian insurgency that the Party might well recommend as supplementary grade school reading. The sequence begins with Stenka Bazin, the leader of the seventeenth-century peasant revolt, who was executed on the Red Square and whose severed head "guffawed at the Tsar," and it ends with the man "dear to us all": Lenin. He is the central, dominating figure in *The Bratsk Hydro-Electric Station*. Thus we are told:

> Communists are advancing over the earth
> Like a million-visaged Lenin, . . .

The author is aware of the many ills of the age, but he has a panacea for them all: to fight under Lenin's banner. The penultimate section of the epic ends thus:

> Through wars,
> through crimes
> but still without retreating
> mankind is on its way
> to Lenin,
> mankind is on its way
> to Lenin.

"A Night of Poetry" is the heading of the last section. It describes an outing of the power station crew within sight of the "sea" formed by the dam. While they are gathered around a bonfire, one man brings out his accordion, and a middle-aged couple, both local poets, read their verses to the accompaniment of lively music. Everyone, including Yevtushenko, is delighted. Asked to recite verses of his own, he obliges, but the public is not impressed. Down deep he feels that he lacks "something basic, that is needed by these people and," he adds, "by myself." The persistent note of self-dissatisfaction is also heard in the cycle of lyrics—written after the epic—which was prompted by Yevtushenko's trip to Russia's Far North, a harsh, challenging land. From "The Ballad of Salvation," a long, fuzzy poem, we learn that there is "only one thing I neither did nor will betray": the Revolution. Yet in another piece Yevtushenko describes himself as "superstitiously uncertain," apparently of everything. Again, he says that he has a vital message to the citizenry and is eager to deliver it, but is unsure of its worth. Elsewhere he writes:

> All the time I keep repeating to myself:
> Why, why do I lie to people?

He sees himself as a schooner trapped by ice floes, and he asks:

> Can it be that, crushed by my own ice,
> cracking along the seams in fighting the floes,
> I shall angrily spit, and surrender,
> worn out, not having broken through to myself?

Several poems, particularly "The Stranger," an unpretentious lyric, one of his most engaging, are good enough to suggest that he may yet "break through" to maturity as a person and as a poet.

Andrey Voznesensky began to publish verse a decade later than did his contemporary, Yevtushenko, whose first book of poems appeared when he was nineteen. In his early youth Voznesensky wanted to be a painter. In this ambition he was perhaps to some degree affected by the little book of reproductions of Goya's etchings that his father, home on leave from the Front, had (with nothing else but food) in his knapsack. Did the boy's memory of those etchings ultimately find expression in the man's "Goya"? This is justly one of his better known poems. Here, reviving "The Disasters of War," he drives "strong stars like nails into the memorial sky." He was a senior at the Architectural Institute when a fire there destroyed the design he was to submit at the finals. He decided that the conflagration was symbolic for him: "I understood," he said, "that architecture was burned out in me. I became a poet." He was then twenty-four. Soon thereafter he sent some of his verse to Pasternak, and was invited to visit him. Their meeting was pregnant for Voznesensky. He settled in Peredelkino, the Moscow suburb where Pasternak lived, and stayed with the man he called his "only master" until his end. The year of Pasternak's death (1960) was marked by the appearance of the young man's first two books of poems. They were followed by four more collections.

Concern with painting and architecture is clearly reflected in his work. As for the influence of his "only master," it was the early Pasternak who left his mark on the young poet's style by encouraging him to use language freely; in his allegiance to moral, spiritual, quasi-religious values, above all in his affirmation of inviolate selfhood, the novice followed the Pasternak with whom he had had the privilege of personal contact. It is notable that from the first Voznesensky's writing was in an idiom all his own. He is a true craftsman, a verbal virtuoso, in full command of the tools of his trade. He puns happily (to the distress of his translators), juggles with words, plays with the aural elements of language: alliteration, assonance, consonance, dissonance, pitch, rhythm. In his use of internal rhyme and the near rhyme that the Symbolists had legitimized, he is extremely ingenious. "Art, like physics," declares this innovator, "cannot develop without experiment." He coins words, shifts his tone rapidly from one key to another, allows himself a deliberate anachronism, juxtaposes sophisticated diction with slang. His fooling with language is obsessive and sometimes seems mechanical. As with other incantatory versemakers, melody is of first importance to him. "Music in verse is indispensable," he wrote to a friend, "it is a signal, a siren, directing the reader's attention to the highest meaning of the poem."

On occasion he can be direct, clear, explicit. More often he employs language that is figurative, oblique, allusive, elliptical— a kind of metaphoric shorthand. At their best the poems are a highly charged compound of fantasy, feeling, humor, irony, the product of an ebullient, independent nature. He has, to use his own apt phrase, an "Achilles heart." His poems testify to his sense of here and now, and to the self-confidence of a leader of the poetic vanguard in his country. It is plain that he lives in the atomic age and that he readily, if temporarily, succumbed to the fascination of the technological marvels that are among its prominent features. His public readings—he is an accomplished reciter—have attracted great crowds, chiefly of the young, and the sales of his books have been fabulous.

The body of his work—he has been publishing verse for a decade—is not large, but the scope of the subject matter is unusually so. It ranges from the exuberant depiction of a Brueghel-like scene to a subtle love lyric. He writes out of the experiences of a wide-awake, educated, greatly gifted young Muscovite who has traveled far and wide both at home and abroad, including the United States. Voznesensky is attracted by such matters as Siberian bathhouses (peasant women jumping from a native variety of a Turkish bath into a snowdrift); the New York airport at night ("The monument of an era," "the accredited embassy of ozone and sun"); the hunting of a hare (in dying it has "the distorted and luminous visage of angels and cantatrices"); a strip-tease dancer who removes her clothes "the way you peel an orange"; the monologue of a beatnik in flight from revolting "cybernetic machines"; the beheading on the Red Square of a foreign spy who had been the mistress of Peter the Great and whose severed head delivers a self-revealing speech. Other subjects include a Roman garage (a hymn to speed); the "Marché aux Puces" (the wares look like victims of an atomic war); "A Woman Takes a Beating" and "A Woman Gives a Beating" deal with the war of the sexes—the speaker is on the side of the woman. Among the "far-out" pieces is one in which the poet in a New York hotel room dreams of an aluminum bird with a cigarette in its beak, a creature perhaps begotten by a flying saucer on a queen of the blues, and wakes up screaming.

In sharp contrast to this are the poems dictated by the Social Muse. Such is the piece which commemorates half a dozen victims of fascism, including Jews, each mentioned by name. The situation could be clearer, but these lines are free from the rhetoric that the subject might have called forth, and, indeed, have emotional force.

A number of lyrics are variations on the perennial themes of poetry: the miseries inherent in the human condition; the sanctuary of Nature and of silence; love, its vicissitudes and joys. Such poems as "Autumn," "The Party," and an untitled piece about a pregnant girl show the mingled power and tenderness that belong to love lyrics. In yet another poem Voznesensky offers this memorable image:

> We shield with our shoulders
> what is arising between us,
> as a flame is shielded between palms.

Among the motifs on which he dwells is the inner being and role of the artist, specifically the poet. He is exalted as at once a tribune and a rebel, one who smashes dogmas and shakes thrones, so that tyrants have reason "to take Pegasus for the Trojan horse."

Seizing upon the recent physical theory of anti-matter, Voznesensky chooses to have it underline the dualism built into the psyche. The problem of personal identity is the theme of several lyrics. Thus he writes in a light vein:

> In me, as in a spectrum, live seven "I's" . . .
> In springtime
> I dream
> > that I—
> > am the eighth.

Another poem ends:

> Like the Abominable Snowman
> I am absolutely elusive.

And indeed he is. It is hard to reconcile the author of his engaging, moving, or amusing poems with that of the tiresome pieces, such as the one in which he illustrates at great length the familiar proposition that everything flows, or the pointless fantasy that he claims to be realistic in the tradition of Gogol and Swift. Prompted by the "cleaning" of Paris, which merely removes the grime from the façades, he takes the operation one step further and shows the inhabitants and buildings of the city divested of their exteriors. A strip-tease performer has removed her skin; their walls gone, rooms hang over streets like clusters of balloons; the skull removed, thoughts warble like birds in wire cages.

Voznesensky's probably most ambitious and certainly longest composition is "Oza," first printed in an issue of a Moscow monthly in 1964. It is a medley of verse and prose, purported to be the contents of a notebook found in a hotel room in Dubna, a town that houses a cyclotron. The text opens with the hero bidding farewell "through the grating of the lines" to his fair-haired love, the girl who gives the piece its title. The rest is a sequence of disconnected flashbacks. Oza, a seventeen-year-old, is "encaged in immortality" like Beatrice. "When we are together," runs a prose observation, "I feel the future passing from you into me and the past from me into you, as if we were an hourglass." When she frees herself from his arms, she "blurts out, as though speaking a foreign language: 'I have received wonderful esthetic pleasure.' "

There is also an older girl involved, a physicist, called Zoya. A tender passage about her is interrupted by a digression, followed by the line:

> Farewell, Zoya.
>
> Hail, Oza!

"Ave, Oza" is the refrain of the last of the poem's fourteen sections (one of them consists of a single line). Therein the poet admits that, "a cynic and a clown" he had not suspected that love would entail "a great dread"; he implores microbes, people, locomotives not to harm the girl. Without anything to lead up to it, he concludes:

> I do not reproach you with having gone,
> I thank you for having come.

The author is at pains to mystify us as to the identity of his beloved. The impression is that he is uncertain of her name. Is the cyclotron back of the confusion? The device, we are told, takes people apart and rearranges the pieces, sometimes with awkward results (a woman complains: "They have forgotten to put in my heart"). Furthermore, by shifting the atoms, it brings about transformations, making objects and presumably people unrecognizable. Now Oza, "shockingly ignorant," has never heard of the cyclotron, but Zoya, the scientist, for an unknown reason, exposes herself to its effects. Can it be that Zoya is changed to Oza? (Significantly, the two names are almost anagrammatic). This is admittedly a far-fetched theory. In any event, the love affair is shrouded in mystery.

The fog lifts over the abundant digressions from the romantic theme. They are enlivened by flashes of humor and irony. The poet entertains Oza with a time game in which the future precedes the past, and he has fun with a mirror on the ceiling of a restaurant. But he also makes pronouncements that sound like solemn banalities to Western ears, if perhaps not in the land where he lives "among snows and saints." In a parody of "The Raven" the bird is a cynical rotter whose refrain is a euphemism for a three-letter word unprintable in Russia. The dialogue concludes with the admission that there is no way of making clear to the wretch that we live not in order to "croak" but so that our lips may know "the miracle of the kiss and of the clear brook." Elsewhere, watching "the crowds of automata trooping to automats" and noting "the robotization" of man, the poet cries:

> Horrible! Mama,
> enwomb me!

He curses cyclotrons and indeed himself for having been blind to the depersonalizing effect of automatic technology. Machines rust away, empires vanish, he has it, only one thing endures: "the radiance they called 'the soul.'" The further emphasis on humaneness as a cardinal quality is an echo of a statement in the foreword, that his intention was to produce a phantasmagoria against "programmed beasts."

A reader of Voznesensky is apt to be taken aback by his cycle of poems published a year before "Oza" under the title "Longjumeau." This is the name of a suburb of Paris where in 1911 Lenin lectured on revolution to a number of future pillars of the Communist Party. The piece outdoes in uninhibited extravagance the adulation lavished on Lenin over the years—no small feat of inventiveness. The author asserts *inter alia* that Lenin "answers all questions," that he "x-rays" those who enter the Mausoleum, and that the mummy's

                         transparent brow
          burns lamp-like sunnily and passionately.

There is nothing in the text of this panegyric to suggest that the poet was jesting. Early in 1963 he was attacked in the press on the ground of his "formalism" and other signs against "socialist realism." He also received a severe tongue-lashing from Khrushchev himself. Though he suffered neither imprisonment nor deportation, this was a humiliating experience, which was touched on in "Oza" and in some lyrics. "Longjumeau" does not, however, read like an attempt to appease his detractors. It is by no means an example of stylistic orthodoxy. Besides, when the cycle appeared— it is dated 1962–63—the campaign against Voznesensky had for months been a matter of the past.

The image of the poet as an intelligent, civilized, decent man, a champion of an open society, who loves his country but may be presumed to abhor blind, bigoted patriotism, is further damaged by a more recent work. His cycle of poems entitled "Walkie-Talkie" contains a diatribe against China. Oddly enough, not a native of the celestial empire, but a sixteenth-century Tartar khan, routed by the Russians, is the symbol of the country. His name was Kuchum, and the author seems to have chosen him so as to play with some unsavory words, like *chuma* (plague), which have the syllable *"chu."* Voznesensky is careful to avoid any suggestion of racism or militarism:

> Russia, my mama,
> do not think of clenching your fist.

His target is the regime of Mao Tse-tung—whom he does not name—with its "nonsense about military communes," its savagery that would wipe out centuries of history and have us walk on all fours, its expansionist greed:

> I hear: "We want the caviar! I hear:
> Give back Baikal!"

This Chinese pseudo-communism is an avatar of fascism, threatening war, "a wave of owlish chauvinism." In the next breath, however, the poet indulges in an outburst of chauvinism on his own. He asks:

> Can it be that we shall again have to carry the planet
> on our back alone?

This is an amplified echo of Yevtushenko's assertion that in the Second World War, Russian bodies protected Paris and New York from slavery. He goes on:

> Time!
> Worship Russia
> for its unprecedented destiny!
> For our selflessness, eternal as the heavens . . .
> Russia the Savior!
> Again Russia.
> Always Russia.

This surpasses even Dostoevsky's messianic nationalism. The novelist held, among other fantastic notions, that throughout its existence Russia had exemplified "political disinterestedness." The poet has it that his country's freedom from selfish motives will endure forever. Viewed in the light of Soviet foreign policy and of the hideous subjugation of Czechoslovakia, the idea seems particularly weird. Incidentally, Yevtushenko is reported to have sent a telegram to the Soviet Premier and to the head of the Party denouncing the invasion as "a tragic mistake," of unforeseeable harmful consequences to the Communist cause. The author of "Walkie-Talkie" has remained silent.

It is no secret that since the turbulent year 1956, if not earlier, clandestine writings have been circulating, at serious risk to authors and readers, in Moscow, Leningrad, and presumably in other population centers with institutions of higher learning. In the second half of the fifties handwritten or mimeographed copies of severel ephemeral sheets were passed from hand to hand in student circles, mostly radically minded followers of Yevtushenko. In 1959 and 1960 three issues of *Syntax,* an underground periodical consisting of contributions from young Moscow and Leningrad versifiers, came out.

There is much chaff in this substantial collection, but also some unhackneyed work. It is puzzling to note the tame character of these secretly circulated productions. There is no overt dissent here, no call for insurgency. In only one piece is there reference to a new revolution, in fact, to more than one. The young authors come close to heresy only indirectly by painting pictures of the drabness and vulgarity of everyday Soviet life. There is some clowning, irony, an eroticism unusual in Soviet writing. By and large the verse reflects the attitude of dejected, sometimes cynical people who see no escape from the society in which they are trapped. Forlorn as they are, however, they do show defiance by appearing in these uncensored pages. The authorities retaliate by sending the editor to a forced labor camp for two years.

Other clandestine, short-lived periodicals sprang up. One of them was called *Boomerang*—its editor was put behind bars; another bore the sanguine title *Phoenix.* Its first issue, dated 1961, is provided with an epigraph demanding of writers merciless truth. The product of the efforts of a score of tyros, it, too, is largely verse. The medium is as popular *sub rosa* as it is in the open. The initial poem is a translation of Stefan Zweig's "Polyphemus." The legend of the one-eyed giant who devours a group of prisoners in a cave one by one is an allegory, obvious if strained, of Russia under Stalin. There are pieces voicing forebodings of catastrophe and atomic war, or giving vent to anger, indignation, hunger for a new faith. Harsh judgments are passsed on Russia and the Russians of the day, including the versifiers' own generation. One of them speaks of suicide, others, overreacting to "socialist realism," escape into dreams and the irrational. A poem in prose is an amateurish exercise in surrealism. The impulse to face life, the world, also finds expression. And there are defiant lines like these:

> Russia is struggling in a strait jacket,
> But it will never be subdued.

The call to and prediction of rebellion, in which the poets expect to play a vital part, recur. Indeed, in a lengthy letter a former admirer of Yevtushenko dismisses him as a "new kind of chameleon" and berates him for traitorous opportunism.

In 1965 a collection entitled *Sphinxes,* and containing some verse, made its appearance. The following year *Phoenix* was re-born in the form of a bulky miscellany. An editorial note apostrophizes the authorities thus: "You will win this battle, but you will lose the war we are fighting for democracy in Russia." The 376 typewritten pages include literary criticism and discussions of sundry topics, philosophical, historical, political, as well as some fiction and poems. One of the latter is a powerful evocation of a fight between a wolf and a wolfhound, in which the hound is killed. Some of the other verse has a touch of religious feeling —an example is a variation on Psalm 137—which puts these efforts on the Index. Shortly after *Phoenix 1966* started circulating, four of the persons involved in its production were arrested and eventually given prison terms.

These underground publications, and some others, are said to have been prepared by a group of writers, painters, sculptors, known as SMOG, a name made up of the initials of the Russian

words for "word," "thought," "image," "depth." The aim of
the coterie, as defined in its manifesto, is the revival of literature
and art in the spirit of the country's "immortal heritage." It is
not surprising to find that the style of underground verse faintly
echoes Blok, Bely, Tsvetaeva, Pasternak, the early Mayakovsky,
Khlebnikov, Mandelshtam.

Admittedly, the poems that appeared in the clandestine pages
are of scant significance as literature, but one admires the underground authors' courage and dedication.

As noted above, during the first post-Stalin decade, poetry, literature generally, achieved a *modus vivendi*. Those years brought
writers of verse, and also of fiction and plays, a limited freedom
of expression. It was grudgingly granted by the authorities and,
with the exception of a short period, merely tolerated—the writers'
loyalty to the regime being assumed. At the Congress of the Party
held in 1961 Tvardovsky deplored the timidity of his fellows in
failing to take advantage of the permissive atmosphere. As the
sixties rolled on, the situation underwent a change. The numbing
effect of the Terror having been dissipated, not a few members of
the profession made the most of the relaxation of control. Among
them were several older poets and a number of young practitioners,
men and women who had either made a distinctive contribution to
the art or who gave promise of doing so.

Ever since Khrushchev was replaced by a collective leadership,
a less negative view of Stalin's rule has prevailed in high places.
And now a kind of neo-Stalinism is in the saddle as regards both
domestic and foreign policies. At the same time the ferment of
dissent is at work among the intellectuals and some of the young.
On the eve of the invasion of Czechoslovakia, an eminent physicist
circulated an appeal as long as an essay, addressed to the leadership
and the citizenry, in which he called for a wide range of liberal,
indeed revolutionary measures. Among the changes that he advo-

cated was one long desired by the anti-Stalinist writers: the abolition of censorship, which, he claimed, was killing "the living soul" of Soviet literature. The author of this astounding document must have been the spokesman of Russia's scientific elite. Some time before its appearance the Party had launched a campaign to tighten its control of cultural activities and combat ideological disaffection. Early in 1968 Tvardovsky described the atmosphere in literary circles as one of "gloomy silence." It is likely, though the wish may be father to the thought, that the partial refreeze will be followed by a resurgence of the liberal trends. Pasternak, Anna Akhmatova, Zabolotzky survived the years of the Terror. Under the ice the stream flowed. The springs of native talent are not apt to dry up. And the talented should continue to find a large, enthusiastic audience. Russian versemakers, it must be recognized, have that historical sense which, in Eliot's phrase, "makes a writer most acutely conscious . . . of his own contemporaneity." By the same token, they have a humane tradition marked by an inveterate concern for the individual as well as for the collective; and, currently frowned upon by the authorities though it be, an increasing devotion to formal excellence.